# COUNSELING OUTSIDE THE LINES

## Creative Arts Interventions for Children and Adolescents

### Individual, Small Group, and Classroom Applications

Ann Vernon & Kathryn L. Barry

RESEARCH PRESS
PUBLISHERS

2612 North Mattis Avenue, Champaign, Illinois 61822
800.519.2707 / researchpress.com

RESEARCH PRESS
PUBLISHERS



5 4 3 2 1 13 14 15 16 17



Copies of this book may be ordered from Research Press at the address given on the title page.

Composition by Jeff Helgesen
Cover design by McKenzie Wagner, Inc.
Printed by Edwards Brothers Malloy, Inc.

ISBN 978-0-87822-677-1
Library of Congress Catalog Number 2013939076

*To my 94-year-old mother, Ethyl Suhumskie, who nurtured my imaginative play throughout my childhood. As noted several times throughout the book, I have vivid memories of those times when I assumed various roles as gas station attendant, teacher, mother, nurse, pioneer, and so forth. So I thank you, Mom, for being such a wonderful influence in my life. —A.V.*

*To my Dad, Corky Stevens. He always encouraged my love of the arts by finding teachers for me, paying for lessons, and sitting through recitals for everything under the sun. But most important, he took time to make music with me. I have very fond memories of our times together, singing with the guitar, whether for an audience at a Christmas party, at a nursing home, or just on our own front porch. Thanks for the music, Dad! —K.L.B.*

# Contents

*Forms and Handouts* xi

*Foreword* xv

*Acknowledgments* xvii

*Introduction* 1

**Chapter 1: Counseling Through Play and Games** 9

**Individual Interventions: Elementary**

1 Roaring for Clues *(Friendship skills)* 23

2 Race for Results *(Underachievement)* 29

3 Pathways to Peace *(Anger management)* 33

**Individual Interventions: Middle School**

1 Knock Down Anxiety *(Anxiety)* 42

2 Predictable Anger *(Anger management)* 45

3 Grand Slam! *(Interpersonal relationships)* 49

**Individual Interventions: High School**

1 Fact or Fiction Tic-Tac-Toe *(Anger management)* 54

2 POSITIVE Hoops *(Overcoming negative thinking and behaving)* 58

3 Strategy Match *(Anxiety)* 62

**Classroom or Small-Group Interventions**

Elementary—Who Knew? Me and You! *(Peer relationships)* 66

Middle School—Treasured Hunting *(Peer relationships)* 68

High School—Shift *(Overcoming negativity)* 75

**Chapter 2: Counseling Through Music** 83

**Individual Interventions: Elementary**

1 Give 'em Five *(Teasing and name calling)* 93

2 Music Makes the Medicine Go Down *(Procrastination)* 96

3 Think It Through *(Tattling)* 98

**Individual Interventions: Middle School**

1 Relationship Rationality *(Relationship problems)* 101

2 Rap It Up with Respect *(Perspective taking and respecting others)* 104

3 Me Music *(Self-awareness)* 107

**Individual Interventions: High School**

1 Rights, Privileges, and Responsibilities *(Rights and responsibilities)* 109

2 Re-Solution Revolution *(Underachievement and goal setting)* 112

3 A Song a Day Keeps the Blues Away *(Negative emotions)* 116

**Classroom or Small-Group Interventions**

Elementary—Time and Place *(Behavior awareness)* 117

Middle School—Building Bridges *(Peer relationships)* 120

High School—Stress Relieving Rhythms *(Stress management)* 123

**Chapter 3: Counseling Through the Visual Arts 127**

**Individual Interventions: Elementary**

1 Look at Me *(Self-awareness)* 137

2 Picture Perfect *(Perfectionism)* 138

3 Show Me How You Feel *(Identifying and expressing feelings)* 142

**Individual Interventions: Middle School**

1 That's How I See It *(Perspective taking and problem solving)* 145

2 Who Do You See? *(Self-awareness)* 147

3 Picture Your Peers *(Peer relationships)* 150

**Individual Interventions: High School**

1 As I See It *(Career decision making)* 153

2 Photo Friends *(Friends and transitions)* 155

3 "Snap" Out of It *(Depression)* 157

**Classroom or Small-Group Interventions**

Elementary—The Me We See *(Self- and other awareness)* 160

Middle School—See the Options *(Problem solving and group cooperation/collaboration)* 161

High School—Mask It *(Self-identity)* 164

**Chapter 4: Counseling Through Expressive Writing 167**

**Individual Interventions: Elementary**

1 Write About Me *(Self-awareness and self-acceptance)* 178

2 "Write" Choices *(Decision making)* 180

3 Write All About It *(Expression of feelings)* 183

**Individual Interventions: Middle School**

1 Personal Prose *(Expression of feelings)* 185

2 "Write" Through It *(Friendship conflicts)* 187

3 Put It in Writing *(Decision making)* 189

**Individual Interventions: High School**

1 J is for Journaling *(Self-awareness)* 191

2 A Personal Story *(Decision making)* 193

3 Writing Remedies *(Relationships with peers or parents)* 194

**Classroom or Small-Group Interventions**

Elementary—What's "Write"? *(Decision making)* 196

Middle School—Write Around *(Self- and other awareness)* 200

High School—Express It *(Self-awareness and values clarification)* 202

**Chapter 5: Counseling Through Literature 205**

**Individual Interventions: Elementary**

1 What's the Story? *(Divorce)* 218

2 Story with a Happy Ending *(Sad feelings)* 221

3 Bully Books *(Being bullied)* 224

**Individual Interventions: Middle School**

1 Parent Poem *(Relationships with parents)* 226

2 Required Reading About Bullies *(Relational aggression)* 229

3 Dear Abby Letter *(Self-acceptance)* 232

**Individual Interventions: High School**

1 Science Fiction Hits Home *(Trust)* 235

2 Don't Judge a Book by Its Cover *(Expressing emotions)* 237

3 Achievement Autobiography *(Academic underachievement)* 240

**Classroom or Small-Group Interventions**

Elementary—Book Buddies *(Friendship skills)* 246

Middle School—What's in a Title? *(Prejudice and stereotyping)* 251

High School—Cyber-Safety Movie Mystery *(Cyberbullying)* 254

## Chapter 6: Counseling Through Drama 261

**Individual Interventions: Elementary**

1 Curtains on Friendship? *(Friendship and jealousy)* 270

2 Dialogue Duo *(Anxiety)* 275

3 Drama of Conflict *(Dealing with conflict)* 277

**Individual Interventions: Middle School**

1 Mask of Anger *(Anger as a secondary emotion)* 280

2 The Many Roles I Play *(Self-deprecation)* 282

3 Lights! Camera! Empathy! *(Developing empathy)* 284

**Individual Interventions: High School**

1 Lead Role of Worrier *(Anxiety)* 287

2 Curtains on Conflict *(Conflict resolution)* 289

3 Re-"Acting" to Bullying *(Bullying)* 294

**Classroom or Small-Group Interventions**

Elementary—The Eyes Have It *(Listening skills)* 296

Middle School—Dramatic Inflections *(Communication skills)* 300

High School—Cliff Hanger *(Responding to negative peer pressure)* 306

## Chapter 7: Counseling Through Activity-Based Experiential Interventions 309

**Individual Interventions: Elementary**

1 Catch It If You Can! *(Self-acceptance)* 321

2 You've Got a Friend *(Friendship)* 323

3 Feelings Fling *(Identifying and expressing feelings)* 326

**Individual Interventions: Middle School**

1 It's "Up" to You *(Problem solving and decision making)* 330

2 Mood Management *(Managing negative emotions)* 332

3 Fearless Friends *(Peer pressure)* 334

**Individual Interventions: High School**

1 Better Think Twice *(Decision making and consequences)* 338

2 Finding My Way *(Postsecondary planning)* 340

3 Get Out from Under It *(Procrastination)* 342

**Classroom or Small-Group Interventions**

Elementary—Tell It Like It Is *(Communication and assertion)* 345

Middle School—Identify Yourself *(Self-awareness and values clarification)* 347

High School—We Can Work It Out *(Group collaboration)* 351

## Chapter 8: Case Studies 355

**Elementary**

1 Annie *(Divorce issues)* 356

2 Kevin *(Anger management and impulse control)* 360

3 Amy *(Anger/mood management)* 364

**Middle School**

1 Gary *(Anger, aggression, loss)* 368

2 Kyla *(Wellness, weight management, academic achievement, self-esteem, depression)* 372

3 Brittney *(Loss, transition, anxiety, depression)* 376

**High School**

1 Dakota *(Anxiety, depression)* 380

2 Stacie *(Anxiety, codependency)* 384

3 Todd *(Transition, loss, career and college planning)* 387

## Appendix: Game Board 393

*References* 397

*About the Authors* 405

# Forms and Handouts

## Chapter 1: Counseling Through Play and Games

Roaring for Clues Cards 26

Roaring for Clues Message 28

Race for Results Game Cards 31

Pathways to Peace Game Board 35

Pathways to Peace Consequence Cards 36

Pathways to Peace Trigger Cards 38

Pathways to Peace Skills Cards 40

Knock Down Anxiety Cards 44

Predictable Anger Fortune Teller Instructions 47

Predictable Anger Fortune Teller Strategies 48

Grand Slam Pitch Questions 51

Grand Slam Ball Field and Scoreboard 53

Fact or Fiction Tic-Tac-Toe Cards 55

Fact or Fiction Tic-Tac-Toe Board 57

POSITIVE Hoops Situations 60

Tips for Thinking POSITIVE 61

Strategy Match Cards 64

Treasured Hunting Clues 70

Treasured Hunt Invitation 74

Shift Game Board 77

Moving On! Cards 78

Shift Cards 80

## Chapter 2: Counseling Through Music

Give 'em Five Song 95
Think It Through Song 100
Relationship Rationality Song 103
Rap It Up with Respect 106
Rights and Responsibilities Song 111
Re-Solution Revolution Song 114
Re-Solution Revolution Goal Worksheet 115
Time and Place Song 119
Building Bridges Worksheet 122

## Chapter 3: Counseling Through the Visual Arts

Picture Perfect Sentence Stems 140
Picture Perfect Ribbon 141
Show Me How You Feel Cards 144
Who Do You See? Attributes 149
Picture Your Peers Outline 152
"Snap" Out of It Feeling Chart 159
See the Options Group Process Form 163

## Chapter 4: Counseling Through Expressive Writing

Write About Me Activity Sheet 179
"Write" Choices Activity Sheet 181
Write All About It Activity Sheet 184
Personal Prose Activity Sheet 186
"Write" Through It Activity Sheet 188
Put It in Writing Activity Sheet 190
J is for Journaling Activity Sheet 192
What's "Write"? Activity Sheet 197
Express It Activity Sheet 203

## Chapter 5: Counseling Through Literature

What's the Story? Tips 220
Story with a Happy Ending 223

Bully Books Story 225
Parent Poem 228
Required Reading About Bullies 230
Required Reading About Bullies Tips 231
Dear Abby Letter 234
Don't Judge a Book by Its Cover 239
Achievement Autobiography Learning Style Assessment 243
Book Buddies Story 248
Book Buddies Tips 250
Cyber-Safety Movie Mystery Quiz 257
Cyber-Safety Movie Mystery Contract 259

**Chapter 6: Counseling Through Drama**

Curtains on Friendship? Puppet Play 272
Drama of Conflict Scenarios 279
Curtains on Conflict 291
Tips for Listening 298
Listening Song 299
Dramatic Inflections Game Directions 302
Dramatic Inflections Cards: Situations 303
Dramatic Inflections Cards: Phrases 304
Dramatic Inflections Cards: Questions 305
Cliff Hanger Peer Pressure Fact Sheet 308

**Chapter 7: Counseling Through Activity-Based Experiential Interventions**

Catch It If You Can Cards 322
You've Got a Friend Dilemmas 325
Feelings Fling Feelings Cards 328
Feelings Fling Action Cards 329
Fearless Friends Activity Sheet 336
Get Out from Under It Activity Sheet 344
Identify Yourself Role Cards 349
We Can Work It Out Group Process Sheet 353

# Foreword

If you work with children and adolescents as a professional counselor and are looking for ways to expand your interventions and strategies that will positively impact your clients, you have found a wonderful learning experience in this resource. *Counseling Outside the Lines: Creative Arts Interventions for Children and Adolescents* offers a unique, invaluable, hands-on opportunity to use creative arts interventions that are clinically practical and theoretically based. It is a must read, not only for seasoned professionals, but also for new counselors.

Dr. Ann Vernon has dedicated her life to raising awareness and educating professionals in the counseling field on the best ways to work with children and adolescents in a counseling session. Drawing from her experience as school counselor, clinical mental health professional, and parent, she brings an understanding of how to help youth by implementing developmentally appropriate interventions so they might learn positive coping skills, healthy attitudes, and acceptable behaviors in negotiating the stages of growing up. Her philosophy of counseling children and adolescents is embedded throughout the text, emphasizing that standard counseling techniques, mainly just talking, do not adequately address the needs of the young client. Often, this verbal approach leaves a child or adolescent reluctant to speak or participate. However, as both authors agree and purport, the universal nature of creative arts in a counseling session engages the client, is less overwhelming, and is generally more concrete, relating more appropriately to a child or adolescent client. These three characteristics of creative arts activities are noted in Vernon's list of the *Top 12 Reasons for Using Creative Arts,* which she includes in the introduction and which she applies in each of the activities she and her coauthor, Kathryn L. Barry, describe in the book.

One detail that I am most impressed by is the extensiveness of the content, covering the seven most significant types of creative arts: play and games, music, visual arts, expressive writing, literature, drama, and activity-based experiential interventions. Aside from the well-written introductory section in each chapter, Dr. Vernon and Ms. Barry present specific creative arts interventions for three developmental levels: elementary, middle school, and high school. This organization allows a counselor working in a school to quickly search the activities based on a pending appointment with a student.

At the same time, these activities could be used by therapists working in a mental health facility, hospital, or family setting.

The format of this book is easy, convenient, and thorough. You can quickly understand the rationale for each intervention, the materials needed, and all of the steps needed to make the intervention successful. Handouts or teaching aids are included with each exercise and ready to be copied. Each creative intervention is simple, applicable, and practical. All can be used with boys or girls, and most are applicable to children and adolescents from diverse cultures. Most important, each intervention allows young clients to gain skills, develop insights, and suggest actions that assist them in solving their problems. Such problems include handling stress, valuing themselves, and building coping mechanisms and resilience.

This book does not stop with just giving us all the theory and tools of successful interventions. In the final chapter, nine excellent case studies are provided—three for each developmental level—with examples of creative arts interventions developed specifically for each particular case. How fortunate we are to have this expertise to guide us through these examples in seeing how creative arts interventions can make the difference in working successfully with our young clients.

I have incorporated Dr. Vernon's work for more than 25 years in my own roles as a school counselor and counselor educator. I have employed numerous texts that she has written in my school counselor education classes and have used or adapted many activities similar to those suggested in this book. In every case, the interventions she has designed have provided a road map for success with young clients.

*Counseling Outside the Lines* has the potential to become a classic in the field because it transforms theory into practice in a useful and beneficial way. The financial cost of implementing these interventions is minimal, but their flexible use has great potential to infuse the therapeutic setting with creative energy. In brief, this book asks us as counselors to do what its title suggests: to think "outside the lines" in how we approach the needs of young clients. Most of all, it shows us how we can have fun with children and adolescents when we are able to adapt our work to their world in ways that truly make a difference in their lives. And if we can help just one child feel better, see a problem differently, develop a positive coping strategy, become more resilient in the face of adversity, or smile, then our life's chosen profession is worth it.

Toni R. Tollerud, PhD, LCPC, NCC, NCSC, ACS
Distinguished Presidential Teaching Professor
Northern Illinois University

# Acknowledgments

Writing a book such as this is exhilarating, as well as exhausting. But in the final analysis, the persistence and patience pay off, and after reflecting on the total experience, I feel a great sense of accomplishment. As I reread the interventions that my coauthor and I developed, it reaffirms for me how important it is to use expressive arts interventions with young clients: because they are so much more engaging and effective than more traditional methods. On the basis on many years of clinical and school counseling experience with children and adolescents, we are both strongly convinced that young clients have enormous challenges to contend with, so it behooves professionals to employ interventions that will help them cope with developmental, as well as serious situational, problems in constructive ways.

We would like to acknowledge all the young clients we have worked with over the course of many years because they challenged us to "counsel outside the lines" as we developed strategies to help them address their issues. Many of these interventions are included in this book, along with numerous new ideas. We would like to thank our spouses for understanding how important this project has been to us and for supporting us as we had to forego other activities in order to stay focused on the goal. Last but not least, we would like to thank Research Press for enthusiastically endorsing the proposal for this book and Karen Steiner in particular for being a very patient and outstanding editor.

# Introduction

As counseling practitioners, we have all had the experience of being at a loss for words. In fact, I have a vivid recollection of one of my first days on the job as an elementary counselor. I had gone into a fourth-grade classroom to explain who I was and what elementary counselors did. "Counselors help children with problems they might have, such as not getting along with friends or parents, fighting with brothers and sisters, or worrying about doing well in school," I said. Immediately, a hand shot up, and an adorable boy with curly blond hair said, rapidly, "My mom has been married three times and my dad has been married twice, and now they are getting a divorce. Is this a problem?" I have to admit his question really took me by surprise because problems like this were not very common in the early 1970s in the community in which I was working. Consequently, in my counseling internships I had dealt only with typical developmental problems. I literally was at a loss for words, but obviously I couldn't dodge the bullet, so I took a deep breath and said, "Yes, this is something I can help you with. Let's talk after recess."

Our first counseling session became one of many throughout the year, and although Erik seemed to feel better each time we talked, I felt frustrated because I didn't have a magic wand to wave that would make his situation better. I felt inadequate because I wanted to be more helpful, but I hadn't really been trained to do anything except listen and nod my head and occasionally employ a few behavioral techniques as needed. Back then, counselors didn't really have a "toolbox" of techniques, and there wasn't much difference between the interventions used with adults and those used with children and adolescents. Fortunately, counseling young clients is much different today. The profession has gradually recognized that adult models of assessment and intervention should not be extrapolated to children and adolescents because, in many respects, counseling children and adolescents is quite different from counseling adults. In contrast to the "listen and nod" model, counselors who now work with youth also incorporate a wide array of creative arts interventions that enrich the counseling process in numerous ways.

As Gladding (2011) notes, "Counseling is a creative process that focuses on helping clients make developmentally appropriate choices and changes distinctive to their concerns and situations" (p. vii). When creative or expressive arts interventions such as music, movement, writing, literature, drama, play, and games are incorporated into the counseling process, clients of all ages, but particularly children and adolescents, experience the counseling process in a way that enhances the outcome. These types of interventions are more stimulating and meaningful, helping clients gain new perspectives and skills to address both typical developmental problems and more serious issues: parental divorce and substance abuse, poverty and homelessness, eating disorders and self-injury, violence and sexual abuse, teen pregnancy and chronic illness, and so forth. The unfortunate reality is that far too many children and adolescents must contend with issues such as these, in addition to the typical developmental challenges they experience, as they navigate childhood and adolescence.

## RATIONALE FOR USING CREATIVE ARTS INTERVENTIONS

The counseling profession is now acknowledging that for many clients who seem relatively unaffected by the counseling process, standard techniques alone are inadequate. This profession has been dominated primarily by verbal approaches that are insufficient for clients who may be reluctant or nonverbal or who speak different languages. Consequently, over the years the practice of incorporating creative or expressive arts interventions into the counseling process has become much more popular with a wide variety of populations (Degges-White & Davis, 2011; Malchiodi, 2005).

Degges-White and Davis (2011) stress that "the expressive arts are exceptional in their effectiveness for individuals who represent a wide array of diversities and differences" (p. 4). And because of the universal nature of the creative arts, they can be used with any client, "regardless of gender, ethnicity, ability, age, language, cultural identity, or physical functioning" (p. 5). Expressive arts approaches, like verbal therapies, attempt to facilitate change and problem solving, as well as increase well-being. Furthermore, using nontraditional approaches can expedite diagnosis, prevention, and intervention.

As opposed to more traditional "talk" methods of counseling, creative arts interventions get clients "doing," which helps them experience things from different perspectives and enhances emotional, social, and behavioral growth. Deviating from more traditional counseling approaches increases the probability that the counselor and client will connect in a more meaningful manner, which in turn results in more effective outcomes.

There are several reasons that creative arts interventions are effective with children and adolescents, as described in the following "Top 12 Reasons for Using Creative Arts in Counseling Children and Adolescents":

1. First, children and adolescents are often referred by others, so they may be resistant, reluctant, or anxious about engaging in the counseling process. Imagine being six years old and going to a mental health counselor because your father just abandoned the family. Suppose the counselor asks you how you feel about your dad moving across the country. Perhaps you can't put your feelings into words, and you might not trust this person that you have never met before, so you just clam up and say nothing. But suppose the counselor first puts you at ease by introducing herself through a puppet or suggesting that the two of you play a game to get better acquainted. Wouldn't you feel much more comfortable?
2. Another reason to use creative arts interventions relates to developmental considerations. Because thinking gradually progresses from concrete to abstract, it is essential to employ interventions that are more concrete, even with adolescents, because many youth do not achieve formal operational (abstract) thinking until later in adolescence (Vernon, 2009). Consider the difference between just talking to a 13-year-old girl about emotional ups and downs and sharing a story written by another teenager about riding the emotional roller coaster. When I used the exercise "Like a Yo-Yo" (Vernon, 1998b, p. 185) with my client, she immediately said that this was exactly how she felt and proceeded to give me a more detailed description of her up and down moods. Reading the story enhanced her understanding of what she was experiencing and facilitated her self-disclosure.
3. Anyone working with children in particular knows that their attention spans are limited, so it is much more effective to use interventions that are motivating and engaging. I remember that during my first year as an elementary counselor it was difficult to bring my language down to the level of a seven-year-old who had anger management problems, but it was also challenging to keep him focused during the counseling session. I didn't have many techniques in my toolbox in those days, but now I know how much more effective it would have been to read *Moody Cow Meditates* (MacLean, 2009), a story about how the moody cow used his mind jar to reduce his anger, or to play a hopscotch game called "Adios Anger" (Vernon, 2009, p. 206) to help this child identify ways to manage his anger.
4. Children's ability to remember concepts between sessions may also be limited, and for this reason, creative arts interventions, which are more concrete, are especially effective. Engaging clients in the session through music, games, art, or metaphors helps anchor the concepts in their heads. I recall working with

a 16-year-old who was very upset that his girlfriend hadn't called him the previous night as she had promised. In his mind, she didn't call because she no longer cared about him, she most likely had been out with someone else, and she would probably break up with him. His overgeneralizations blew the problem way out of proportion, and he was unable to entertain the notion that there might have been other reasons that prevented her from calling. As he talked about the problem, he was staring out the window, where there was a bug zapper hanging from the tree. I asked him to imagine that his head was a giant bug zapper and that it "zapped" the negative thoughts before they entered his brain and became entrenched. In this way, he would be more likely to look just at the fact, which was that she hadn't called him, rather than make assumptions. This metaphor was exceptionally helpful to him, and he continued to use it throughout adolescence, in college, and even as a newly married young man! The fact that he had a concrete image facilitated his ability to think more clearly and deal more effectively with his problems.

5. Another compelling reason to use creative arts interventions is that, because of the variety of techniques, it is very easy to address different learning styles. Whereas traditional counseling is characterized by a verbal/auditory approach that can be very limiting, creative arts interventions are visual and kinesthetic in addition to being auditory and verbal. With clients who learn best by doing, engaging them in a role-play, a game, or music and movement is much more effective than just talking. Indeed, in schools, very often the clients who are referred to a school counselor are those whose learning styles are more kinesthetic and tactile as opposed to auditory or visual. These students often experience behavior problems in the classroom due to the fact that most learning environments are structured for the more dominant visual/auditory learner. I remember working with eight-year-old Marcus, who figuratively bounced off the walls when he entered my office after school. I quickly learned that the most effective way to work on his behavior problems was to have him do something active, such as tossing a beanbag into a red bucket if he thought the scenarios I read illustrated positive classroom behaviors or acting out positive and negative ways of responding to his teacher's requests.

6. Not only are creative arts interventions effective in addressing various learning styles, they are also very culturally responsive. As Gladding (2011) states, "The creative arts are truly global and relevant to counselors from multiple settings and backgrounds" (p. ix). This relevance applies to clients from diverse backgrounds as well. Because of the ethnic and racial changes in the fabric of our society, being culturally responsive is impera-

tive. It is a given that clients from diverse cultural backgrounds respond well to the creative arts. For example, the Latino culture uses *cuentos* (short stories) to teach values and social principles, as well as to increase self-esteem and achievement (Ramirez, Jain, Flores-Torres, Perez, & Carlson, 2009). The visual arts also transcend culture and have been used throughout time, as evidenced by ancient cave drawings and Egyptian hieroglyphics. Gladding notes that creative arts interventions that are culturally appropriate help clients develop self-awareness as they learn to express themselves in symbolic ways and that concrete experiences give clients something that helps them relate better to themselves and others.

7. A further reason for employing creative arts interventions with young clients is that they facilitate expression of concerns that may be difficult for them to express. Imagine that you are a five-year-old whose mother just had a baby. You might not be able to tell your counselor how you feel about this, but when he takes you to a play area with a playhouse, dolls, baby strollers, and so forth, you immediately begin to convey how you are feeling about this new addition to your family. Art, music, bibliotherapy, and play techniques are very useful in facilitating expression of concerns that may be hard to articulate, especially for younger children.
8. Creative arts techniques are more interactive, which is very important with children and adolescents, who often need more incentive to engage in the counseling process. I remember working with a very resistant 12-year-old, who sat and stared out the window while I floundered around trying to get a sense of what I could do to help her. It didn't take me long to realize that the "talk and nod" approach wasn't working because I was the only one talking and she wasn't nodding! The one thing I had learned very well over the years was that when something isn't working, don't do more of the same, so I brought out the checkerboard and invited her to play with me, adding that before either one of us could make a move, we had to draw a card from a box and complete an unfinished sentence written on it. The interaction during the game facilitated self-disclosure, as well as helping us to develop rapport.
9. The "hands-on" approach that characterizes many of the creative arts interventions has more impact and is more meaningful than talk. Rather than talking about perfectionism with an eight-year-old, I gave him a tennis ball and asked him to juggle first one, then two, then three balls. After trying this experiment, we then talked about how difficult it was to do this and that it would be hard for almost anyone to do it perfectly. This conversation segued into a discussion about his issues with perfectionism.

10. Especially when working with younger clients, have you ever felt that they were lost or overwhelmed by words? Many times a mismatch occurs when the counselor relies too much on talking. Clients might not be proficient in the language, either because of diversity factors or developmental limitations. Integrating the creative expressive arts into counseling has limitless possibilities for overcoming this mismatch.
11. Being a counselor can be incredibly rewarding, but it is also hard work. It is easy to get overinvolved with your clients' problems. Furthermore, many counselors don't know how to say no, and they try to help everyone who needs it, often at the expense of their own needs. Burnout is not uncommon in this profession, but using creative arts techniques can help prevent this from occurring because the counseling sessions are more engaging and the variety puts some spice into the process.
12. Although all of the preceding reasons justify the use of the creative arts in counseling, we would be remiss not to mention that they are more engaging for both client and counselor! Of course counseling is serious work, but it can also be fun. Years ago I worked with a teenager who had been referred by her teacher because she had horrendous problems with procrastination. Although she was very bright, her grades did not reflect this because she simply did not turn in assignments. During one session I had her pretend that she was the president of the Procrastinators Club. As president, her job was to recruit nonprocrastinators to join her organization. To do that, she needed to make up a brochure listing all the advantages of being a procrastinator. At first she resisted, but I assured her that this could be fun. Once she started thinking of reasons to join, she really got into it. Then I asked her to imagine that she actually was not a procrastinator and that as president of the Non-Procrastinators Club she needed to recruit the procrastinators by coming up with compelling reasons why it is best *not* to procrastinate. After she shared both sets of reasons, I then asked her to make a list of things she procrastinated about. Once that was complete, I asked her to lie down on the floor, and as I read off each item on her list, I placed a large pile of newspapers on her chest to symbolize how things "build up" when you procrastinate. After asking her how she felt under this pile of procrastination, I then told her that she could reduce the pile by identifying something that she could think or do to overcome her reasons for procrastinating. We both ended up laughing throughout the session, and the "out of the box" intervention made the point.

In summary, effective interventions follow the "innovative model," developed by Vernon:

**I** = Innovative

**N** = Need to match the client's learning style

**T** = Target the identified problem

**E** = Engaging and energizing for the client

**R** = Relate to the client's culture and developmental level

**V** = Varied, to keep clients motivated

**E** = Educational and skill oriented

**N** = Need to facilitate change

**T** = Teach emotional and behavioral self-control

**I** = Interesting and intriguing

**O** = Out of the ordinary, as in the creative arts

**N** = Nontraditional, as in the creative arts

## OVERVIEW OF THIS BOOK

The purpose of this book is to facilitate understanding and application of the creative arts in counseling, with specific applications with children and adolescents. Each chapter presents an overview of one of seven creative arts approaches, with numerous examples and suggestions for incorporating each approach with other expressive arts modalities. The following areas are described:

1. Play and games
2. Music
3. Visual arts
4. Expressive writing
5. Literature
6. Drama
7. Activity-based experiential interventions

Following each introductory section, which I wrote, related interventions developed by myself and my coauthor, Kathryn Barry, are presented for specific age groups: elementary, middle school, and high school. There are three interventions for each age group, as well as three for small-group or classroom settings, for a total of 84 interventions. Specific interventions are presented on separate pages in an easy-to-read format that includes the topic addressed, a brief rationale, materials needed, and a step-by-step procedure for implementing the intervention. These interventions address a wide variety of topics, such as dealing with anxiety, anger, depression, underachievement, bullying, peer relationships, self-awareness, behavior awareness, problem solving, goal setting, and much more. For each chapter, the expanded table of contents indicates the developmental level and topic area, providing easy access for counselors looking for a specific topic suitable for a client of a certain age.

Many of these interventions have been used with clients in both mental health and school settings. Experience tells us that these methods work and that clients are more invested in the counseling process when these types of techniques are used. Although these methods are engaging and fun for both client and counselor, it is important to point out that the counseling session is not just "fun and games"; these interventions target specific problems and have been developed to increase the young client's ability to more effectively address both developmental and more serious situational problems.

The last chapter of the book presents nine case studies based on actual clients' problems, with names and other information changed to protect their identity. There are three case studies for the elementary level, three for middle school, and three for high school. Practicing school and mental health counselors have contributed the case studies and background information. I developed interventions to address the targeted problems for each case study, using all seven creative arts approaches in each case to illustrate the versatility and wide applicability of this method of counseling.

*Counseling Outside the Lines* is intended for school and mental health counselors, social workers, school psychologists, and family counselors who work with children and adolescents and are searching for unique and effective interventions to employ with this population. It should also be an invaluable resource for graduate students who want to enhance their expertise and leave their program with a plethora of techniques to use with future clients. It is our hope that the practical information and the numerous interventions presented in this publication will be welcome additions to counselors' toolboxes and that the strategies will be motivating for young clients. As Jacobs (1992) has noted, counseling is a creative process that *can* be and *needs* to be more than just talking. Start "doing" by reading more about counseling and creative arts applications with children and adolescents.

## CHAPTER 1

# Counseling Through Play and Games

Play is a universal experience that children from all cultural groups enjoy. As many experts have claimed, play is the natural language of children (Coker, 2001; Henderson & Thompson, 2011; Kottman, 2009). According to Landreth (1991), "Toys are children's words and play is their language" (p. 116). Through play, children are able to act out conflicts, express thoughts and feelings, develop self-acceptance, learn to solve problems and make decisions, and develop self-efficacy and competence (Kottman, 2009). Play can be a healing as well as a growth process that helps children overcome barriers and cope more effectively with issues that affect their well-being. As Landreth (2002) notes, play is flexible, allowing children to express themselves in a natural way. Consequently, it can "enhance normal development and alleviate abnormal behavior" (Henderson & Thompson, 2011, p. 559).

Think back to your childhood and reflect on your own experiences with play and games. Did you have a vivid imagination as a child? If so, you probably "became" many different people in a given week. One of my mother's favorite recollections is of when I became my best friend's father, who ran a filling station. I dressed up in boots, a raincoat, and a hat and "came home" from the station rubbing my hand over my forehead. When my mother asked me what was wrong, I said I had had a bad day at the station and had a terrible headache! And there was the time when she was coming down to the basement, where my sister and I were playing school. "Out of the way," we shouted as we rushed up the steps. "It's a fire drill . . . we have to get all the kids out of here." We also played house by the hour. In addition to being parents, we were nurses, secretaries, and even pioneers who set up camp when we circled the wagon trains for the night. Fortunately, my mother encouraged this type of play, and I still have vivid memories of these fun-filled times.

I also played games with my siblings and my friends—board games such as Clue or Monopoly, card games such as hearts, or outdoor games such as hide and seek, tag, Red Rover, and so forth. Through these activities, we learned about cooperation, competition, conflict resolution, and compromise. We developed relationships and leadership and communication skills, all of which helped prepare us for life. It is concerning that television, computers, video games, and other forms of technology consume so much of children's time that many don't engage in as much spontaneous or imaginative play as did children in previous generations. And in difficult economic times, when parents are working overtime to make ends meet, it is often easier to park children in front of a machine that entertains them than to interact with them through creative play activities. Consequently, children and adolescents have the expectation that they will be entertained, not only in school but also in counseling sessions. Employing creative arts interventions is a good "hook" to keep young clients motivated while addressing their issues effectively at the same time.

Although we typically think of play as being appropriate for children younger than age 12 (Schaefer, 2002), adolescents as well as adults may benefit from play, especially since individuals of all ages sometimes find it difficult to express themselves verbally (Gallo-Lopez & Schaefer, 2005) or may have learning styles that are more suited to play approaches. And as Cerio (2000) notes, play allows older clients to regress to earlier developmental levels, which is another reason that this approach is not limited to young children. Obviously, the counselor must use play judiciously with adolescents so that they don't find it condescending. As Kottman (2009) has suggested, it might be good to ask older elementary-age children, preadolescents, and young teens if they would rather play a game, play with toys, or discuss their situation. It is also important to point out that the play activities selected for adolescents would be different from those used with younger clients, even though the underlying principles of the approach are essentially the same, according to Cerio.

## ADVANTAGES OF USING PLAY AND GAMES IN COUNSELING

Think back to one of your early experiences with play or games. What were you doing? Not only do I have many memories about my imaginative play, but I also remember other types of play: jumping with my brother and sister for hours on a large tractor tire inner tube, playing jacks with my friends and learning many different techniques for picking the jacks up, and jumping rope to various jump-rope chants. There were rules to follow in jacks, and even in jump rope, such as not stepping on the rope when playing with friends. I had to work hard and practice a lot to be good at these things, so along with being fun and exciting, there was a bit of challenge to these activities.

Obviously, there are many advantages to using play and games in counseling, not only for intervention but also for assessment. Play can make the assessment process much more pleasant for both client and counselor. Rather than drilling the client with a series of questions from an inventory or taking a longer period of time than is preferred to gather the needed information, the counselor can write required questions on game cards and have the client draw them as he or she takes a turn in Jenga, for example. Wagner (2003) stresses that because play is such a fundamental way for children to express themselves, practitioners need to consider the importance of play in assessment. Dolls, puppets, and family figures are invaluable for assessing family dynamics; scary toys such as fierce animal figures facilitate identification of fears; and bop bags, toy weapons, and so forth can be used to assess aggression (Kottman, 2009).

In addition to assessment, other advantages of using play and games interventions include the following:

- Play is engaging and enjoyable (Henderson & Thompson, 2011).
- Play helps children overcome resistance (Kottman, 2001).
- Play helps children work out problems (Bradley, Hendricks, & Crews, 2009; Kottman, 2009).
- Through play, children can practice productive behaviors (Bowman, 2004).
- Children learn communication and social skills through play (Brems, 2002; Kottman, 2009).
- Children can test reality by trying on different roles and selecting solutions (Bradley et al., 2009).
- Games can be challenging and thought provoking and can teach mastery (Bradley et al., 2009).
- Games provide an alternative way of connecting with others (Gladding, 2011).
- Toys provide a safe way to "show" what happened when a child may have been told not to "tell" (Homeyer & DeFrance, 2005).
- Through play, children can act out confusing or conflicting situations and learn to make choices (Thompson, Rudolph, & Henderson, 2004).
- Games are safe and nonthreatening (Gladding, 2011).
- Play and games can be used for assessment as well as intervention (Vernon & Clemente, 2005).

## TYPES OF PROBLEMS AND POPULATIONS THAT BENEFIT FROM PLAY AND GAMES

Although there are some limitations, given the age of the client, to the use of play, counselors are beginning to think outside the box and are more frequently using play media and games with clients of all ages for many different types of problems. Several examples of the benefits of this approach with problems and client populations follow:

- Games can help children and adolescents develop social skills (Henderson & Thompson, 2011; Vernon, 1998a).
- Children and adolescents can learn to deal with grief through play and games (Bullock, 2007; Lowenstein, 2006).
- Games can help adolescents learn effective ways to cope with the transition to high school (Teeter, Teeter, & Papai, 1976, as cited in Gladding, 2011).
- Children can find better ways of coping with fears and separation anxiety through play (Kottman, 2001, 2002).
- Through play, children can work through the feelings and issues resulting from abuse and neglect (Gil, 2006).
- Play can be an effective approach with clients with selective mutism (Spasaro & Schaefer, 2004) and autism (Rogers, 2005).
- Play therapy has been used to help children and adolescents deal with anger and aggression (Johnson & Clark, 2001).
- Play therapy helps children with learning disabilities and improves academic performance (Blanco & Ray, 2011).
- Children and adolescents can develop self-awareness and learn more about family dynamics through play involving dolls, dollhouses, and other family artifacts (Graham & Pehrsson, 2011).
- Play therapy has been used to successfully treat young children with night terrors (Malchiodi, 2005).
- Play therapy can help children deal with trauma and posttraumatic stress disorder (Baggerly, 2007; Gil, 2006).
- Play therapy is an effective approach with children who have chronic or terminal illnesses (Jones & Landreth, 2002).

## PLAY MEDIA AND GAMES VERSUS PLAY THERAPY

It is important to distinguish between play therapy and using play and games to facilitate the counseling process. Play therapy necessitates further study and training (Vernon & Clemente, 2005), and there are specific certification requirements, whereas using toys and games in counseling does not require this degree of preparation. Play therapy is a form of therapy that helps children learn about their experiences in a safe, nonthreatening environment. Kottman (2009) describes play therapy as using "toys and play as the primary vehicle for communication with young children" (p. 123). She stresses that professionals who use play therapy need to think differently so that they can help children communicate effectively using toys and games. According to Kottman, goals of play therapy include increasing clients' self-confidence and self-acceptance, helping them to explore and express their feelings, increasing their decision-making skills, helping them to practice self-control and self-responsibility, and examining alternatives and practicing problem solving with them. Readers interested in learning more about play therapy can consult the website for Play Therapy International (www.playtherapy.org).

Anna Freud was one of the first people to use play therapy with children. Freud's model was based on psychoanalytic theory, and her work was followed by Virginia Axline, who developed nondirective play therapy based on Rogers's client-centered therapy (Homeyer & DeFrance, 2005). Today, there are several different theoretical approaches to play therapy. The first is child-centered play therapy, which is nondirective. In this approach, the counselor's primary role is to convey acceptance and belief in the child. The second approach is Adlerian play therapy, developed by Kottman and based on Adlerian theory. This approach is a combination of nondirective and directive aspects. The play therapist uses a variety of techniques to help the client develop insight into his or her lifestyle and then reeducates the client to help him or her learn new skills (Kottman, 2009). A third approach is cognitive-behavioral play therapy, a more directive method involving diagnosis and structured play to address the issue (Homeyer & DeFrance, 2005). The cognitive-behavioral play therapist's role is to focus on a problem and, through play, help the client learn more adaptive thoughts and behaviors that will result in better problem-solving skills (Kottman, 2009). Two more recent approaches include ecosystemic play therapy and prescriptive play therapy. Ecosystemic play therapy is a developmental and systemic approach that takes into consideration the impact on the client of ethnicity, culture, family, peers, school, and religion (O'Connor, 2000). In prescriptive play therapy, the play therapist prescribes the play therapy technique to meet the child's needs (Homeyer & DeFrance, 2005).

According to Kottman (2009), as well as Landreth, Ray, and Bratton (2009), play therapists use several specific skills. The first is tracking, in which the counselor describes the child's behavior in order to communicate caring. This helps build the relationship with the child. A second skill is restating content, which is similar to paraphrasing. This also helps develop the relationship and conveys understanding to the child. A third skill is reflection of feelings, which helps the client develop a better understanding of his or her emotions. A fourth skill is returning responsibility to the child, which enhances self-reliance and facilitates mastery and self-control. A fifth skill is using the child's metaphor, by which the counselor tracks, restates content, reflects feelings, and returns responsibility to the child through the metaphor. A final skill is limit setting, which is done to protect the child in the environment and helps the child develop a sense of social responsibility.

Play therapists use specific types of toys to facilitate expression of feelings and thoughts and to provide opportunities for reality testing. Kottman (2009) has identified the following categories of play materials:

- Family and nurturing toys, including dolls of different ethnicities; dollhouses and furniture; play dishes; baby bottles and clothes; people puppets, stuffed toys, animal families; and play kitchen appliances. These toys help the child explore family relationships.
- Scary toys, including plastic monsters, snakes, insects, alligators, dragons, and animal puppets such as wolves and bears, to help clients learn to deal with their fears.
- Expressive toys, such as an easel, all types of paints, crayons, fabric scraps, scissors, tape, pipe cleaners, glue, clay, and materials for making masks. Expressive toys help clients express their feelings and their creativity.
- Aggressive toys, including toy weapons, toy soldiers, foam bats, plastic shields, handcuffs, and small pillows for pillow fights, which facilitate expression of anger and aggression.
- Pretend or fantasy toys, which help children explore roles and experiment with different behaviors. Toys in this category include masks, magic wands, dress-up clothes, blocks and building materials, purses, telephones, doctor kits, kitchen items such as pots and pans, puppets and a puppet theater, and jewelry.

Cerio (2000) adds an additional category, rule-oriented toys, which includes board games, darts, skill games, and sports.

Given that the focus of this chapter is on the use of play and games in counseling as opposed to play therapy, which requires specific training, the remainder of this chapter describes how counselors can incorporate play and games into their counseling sessions to promote young clients' abilities to more effectively address troubling issues. As Brems (2002) notes, "Play is perhaps one of the most common techniques utilized by child therapists" (p. 248).

## EXAMPLES OF PLAY AND GAMES INTERVENTIONS

Counselors who use play and games as counseling interventions are limited only by their own creativity. Granted, companies such as Child Therapy Toys, Childswork/Childsplay, the Self-Esteem Shop, and YouthLight, Inc., have excellent games for helping children and adolescents deal with anger, anxiety, bullying, decision making, self-control, divorce, and friendship, for example. However, it is much less expensive and often more effective to think imaginatively and create a game that specifically addresses the issues your client is dealing with. Several general strategies illustrating how to use play and games are subsequently described, followed by more specific and detailed interventions for children and adolescents of various ages.

Interventions intended for use in classrooms and small groups are also presented.

## Rapport Building

Children and adolescents are often reluctant to see a counselor for a variety of reasons, including being embarrassed that they have a problcm, resentful about being referred, or anxious about what will take place. Put yourself in their shoes, and you will understand why play and games are excellent approaches with both children and adolescents. Puppets and stuffed animals work well with younger children. Puppets provide a safe way for children to share feelings, and through puppetry children tell stories and "play out their fantasies" (Orton, 1997, p. 230). Puppets can be used to help children develop communication skills, express feelings, make decisions, and facilitate behavior change. Several different types of puppets can be used: finger puppets, cardboard cutouts, or hand puppets. It is important to consider the ethnicity of the client and select puppets appropriately (Vernon & Clemente, 2005).

In developing rapport with younger adolescents, playing a simple game called "People, Places, and Things" works well (Vernon, 2002, pp. 22–23). Just attach a spinner to the center of a paper plate that is divided into three parts, labeled "People," "Places," and "Things." Take turns spinning the spinner, and when it lands on one of the categories, the "spinner" shares something about himself or herself relative to that category. A good deal of information can be gleaned from this simple strategy.

## X or O?

Another easy game that can be played with children or young adolescents involves drawing a tic-tac-toe board on a sheet of paper. One player (the counselor or client) is X, and the other is O. Before putting a mark on the board, each player must draw a card and answer a question. Questions can be developed specifically to address the client's issues. For example, if the client is having problems with anger, questions can include the following:

- What do you do that lets other people know you are angry?
- How long do you stay angry?
- What's something you do that helps you deal with your anger?
- What do you usually get angry about?
- What do other people do when you get angry with them?
- Do you think you can control your anger, and, if not, what makes it difficult?

The first person to get three Xs or 3 Os in a line is the anger "expert." Several rounds can be played.

### Pick 'em Up

In this game, players take turns picking up straws that contain unfinished sentences written on very narrow strips of paper and slipped into the straw. Depending on how many people play, you might need 20 to 25 straws. Once again, it is best to tailor the sentences to problems the client is dealing with. For example, if a client is struggling with her parents divorcing, sentences such as the following can be used:

- When my parents told me they were getting a divorce I felt . . .
- The worst thing about my parents getting divorced is that . . .
- When I feel very sad about what is happening in my family, I . . .
- Some feelings I have about my parents getting divorced are . . .
- Something that helps me when I feel sad or angry is to think . . . or do . . .
- I wish my parents would . . .

Straws are tossed randomly on a table, and a player needs to pick up one straw without touching others. If successful, he or she takes the question out of the straw and responds to it. If the player touches another straw, he or she forfeits a turn but is asked to share something about himself or herself that the counselor (or others if this is done in a small group) can't tell by looking at him or her. The game continues until all the straws have been picked up. The sentences can be readily tailored to the age of the client.

### Think It Through

This strategy, which is similar to the game Concentration, is a good way to build a relationship, as well as a technique to address specific problems. First, make pairs of cards that you and the client will take turns trying to match up. If there is no match, play is turned over to the other person to try to make a match. When there is a match, the person who turned over the cards responds to the question, takes those cards and puts them in his or her discard pile, and takes another turn, answering the question if there is a match or turning play over to the next player if there is no match. The player with the most cards in his or her discard pile at the end of the game is the "Think It Through" champion. Examples of cards for young adolescents dealing with friendship problems include the following:

- When my best friend doesn't call me, I feel . . .
- If I see my best friend whispering to others, I think . . .
- I get upset if my friends . . .
- One of the best ways to handle conflicts with friends is to . . .
- I think good friends should . . .
- It is important to me that my friends . . .

## Roll It

For this game, you will need one die and 24 index cards numbered 1 to 6 (there will be four cards per number), which should be separated into six piles, with the 1s in a pile, the 2s in another pile, and so forth. To play the game, you and the client (or two or more clients can play instead if you are using this in a group) take turns rolling the die. The player looks at the number on the die and then picks up a card with a corresponding number from one of the six piles. After reading the card out loud, the player responds to the question and puts the card in a discard pile specifically for that number. If during the game a player rolls a number and all the cards have been used, he or she then draws from the discard pile corresponding to the number rolled on the die. In addition to being a good rapport builder with general get-acquainted questions, cards can be tailored to a specific problem. Examples of cards developed for a child with academic problems include the following:

- What is the subject that is most difficult for you?
- How do you feel when you have homework to do?
- What is it like for you when the teacher hands papers back to the class?
- What is one thing you do that helps you concentrate on your schoolwork?
- How do you feel when you try to do something, but it is too hard?
- If you have to stand in front of the class to answer questions, how do you feel?

## Let's Bowl

For this game, most appropriate for children, you will need a plastic bowling set and 35 cards made out of construction paper to match the colors of the bowling pins (7 cards per color, assuming that sets have 2 pins of the same color, 10 pins total). The cards can be tailored to a specific problem, or they can be generic get-acquainted cards, as illustrated by the following:

- One of my favorite things to do is . . .
- Something that makes me laugh is . . .
- Something I don't like to do is . . .
- If I had three wishes, I would wish for . . .
- When I grow up I want to be . . .
- Something that I feel proud about is . . .

To play the game, the client rolls the ball. If one or more pins are knocked down, the client notes the color of the downed pins, picks a card representing each color, and responds to the questions on the cards. The game ends when all the cards have been played, but it can be repeated by reshuffling the cards.

## OTHER EXAMPLES OF PLAY AND GAMES INTERVENTIONS

Children naturally gravitate toward toys and games, so having a basket with puppets, stuffed animals, and various other toys—such as a telephone, dress-up clothes, a magic wand, and so forth—is often an invitation in itself to engage in play. I recall working with a kindergarten child who lived with his grandmother. One day he came into the counseling office and immediately picked up the toy telephone and "called" his father, who didn't come for a weekend visit as he had promised. I learned a great deal about this child's hurt and anger through that conversation and was able to structure some additional interventions to help him deal with the rejection.

Bradley and colleagues (2009) describe the "Name Game" as an intervention that can be used individually or in a small group. On individual index cards, the counselor writes statements that have some relationship to the problems the young client is experiencing. For example, if the child has problems with his or her parents, examples of sentences could include the following:

- When my parents make me do things I don't like to do, I feel mad.
- When my parents let my sister do something that they won't let me do, I feel sad.
- When my mother makes me go to bed early, I feel happy.
- When my dad takes me bike riding, I feel scared.
- When my brother and I fight, I feel excited.

The counselor reads each card, and if the child agrees with the statement, he or she can say, "Me, too" and keep the card. If the client doesn't agree, the card can be discarded. The counselor, of course, encourages discussion about the statements written on the cards.

Gladding (2011) suggests using an "anger ball." When the ball is thrown, the client releases anger by verbalizing something he or she is angry about. This could be followed up with more discussion about the anger and positive ways to cope with it. Vernon (2002, pp. 272–273) has created a game to help clients deal with moving, involving a generic game board and cards such as the following:

- You are moving to a brand new house in a different neighborhood and a different school. You feel . . . because you are thinking . . .
- You are moving from your house to an apartment. You feel . . . because you are thinking . . .
- You are moving from the city to the country. You feel . . . because you are thinking . . .

- You will be leaving behind several good friends when you move. You feel because you are thinking . . .

Each card indicates the number of spaces the client can move after responding, and the counselor encourages discussion about the client's thoughts and feelings.

Sand tray therapy is another variation of play that is used to connect with clients and to help them deal with intrapersonal and interpersonal issues (Henderson & Thompson, 2011; Homeyer & Sweeney, 2005). Counselors using this approach need two sand trays (20 × 30 × 3 inches), one containing wet sand and one containing dry sand. The trays should be painted blue on the inside to simulate water and sky. In addition, they need to include miniature toys representing different categories, such as people, animals, buildings, vehicles, and structures; natural objects such as sticks and shells; and symbolic items. According to Homeyer and Sweeney (2005), the sand tray is a safe medium that facilitates emotional expression and is especially useful for resistant clients or those with poor verbal skills. Through this approach, clients consider possibilities, further their self-exploration, and experience some sense of control.

This kinesthetic and primarily nonverbal experience begins when the counselor invites the client to play with the sand and select from a variety of miniatures. This invitation can be directive or nondirective. For example, the counselor could ask the client to create a scene in the sand or ask the client to work on a specific scene based on a recent event or troubling emotion (Homeyer & Sweeney, 2005). However, what the client creates is entirely of his or her own design. As the client works, the counselor may ask questions, reflect on what he or she is seeing, or remain silent. Homeyer and Sweeney prefer to have more interaction and discussion, using the sand tray creation as a springboard for conversation. According to Gladding (2011), clients typically progress through three stages—chaos, struggle, and resolution—and it is helpful for counselors to track progress by taking pictures of the sand trays at each session. Readers interested in more about this approach should consult Homeyer and Sweeney (2011), *Sandtray Therapy: A Practical Manual.*

## INCORPORATING PLAY AND GAMES WITH OTHER CREATIVE ARTS TECHNIQUES

Play and games can readily be incorporated with other creative arts techniques. For example, after playing a counseling game geared to a client's specific problem, the counselor can invite the client to write about what he or she learned through participating in the game. As a follow up, the counselor could suggest that the client go a step further and take something that he or she learned and put it into action. I recall working with a 10-year-old who was having difficulty anticipating consequences of decisions; some of the choices he was making had far too many negative consequences. Because he wasn't motivated to talk about this problem, I developed a game called "Cross the Line." I put two long lines of masking tape across both ends of the room. I explained to the client that I was going to read some behaviors related to decision making and consequences. His job was to decide whether what I read on a card was a good decision that would help him cross the line or whether it was a decision that could have negative consequences. If he thought it was a good decision, he could run to the line opposite where he was standing and cross it; if he thought it was a bad decision, he had to identify at least one negative consequence and stay where he was. When he was able to cross the line, I put that card in an envelope so that at the end of the game he would have a tangible reminder about which decisions he thought were good ones. For example, he had to decide whether lying to his parents about doing his homework, feeding his dog without being reminded, or taking his brother's favorite toy without asking were good or bad decisions. After he played the game, he wrote a short story describing what he had learned and how it might affect his future decision making.

Play in and of itself engages the client on multiple levels, and often several creative arts interventions are incorporated within the play. If a child is using toys in a play therapy session, he or she may also be role-playing at times. I recall working with a young child to help her deal with her fears about being in the dark. At one point, she was playing with dolls and putting them to bed, role-playing her mother as she explained to her dolls that they didn't need to be afraid because there weren't any monsters in the neighborhood.

Music can also be used in conjunction with play and games. For example, children can play musical chairs as they expand their feelings vocabulary. As in musical chairs, a chair is taken out of the circle each time the music stops, and the person left standing draws a feelings word from a box and describes a time when he or she felt this way. If the feeling is negative, the child talks about how he or she handled the negative feeling (Vernon, 2006, p. 127).

## CLASSROOM OR SMALL-GROUP APPLICATIONS

Using play and games in a small-group setting is an excellent way to introduce concepts that will not only have appeal but will also facilitate acquisition of skills. Bradley and colleagues (2009) have suggested using "Diversity Bingo" to help group members develop awareness about cultural diversity. Lowenstein (2010) has described a game to use during family group sessions that helps family members identify strengths and needs, as well as the "Beach Ball Game," which facilitates communication and understanding among family members as they toss a beach ball back and forth and respond to color-coded questions about life in their family.

Games are also highly applicable in classroom guidance because they are engaging as well as instructional. Consider the difference between talking about cooperation and playing a game that involves cooperation. It doesn't take much to realize that the latter approach is likely to be much more successful because participants are learning as they are doing. For example, children in a classroom can be divided into teams of five to six members and given the task of using a spoon to move three Ping-Pong balls to a bucket at the other end of the room, one ball at a time. To complicate things, each player must place one hand behind his or her back and pass the ball to the spoon of the next team member. If the ball is dropped, team members must discuss what to do and work together to get the ball back on the spoon. Content questions encourage discussion about how team members cooperated to complete their task and how things would have been different if they hadn't cooperated, and personalization questions help them think about their own behavior: Are they generally cooperative or uncooperative (Vernon, 1998a, pp. 291–292)?

Another game that has been used successfully in classroom settings with middle school and high school students is an activity that focuses on decision making and communication skills. Class members are divided into teams of six and are instructed to build a tower that is at least three feet tall. It cannot be anchored to anything except the floor. The only materials are piles of newspapers and magazines and rolls of masking tape. The teams have 10 minutes to plan their project, during which time they can talk but cannot touch any of the materials. Following the planning session, they have 20 minutes to build the tower, but they cannot talk. Once each group has had a chance to showcase its product, discussion centers around how group members felt about doing this, how they communicated when they couldn't talk, how they decided what to do and who would do it, and what roles group members assumed: leader, follower, blocker, supporter, and so forth. Group projects such as this promote team building, cooperation, communication, and problem solving.

## SUMMARY

Countless ways exist to incorporate play and games into individual, small-group, and classroom guidance sessions. As noted, there are numerous advantages to this type of approach with young clients, whose words might best be expressed through toys, puppets, sand tray play, or various games. In fact, because play is the child's language, asking young clients to express themselves verbally can be like asking them to speak a foreign language. As counselors use different play techniques to help clients develop greater self-awareness and skills, healing and growth occur. Consequently, young clients are better equipped to deal with typical developmental issues as well as more serious problems. The interventions described on the following pages—addressing interpersonal relationships, underachievement, anger management, anxiety, and overcoming negative thinking—will, it is hoped, be an asset in your work with children and adolescents.

# Roaring for Clues

**TOPIC** Friendship skills—specifically, being bossy

**RATIONALE** There are times when children get their way when they behave aggressively, especially if their peers are afraid of them. However, this can lead to a pattern of bossy behavior that is not conducive to maintaining friendships. This activity is intended to help the client become more aware of aggressive behaviors and more sensitive to others' feelings.

**MATERIALS**

A lion puppet

A set of Roaring for Clues Cards

An envelope for clue card 1

Roaring for Clues Message

A small box labeled "ROAR," containing a jelly bean or other piece of candy and the Roaring for Clues Message

**PREPARATIONS**

*Clue cards:* Copy the clue cards, glue them to tagboard, then cut apart. At the bottom of each card, on the line provided, indicate where the client can find the next clue (throughout the building or all in one room—for example, clue 2 could be under a chair or outside under a tree; determine this based on the client's age and available time and space). Hide the clues before meeting with the client.

*"ROAR" box:* Put a "pill" (jelly bean or piece of candy) in the box. Also copy the message and put it inside the box. The client can give Leo the pill to get his roar back, and she can refer to the message to help her remember what to do instead of roaring at her friends.

**PROCEDURE**

1. When working with a client who has problems with aggressive behavior, especially around peers, introduce her to Leo the Lion (puppet) and explain that Leo is going to tell her the following story:

> My name is Leo. I am a lion, and I really, really need your help! You see, I have lost my roar, and I am afraid that if I don't find it soon, I will also lose all my friends. I am not just Leo the Lion. I am Leo, the King of the Jungle! I am powerful and in charge, and if I can't roar, no one will be my friend or play with me or know what I want them to do! This is horrible, just horrible! You must help me. Though I could not find my roar, I did find an envelope. Maybe there is something inside it that will give me a clue about where to find it.

2. Have Leo hand the envelope with clue 1 to the client and tell her to open it. Inside she will see the first of a series of clues that will lead her on a scavenger hunt to help find Leo's ROAR, as well as to learn some things about being a better friend. Each clue will give her an example of an inappropriate behavior that Leo is guilty of with friends, most often being too aggressive and bossy, and which Leo has come to believe is what friends expect and prefer.
3. Begin by having the client (or Leo if the client is too young) read clue 1 and discuss what she thinks it means that Leo needs to be more sensitive and listen to others. Ask her if she or anyone she knows ever has problems like this, encouraging her to elaborate so that she will personalize the messages inherent in the scavenger hunt clues.
4. Then have her read where to find clue 2 and go to that location. Have her read this card and encourage discussion about the question posed in the clue. Then have her read where to find clue 3 and go to that location. Proceed in this manner with the remainder of the clues, involving the client in discussion about the content of each clue before moving on to the next.
5. When she finds the box labeled ROAR, tell her to open the box and read the instructions inside, which indicate that she should pretend to give the "pill" to Leo to help him get his ROAR back. Then Leo should say:

   > I thought I would be really happy when I got my roar back, but now I am a little nervous about it. I always thought everyone liked the way I roared about, making them do things my way. But now I am not so sure. What do you think?

6. At this point, engage the client in a discussion about Leo's question. Ask what she learned about friendship from Leo and encourage her to share how she might be able to use these ideas to help her get along with her friends. As much as possible, get her to personalize and apply the concepts to herself. In closing, give her the box with the message and put all of the other clues inside as

well. She can take this with her to help her remember what she learned about getting along with friends based on Leo's experience.

# Roaring for Clues Cards

**CLUE 1**

Leo thinks he must find his roar
Or he'll lose his friends forevermore!
But the truth he will learn as his search follows through,
And he listens to and solves each clue.
Roaring is not all it's cracked up to be.
Leo needs to be sensitive
And listen to others, you see!

You will find CLUE 2 here: ______________________________

**CLUE 2**

Leo is a really good runner, and he is really funny. He makes everyone laugh a lot, and when he wants to, he can be very kind. But when he roars he is very scary! He thinks everyone likes him and wants to be his friend because of his big roar and because he is King of the Jungle. Do you think that's how his friends feel about his roar? Do you think they like him because of his roar?

You will find CLUE 3 here: ______________________________

**CLUE 3**

Leo picks who he wants to play with each recess and before and after school. If that person says he or she wants to play with someone else, he ROARS, "You will play with ME this recess or else you will NEVER, ever be my friend again!" What do you think about Leo saying this? What would be a better way to respond to his friend?

You will find CLUE 4 here: ______________________________

**CLUE 4**

When Leo wants to play something different from what his friend wants to play, he just ROARS loudly, "NO WAY! WE WILL PLAY WHAT I WANT TODAY!" Tell Leo how you would feel if you always had to play what your friend wanted to play and he or she would never do what you wanted.

You will find CLUE 5 here: ______________________________

**CLUE 5**

If friends play four square or another game with Leo and Leo doesn't win, he gets mad and says that they cheated, even though they didn't and he knows it. It really hurts their feelings. Can you tell him how you would feel if he said that to you? Maybe Leo will talk to you about why he does this.

You will find CLUE 6 here: ______________________________

**CLUE 6**

When the bell rings at the end of recess, Leo ROARS, "Get out of the way! I am first!" and everyone lets him go first. Leo thinks they let him go first because they like him. Do you think that is why they let him go first? After discussing this last question,you will find a box with some advice about how to help Leo get back his roar.

You will find the box here: ______________________________

# Roaring for Clues Message

**ROAR!!**

**R**esist

**O**verpowering

**A**nyone by

**R**oaring!!

**INSTEAD—BE KIND!**

**B**efore you speak, think of others.

**E**veryone likes different activities, so let others choose, too.

**K**ids don't like to play with "sore losers," so congratulate them when they win.

**I**n lining up, remember: Everyone likes to be first, not just you.

**N**ever forget: You can't force people to like you. You have to earn it.

**D**on't forget to treat others the way you would like them to treat you!

# Race for Results

**TOPIC** Underachievement

**RATIONALE** During the elementary school years, children are continually learning new skills, which can be overwhelming for some. They may develop poor study habits or not have the persistence it takes to achieve well in school. They may not know what will help them improve their performance. This game, adapted from Vernon (2002, pp. 202–203), focuses on habits that affect achievement, both helpful and unhelpful.

**MATERIALS** Game board (copy and use the generic version in the appendix or create your own)

A small toy car, used as a game marker

A set of Race for Results Game Cards

**PREPARATIONS** Copy the game cards, glue them to tagboard, then cut apart. Reproduce the game board in a larger format if you wish.

**PROCEDURE**

1. It is helpful for an underachieving client to learn to distinguish between helpful and unhelpful study habits, which he will have an opportunity to do as he plays the Race for Results Game.
2. To begin, explain to the client that he will be playing a game that involves moving his car around the race track. First, he should put his car on the start space, draw one of the cards from the pile, and read it out loud. He needs to think about whether the card describes something that will help him get his schoolwork done well or whether it won't. If he correctly identifies it as a helpful skill, he can move ahead two spaces. If it isn't a helpful skill, he puts that card in a separate discard pile, stays at the START line, and draws other cards until he is able to move forward for the first time. Then he follows this same procedure, moving ahead two spaces if it is a helpful skill and moving back one space if it isn't, until he reaches the finish. Throughout the game, engage him in discussion about how he decided whether it was a helpful

or unhelpful skill, whether these are skills he uses and, if so, with what results, and so forth.

3. If, after all the cards have been drawn, the client still is not at the finish line, he can take the cards from the unhelpful-skills discard pile and suggest a better skill, thus advancing another space. The game continues until he reaches the end.
4. Debrief by asking the client what he learned about helpful versus unhelpful study skills and suggest that he identify two skills he would like to work on to help him achieve better in school.

## Race for Results Game Cards

| | |
|---|---|
| The assignment looks hard, so you just give up. | The assignment is boring, so you do some of it, take a short break, and do the rest. |
| The assignment is so boring you watch television instead. | You keep your assignment sheet in the front pocket of your backpack. |
| You lose your assignment sheet. | You listen to what the teacher says. |
| You forget to take home your back-pack. | You keep your papers neat and orga-nized in separate subject folders. |
| Your writing is sloppy, but you don't correct it. | You study hard for tests. |
| You don't do your homework. | You take time to proofread your papers. |
| You rush through homework so you can play. | You do all your homework each day so you won't fall behind. |
| You stuff all your papers into the same folder. | You take your time to do your home-work, even though you would rather be done so you can play. |

| | |
|---|---|
| You don't study for tests. | You usually remember to take your backpack home. |
| You don't proofread the work you hand in. | You ask for help if you don't understand something. |
| Your neighbor is talking to you, and you send him a note back instead of paying attention to the teacher. | You ask your parents to go over your spelling words with you. |
| The work looks hard, but you keep trying. | You take your time when you write so that it is done neatly. |

# Pathways to Peace

**TOPIC**

Anger management

**RATIONALE**

Children need to understand that anger is a commonly experienced emotion but that keeping anger bottled up or expressing it in unhealthy ways can be problematic. This game will teach clients some strategies for recognizing and expressing their anger.

**MATERIALS**

Pathways to Peace Game Board

A game marker and a die

A set of Pathways to Peace Consequence Cards

A set of Pathways to Peace Trigger Cards

A set of Pathways to Peace Skills Cards

Several puppets for role-plays

**PREPARATIONS**

Copy the game board and game cards. Glue the cards to tagboard, then cut apart. Reproduce the game board in a larger format if you wish.

**PROCEDURE**

1. When a client is referred to counseling for anger management, ask her if she thinks her life would be more peaceful if she did not get angry and lose her temper so frequently. Explain that there are lots of ways to control her anger, which she will learn while playing a game.
2. Give her a marker and ask her to place it on the START space on the game board. Then have her roll the die for her first turn, moving the designated number of spaces as indicated on the die. As she moves to the various spaces, she needs to follow the dirctions on both the game board spaces and the Consequence, Trigger, and Skills Cards that she will draw when indicated on the game board. When a space directs her to role-play, she may do this with the puppets, with you, or by herself, if that is fitting. She can also use props in your office, such as a telephone, pencil and paper, and so forth, if appropriate.

3. Let her continue to play the game until she reaches the end. Then discuss what she learned about managing her anger and how she thinks she might be able to use these ideas each time she starts getting angry.

# Pathways to Peace Game Board

*Pathways to peaceful changes. Look here for skills and strategies.*

| | | | |
|---|---|---|---|
| You did not stop to think before you re-acted to a trigger! **Go back 1 space.** | Draw a TRIGGER CARD, then draw a SKILLS CARD. Is this a skill you could use for this trigger situation? WHY/WHY NOT? **Move ahead 2!** | Draw a CONSEQUENCE CARD. Role-play the scene with your answer to **move ahead 1 space.** | Give an example of something pleasant and relaxing that you could think about to distract you from your anger. **Move ahead 1 space.** |
| Draw a CONSEQUENCE CARD. Role-play the scene with your answer to **move ahead 1 space.** | Demonstrate how you would take four slow and deep breaths to calm down. **Move ahead 1 space.** | Draw a TRIGGER CARD, then draw a SKILLS CARD. Is this a skill you could use for this trigger situation? WHY/WHY NOT? **Move ahead 2!** | Draw a CONSEQUENCE CARD. Role-play the scene with your answer to **move ahead 1 space.** |
| Give an example of a time when you told someone your feelings (or should have). **Move ahead 1 space.** Act it out and **move ahead 2!** | Draw a CONSEQUENCE CARD. Role-play the scene with your answer to **move ahead 1 space.** | Give an example of a time when you were angry and use an "I-message" to say how you felt. **Move ahead 1 space.** Act it out, and **move ahead 2!** | Draw a TRIGGER CARD, then draw a SKILLS CARD. Is this a skill you could use for this trigger situation? WHY/WHY NOT? **Move ahead 1!** |
| START HERE | Draw a TRIGGER CARD, then draw a SKILLS CARD. Is this a skill you could use for this trigger situation? WHY/WHY NOT? **Move ahead 2!** | How can you tell when you are beginning to get angry? Where do you feel it? **Move ahead 1.** | THE BIG FINISH |

# Pathways to Peace Consequence Cards

### Consequence Card

You told your two best friends a secret and they promised not to tell, but they did, and now the whole class knows. You decide to:

a. Yell at them and tell them off at recess.

b. Calmly tell your friends how you feel.

c. Listen to their story and accept their apology.

d. Cry about it.

### Consequence Card

A kid calls you a loser, so you:

a. Call him a worse name.

b. Threaten to beat him up after school.

c. Tell him, "It takes one to know one."

d. Act as if you don't hear him.

### Consequence Card

You and your brother are watching your favorite TV show. You go to the bathroom, and when you return, he has changed the channel. You:

a. Slug him.

b. Call him a name and go tell a parent.

c. Use an "I-message" to express yourself.

d. Quietly count to 10 to help you stay calm.

### Consequence Card

While you are playing your favorite video game, your mother asks you to take out the trash. You have a really good score and don't want to stop. You decide to:

a. Keep playing until she gets mad.

b. Take out the trash now.

c. Try to finish the game before she gets mad.

d. Ask her if you can just play a few more minutes.

### Consequence Card

You study hard for your spelling test, and you still fail it. Even worse, one of the kids sees your grade and says, "You must be the dumbest kid in the class!" You:

a. Tell her she is the ugliest.

b. Tell her that you feel hurt when she says that.

c. Say you will "shut her up" later.

d. Tell the teacher.

### Consequence Card

A friend promises to play with you at recess, but when recess comes, she is playing with another group of kids, and they say you can't play. You:

a. Use an "I-message" to state your feelings.

b. Say you don't care because they are losers.

c. Tell the teacher they aren't being nice.

d. Ignore them and find someone else to play with.

### Consequence Card

While you are waiting in line for lunch, three older kids cut in line in front of you. You:

a. Tell them how you feel about it.

b. Ignore it.

c. Tell them they are acting like jerks.

d. Tell an adult.

### Consequence Card

Another student in your class broke the school camera but is making you take the blame for it. You know she did it. You:

a. Threaten to beat her up if she won't confess.

b. Tell her how you feel with "I-messages."

c. Ignore her and ignore your anger.

d. Tell someone else what really happened.

## Pathways to Peace Trigger Cards

**Trigger Card**

Your little brother scribbled in your reading book, and you get in trouble for it at school.

**Trigger Card**

You lose the spelling bee to another student. You know the other student was cheating.

**Trigger Card**

Your friend is having a birthday party, but you are not invited.

**Trigger Card**

Several of your friends are not speaking to you. You just found out that it is because someone was spreading a rumor about you that isn't true.

**Trigger Card**

Your big sister borrowed your favorite CD without asking you and put a scratch in it.

**Trigger Card**

You left your homework paper at home, and now you have to stay in at recess to do the work over.

**Trigger Card**

You worked really hard on your homework for an hour and a half last night but lost it on the way to school. Even worse, your teacher doesn't seem to believe you.

**Trigger Card**

The girl behind you was talking, and when you turned around to tell her to be quiet, the teacher yelled at you.

**Trigger Card**

Your uncle teases you in front of your friends about something you did when you were little.

**Trigger Card**

At recess when the kids pick teams, you are the last one to be picked. To make it worse, one of the kids on your team makes a comment, calling you "Last-Time Loser."

| | |
|---|---|
| **Trigger Card**<br>When you are walking home from school, a bully grabs you and throws you into the mud. | **Trigger Card**<br>Your mom made you go change your shirt after breakfast because you spilled milk on it, and then you missed the bus. |
| **Trigger Card**<br>Someone trips you in the hallway, and you fall down in front of all of your friends. | **Trigger Card**<br>The neighbor kid, who is a year older than you and really cool, asks you to go bike riding, but your mom says you have to clean your room up instead. |
| **Trigger Card**<br>An older kid laughs at your new haircut and says you look like a dork. | **Trigger Card**<br>A bunch of kids teased you about your new haircut. One of them called you "Buzzhead," and the name stuck. For the rest of the week that's what everyone has called you. |

## Pathways to Peace Peace Skills Cards

**Skills Card**

Self-talk is helpful when you are beginning to get upset. For example:

- I don't have to handle this alone. I can ask for help.
- I want to be the one in charge of my behavior, not them.

**Skills Card**

Self-talk is helpful when you are beginning to get upset. For example:

- If I don't stop and think before I act, I might regret it.
- Just ignore them! They are trying to upset me, so I won't let them.

**Skills Card**

Ignore the person or the situation: This will often work, especially if the person is just trying to annoy you. If you try this strategy, it often helps to move away from the person or the situation.

**Skills Card**

Learn some conflict resolution and problem-solving skills. For example:

State your feelings by using an "I-message."

I feel ______________ because ______________,
and I would like it if ______________.

**Skills Card**

Don't blame others or make threats. Blame sounds like "You were cheating." Instead, say, "You got in line in front of me."

Do say how you feel and what you want (for example, "Please don't call me names").

**Skills Card**

Distract yourself from your anger. For example:

- Count to 10 slowly: This gives you time to think and takes your mind off your anger.
- Take deep breaths: This helps you calm down.
- Think of something happy and/or relaxing: This calms you down and takes your mind off your anger.

**Skills Card**

Act "as if": Look around for someone close by who is not angry and act like this person. Make your face and body look and act like his or hers!

**Skills Card**

Learn the early warning signs of anger in your body: Where do you experience anger in your body? Do you feel hot? Does your stomach get upset? Does your jaw tighten? Do your shoulders feel tense?

Alternate tensing and relaxing that body part until you have control over it.

**Skills Card**

Express how you feel in positive ways. For example:

- Talk to a friend about how you feel and what you would really like.
- Write down your feelings in a letter to the person you are upset with.
- Write your feelings in a journal or in a letter to someone who might be able to help.

**Skills Card**

Draw a picture of your anger. You can draw a picture of an angry face or something you are angry about. Then you can fold it up and put it aside or throw it away if you think you can let go of some of that anger.

# Knock Down Anxiety

**TOPIC**

Anxiety

**RATIONALE**

Adolescents are often overwhelmed by anxiety, which can prevent them from enjoying new experiences. This intervention uses a familiar game to help the client identify irrational beliefs related to anxiety and then dispute them.

**MATERIALS**

A stacking block game such as Jenga or Tumbling Towers

A set of Knock Down Anxiety Cards

15–20 blank index cards

A pen or pencil

**PREPARATIONS**

Copy the Knock Down Anxiety Card page, glue it to tagboard, then cut the cards apart.

**PROCEDURE**

1. When the client begins to discuss something he is anxious about, help him identify some specific thoughts that lead to his anxiety. For example, if he is anxious about giving a speech in English class, he might be thinking:
   - I know I will mess up and embarrass myself, then I will never be able to show my face again.
   - I will be the worst one in the class! I just know it!
   - The other kids will make fun of me.
2. As the two of you are identifying these thoughts, write each one on a blank index card. When you have identified many or most of the client's irrational beliefs related to this first issue, move on to another issue and identify beliefs associated with that problem. Continue this process with other problems related to the client's anxiety.
3. Next explain that the two of you are going to play a game to help him identify and dispute thoughts that make him feel anxious. Discuss how it is not the events that happen in our lives that cause our anxiety but how we think about those events. For example,

when he has to give a speech in class, instead of assuming that the other kids will make fun of him, he could tell himself that others are probably a little nervous, too, so everyone will be in the same boat. Or he could think that even if someone does make fun of him, it isn't the end of the world because it has happened before and he survived. You might want to have the client practice disputing another thought or two before initiating the play.

4. Then begin the game by asking him to place three blocks flat on the playing surface, adjacent to each other. Then have him place the next three blocks on top of them but in the opposite direction. Have him continue to make layers in this manner until all the blocks are used, creating a tower. When the tower is complete, explain that the two of you will take turns drawing a card with an irrational belief written on it—either one that the two of you identified as he discussed his issues or one of the Knock Down Anxiety Cards, which are more generic in nature but may relate to his issues and give him more practice in disputing in case he didn't identify many of his own anxieties. Before a block is removed from the tower, the irrational belief must be disputed. (By participating in the game, you can model the process.) Stress that blocks cannot be removed from the top level and that any block that is removed has to be placed on the top level. If you are successful, none of the blocks will fall. However, if at any time one of you removes a block and inadvertently knocks down any other blocks, the game is over (depending on time, he can rebuild and start again).
5. When the tower is knocked down, emphasize to the client how he can knock down his anxiety by not thinking that the worst will happen or assuming things without checking out the facts. But even when something he is anxious about actually does happen, ask him if it was as awful as he thought it might be. Point out that the tower that was knocked down can be rebuilt and that when he gets anxious about something, he can "rebuild" by disputing his irrational thinking, which will help him be less anxious.

## Knock Down Anxiety Cards

| | |
|---|---|
| It's awful that I have to do homework every single night. | This is the worst thing that could ever happen! |
| A good friend should always keep your secrets. | I will never understand this subject. |
| It's not fair that my parents expect me to get all As and Bs. | I just know that everyone will laugh at me. |
| I can't stand the way they treat me! | I can't do anything right. |
| I should have gotten a perfect score on my test. | There is no point in trying. |
| If I don't get an A, I am a loser. | If I am not accepted by my peers, then I do not count. |

# Grand Slam!

**TOPIC** Interpersonal relationships

**RATIONALE** Early adolescence is an extremely vulnerable time. Peers are very important to adolescents, and yet they may lack the basic social skills needed to maneuver through relationships when conflict arises. These same difficulties may be present in relationships with adults. This intervention will address social skills deficits and remedies.

**MATERIALS** Grand Slam Pitch Questions

Grand Slam Ball Field and Scoreboard

A deck of playing cards (Remove the aces from the deck.)

At least eight game markers (Client will use a marker each time he draws a card, but the markers will return to home plate when he brings a "runner" in.)

**PREPARATIONS** Copy the Grand Slam Ball Field and Scoreboard and glue it to a sheet of tagboard. Reproduce this item in a larger format if you wish.

**PROCEDURE**

1. As the client begins discussing his relationship problems, explain that one of the things that makes relationships so challenging is that they are complicated and that developing good relationships takes practice. This intervention, which is a game called Grand Slam, will give him an opportunity to learn how to handle challenging relationship issues.
2. Show the client the ball field and place the card deck face down in front of him. Explain that each time he draws a card, he will be "batting," just as if he is playing baseball, using the following guidelines:
   - Drawing a 2, 3, or 4 of any suit is a single.
   - Drawing a 5, 6, or 7 of any suit is a double.
   - Drawing an 8, 9, or 10 of any suit is a triple.
   - Drawing a jack, queen, or king is a home run.

The questions are grouped by topic as follows:

- **Singles:** Recognizing the qualities of good relationships and how to contribute to and maintain good relationships
- **Doubles:** Recognizing bullying and harassment and knowing how to handle issues centered around it
- **Triples:** Handling conflict and solving problems in relationships
- **Home runs:** Handling peer pressure and making good decisions in relationships

3. Have the client draw a card, then "pitch" him a question to answer from the appropriate category on the list of Grand Slam Pitch Questions. Encourage elaboration and role-playing so that he thoroughly addresses each question and fully understands the relationship concepts. When he has answered a question, he may place his game marker on the appropriate base, then draw another card and start with a new marker. Eventually the markers will return to home plate as he continues to move around the board. Be sure to have him keep score as is usually done in baseball, marking the score on the board under "Runs."
4. At the end of the game, discuss what he has learned about relationships and what skills he would be willing to begin practicing.

# Grand Slam Pitch Questions

## Singles (2s, 3s, or 4s of any suit): Recognizing the qualities of good relationships and how to contribute to and maintain good relationships

1. Name a person you admire who makes good choices and has a good influence on you.
2. Think of someone you really care about. Name one way you could show the person you care.
3. Are there rules that should never be broken in a friendship (or other relationship)?
4. How can you tell if someone really likes and cares about you?
5. Name two things that make you a good friend.
6. How can you show someone you like but don't know very well that you would like to be friends?
7. Name two friends and something you have in common with each of them.
8. True or false? A good friend should always listen to you when you have a problem.
9. Think of one of your friends (or adult relationships) and name two of this person's strengths that you admire.
10. What is the most important quality to you in a good relationship?
11. What is the hardest part of making new friends for you?
12. What are some ways that you could meet and make some new friends?
13. What is something you could do to improve your relationship with the adults in your life?
14. Give an example of how people show respect for each other's differences in relationships.
15. What is something you could do to show your parent(s) that you respect them?
16. How might you cheer up a friend?
17. How are you the same as your friends? How are you different? (Restate this question, changing the word *friends* to *parents* or *other relationship partner.)*

## Doubles (5s, 6s, or 7s of any suit): Recognizing bullying and harassment and knowing how to handle issues centered around it

1. What would you think if you saw one of your good friends bullying someone?
2. How do you feel when you see someone being bullied?
3. A new family moved to town from Haiti. A friend made a couple of racist jokes about them. What do you think about this?
4. If someone is continually threatening you and you are afraid, what could you do?
5. If one of your friends was being a bully to someone else, what would you do?
6. If a friend of yours was being bullied, how might you help him or her?
7. You and your friends saw a girl fall into a mud puddle and get her pink sweatpants all muddy. Everyone laughed at her, so you did, too. Someone later said that was bullying. Do you agree or disagree? If it was, what, if anything, should you do?

8. How do you feel when you are being teased?
9. Do you think that teasing and bullying are the same thing? Why or why not?

### Triples (8s, 9s, or 10s of any suit): How to handle conflict and solve problems in relationships

1. Your friend was calling a group of younger students "dweebs," and you were really uncomfortable with it. How could you handle the problem?
2. You heard from several people that one of your good friends has been saying bad things about you behind your back. What should you do?
3. You ask your parents for advice with a friendship problem. Good or bad idea? Why?
4. If you are having problems with a friend and you have tried everything you can think of to solve it (talking to him or her, talking to another friend, giving him or her time to cool off, having a friend talk to him or her, etc.), who is someone you could go to for help?
5. If a friend accused you of something, but you didn't do it, what would you do?
6. "Attack the problem, not the person." This is a familiar expression. What do you think it means?
7. What do you think are the common causes of fights between friends?
8. When kids and parents have problems communicating, some people call it the "generation gap." What do you think this means? Do you agree that there is one?
9. Tell about a time you have had to apologize. Did you find it difficult? Is it important to relationships?
10. What is the most hurtful thing anyone has ever said or done to you?

### Home runs (jacks, queens or kings of any suit): Handling peer pressure and making good decisions in relationships

1. Your friends want you to hang with them at the football game. But you know that you need to stay home and work on the science project you have been procrastinating about. Practice what you would say to them when they ask you to go to the game.
2. You've been invited to a party where there will be drinking. How will you handle it? Role-play what you will say to your friends.
3. One of your friends frequently makes racist remarks or tells racist jokes. You finally decide you need to say something about it, but you don't want to offend him. Practice telling him how you feel. You may find using an "I-statement" helpful—for example:

   I feel____________________ when you____________________

   because____________________, and I would like____________________.
4. Your friend passes you a note in science class and wants you to write an answer and pass it back. But you don't want to get in trouble. What do you do?
5. You just started hanging out with someone recently whom you really like a lot and want to become good friends with. But last night he called and asked you to skip school with him on Friday. You really don't want to do it, but you don't want him to think you are a chicken, and you still really want to be friends with him. How should you handle this?
6. Is there a difference between joking around and harassing? If so, what is the difference?

## Grand Slam Ball Field and Scoreboard

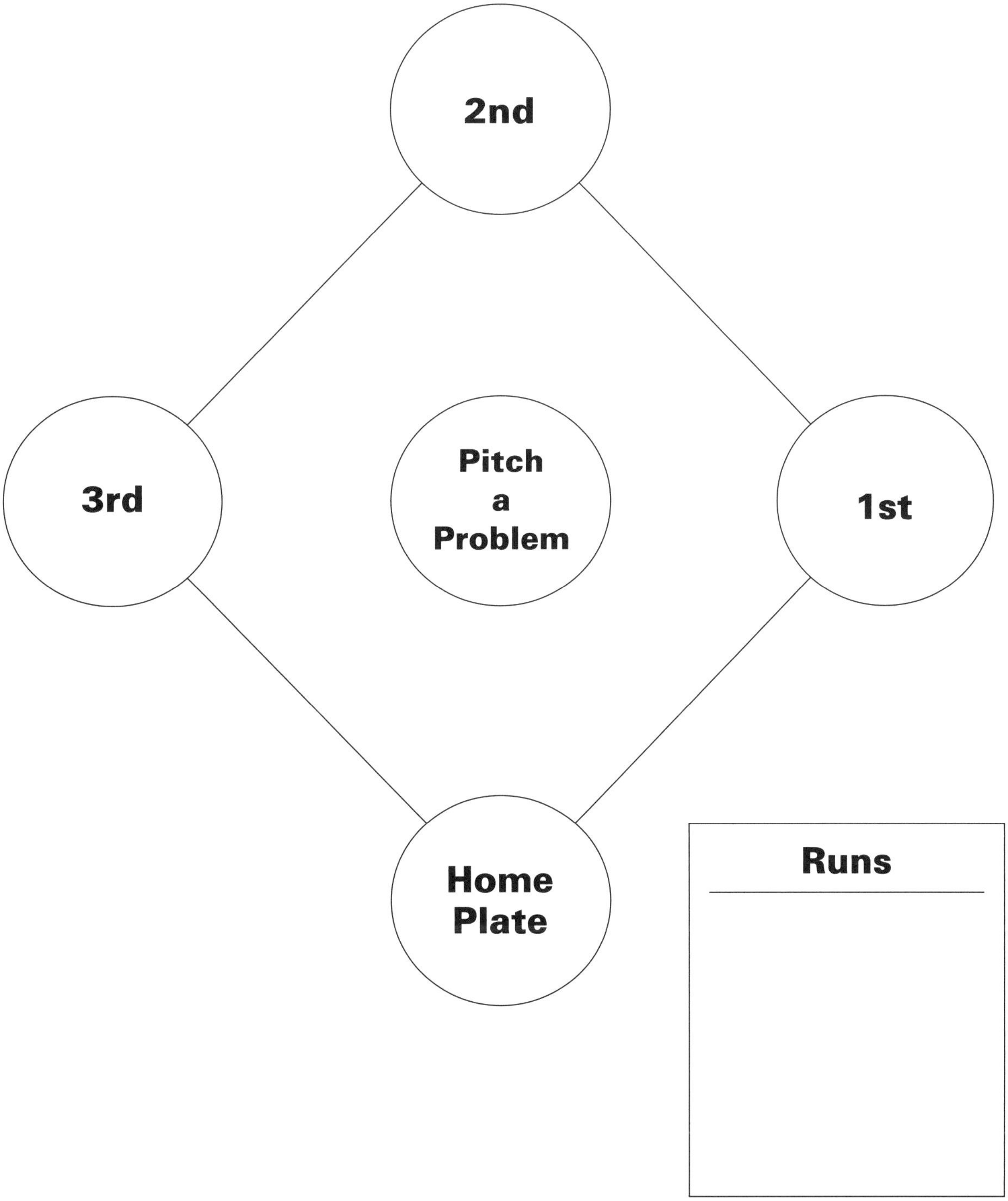

# Fact or Fiction Tic-Tac-Toe

**TOPIC** Anger management

**RATIONALE** Adolescents are often overwhelmed by a roller coaster of emotions during this very turbulent time in their lives. For many of them, the anger they experience can be very frightening because it feels as if they have no control over it. It can be very reassuring to learn some of the facts and myths about anger and to realize that they do have some control.

**MATERIALS** A copy of the Fact or Fiction Tic-Tac-Toe Board

A set of Fact or Fiction Tic-Tac-Toe Cards

A pen or pencil

**PREPARATIONS** Copy the Fact or Fiction Tic-Tac-Toe Board and cards and glue them to sheets of tagboard. Cut the cards apart.

**PROCEDURE**

1. When the client talks about her anger, explain to her that one reason anger is a problem for people is that they lack information—there are lots of myths and misunderstandings about anger. For example, some people think that anger is wrong, but actually it is a frequently experienced emotion. There are, however, unhealthy ways to express it. Ask your client to describe how she experiences and expresses her anger.
2. Show your client the tic-tac-toe board and explain that the two of you will be playing Fact or Fiction Tic-Tac-Toe. It is played the same as the regular game of tic-tac-toe except that, before an X or O can be put down, the player must respond to a question related to the topic of anger.
3. Proceed to play the game, encouraging discussion about each of the client's responses to the questions. When it is your turn, you can provide more information relative to the content on the card.
4. When the game is finished, discuss what the client learned about anger and how she can apply these concepts to her own life.

## Fact or Fiction Tic-Tac-Toe Cards

**Fact or Fiction?**

Talking over and over about the event or someone you are angry with helps you get over the anger.

**Fact or Fiction?**

Sometimes it is best to keep your anger inside so that you don't hurt anyone or anything.

**Fact or Fiction?**

Anger is universal. All people get angry over the same things.

**Fact or Fiction?**

It can be exciting to get angry.

**Fact or Fiction?**

It is possible to learn to control your anger by controlling your thoughts.

**Fact or Fiction?**

Anger is often called a "secondary emotion." This means that there are other feelings such as hurt, fear, and powerlessness underneath it.

**Fact or Fiction?**

Anger can be reduced if you think rational, sensible thoughts.

**Fact or Fiction?**

One strategy for dealing with an anger problem is to get familiar with signals your body gives you.

**Fact or Fiction?**

You can't help getting angry about some things, such as when something happens that you think is unfair.

**Fact or Fiction?**

Some people enjoy being angry because it makes them feel powerful to have people who are afraid of them.

**Fact or Fiction?**

Anger has positive and negative points.

**Fact or Fiction?**

One of the things that helps to control anger is knowing what triggers it.

**Fact or Fiction?**

Techniques for self-calming such as focused breathing, meditation, self-talk, and others can actually be very helpful.

**Fact or Fiction?**

It is important to develop a feelings-word vocabulary so that when you are angry you will have the tools you need to express your feelings without being violent.

**Fact or Fiction?**

There are times when the best thing to do if you are really angry is to get away from your problems—stay away from the person you are angry with until you are calm enough to handle things better.

**Fact or Fiction?**

Coloring mandalas, taking a hot bath, or going for a walk don't help you calm down when you are angry.

# Fact or Fiction Tic-Tac-Toe Board

# POSITIVE Hoops

**TOPIC** Overcoming negative thinking and behaving

**RATIONALE** While trying on various roles in an effort to find their identities and establish themselves as separate from their parents, adolescents will sometimes develop a habit of negativity. No matter how much is right in a situation, they tend to focus only on what is wrong. This can be irritating to those around them, but, more important, it is not a good habit to develop. This intervention will help to raise their awareness of the problem, as well as help them develop strategies for addressing it.

**MATERIALS** An over-the-door basketball hoop with a foam ball (If confidentiality can be maintained, play outside with a real basketball and hoop.)

A copy of the POSITIVE Hoops Situations

Envelopes

A glass half full of water

A copy of the Tips for Thinking POSITIVE page

**PREPARATIONS** Copy and cut the POSITIVE Hoops Situations page into eight strips, one per letter. Put each strip in a separate envelope and label each with the appropriate letter. Put the half-full glass of water on the table.

**PROCEDURE**

1. When your client begins to complain about a situation that has many positives but in which he can see only the negatives, draw his attention to the glass of water. Explain to him that most people would describe the glass of water in one of two ways: either as half full or half empty. The people who say it is half full are usually referred to as optimists; they are people who tend to see the good side of everything. Those who see the glass as half empty are pessimists. Pessimists notice the negative aspects of situations and seldom see the positive. Ask him which he thinks he is: an optimist or a pessimist.

2. Ask your client if he can think of any advantages of being an optimist. Depending on what he identifies, also share the following facts: That optimists live longer, are healthier, have less stress, and are more creative and happier and that others enjoy being around them. Ask how being an optimist might affect his life at present; what might be different?
3. Explain that being an optimist is something that can be learned, so if he is willing to play some basketball, he can gain some insight into being an optimist. Explain that this game is played like HORSE except that it is called POSITIVE. Like HORSE, the game is played by throwing baskets. If he misses a shot, you will give him an envelope containing a situation, starting with the letter P. Before he can try to make another basket, he has to identify something positive about that particular situation, even though the situation may not seem good.
4. Continue to play the game in this manner, making sure to engage the client in discussion about the differences between optimistic and pessimistic thinking, advantages he sees in trying to change the way he thinks, and how he can go about doing that.
5. Give him the Tips for Thinking POSITIVE page, discuss the suggestions, and ask whether he can come up with other ideas that might help him think more positively. Discuss as time allows and encourage him to write these on the tips page. He can also make a poster of these ideas and hang it where he can refer to it often to help him practice his new way of thinking.

# POSITIVE Hoops Situations

**P** I tried out for the play and really wanted the lead part. There were two callback auditions, and I was called back for the lead role both times! But in the end, I didn't get the part. Even worse, one of my biggest rivals got it instead of me. I got a minor role, but I am thinking about quitting because I would have to spend a lot of time watching my rival do "my" part. What POSITIVEs could there possibly be in this situation?

**O** I have been really having a hard time in geometry this semester. When midterm grades came out, I had a D, so I knew my parents would receive a letter. Luckily, I beat them to the mailbox, so they never saw it. I really thought I would be able to bring my grade up by the end of the semester, but instead I flunked the course. My parents are really upset, and they grounded me for the next nine weeks until they see my math grade come up. I will be like a prisoner in my own house for nine whole weeks. What could possibly be POSITIVE about that?

**S** I was planning to go to the prom with my girlfriend, who I have been dating for most of the school year. I had it all planned out. I had reserved the limo, made reservations for dinner, and it was going to be perfect! Then the week before the dance she broke up with me. I do know of a couple of other girls who would go with me, but I am so upset and depressed that I can't even think about going with one of them. What could be POSITIVE about this situation?

**I** My parents have been fighting a lot the last several months. My sister and I have been really worried, and last night our worst fears came true—they told us they were getting a divorce. Our dad is moving into an apartment on the other side of town, and we will only get to see him on the weekends. They told us that they both love us, that it is nobody's fault, but they just don't love each other anymore. How can I find anything POSITIVE about this situation?

**T** During spring break, my best friend is having his birthday party. It is going to be a lot of fun, since all of my friends will be there. We are going out for pizza and a movie and then staying over at my friend's house. But just yesterday my mom told me that I can't go because my family is going on an out-of-state vacation together. And worse yet, we are driving, which will take hours and hours. How boring to sit in a car with my family for that long. I tried to get my parents to let me stay home, but they won't even consider it. What's POSITIVE about this?

**I** I am on the basketball team and have been having a great season. But at the last game I twisted my ankle. The doctor X-rayed it and said it was bad and that I cannot play for the next three weeks. That means I won't be back until the week before the state tournament. Why did this have to happen to me? I know I am supposed to be thinking POSITIVE, but what could anyone possibly find good about this situation?

**V** Last week when my mom came to pick me up at school, I couldn't even believe my ears. She was taking me and my sister to the hospital because my dad had been in an accident. Someone ran into his car and totaled it. He was almost killed, and he won't be able to work for a couple of months, so money is going to be tight. I don't know why this kind of stuff has to happen to our family. What's POSITIVE about this?

**E** There is this girl at school who has a crush on me! She keeps leaving notes in my locker and making me treats in home economics class and stuff like that! It's embarrassing! All my friends tease me about it. What can be POSITIVE about this?

# Tips for Thinking POSITIVE

Practice and pay attention. There are always positives. You just have to be determined and practice, practice, practice.

O—Think of this as a doughnut. There is an expression that says, "Watch the doughnut, not the hole." That means keep your eyes on what is, not what isn't. Don't waste your time worrying and complaining about things that haven't even happened yet.

Surround yourself with positive people, because attitudes tend to be contagious. If you surround yourself with positive people, being positive will be a piece of cake. (Or maybe a doughnut!) ☺

I stands for "I," as in "yourself." Acknowledge that you and only you are in charge of your choice to be more positive. All that awesome power belongs to YOU, so take charge and use it!

Train your mind to see things differently. That's what it's all about. If you wanted to be a weight lifter or a marathon runner, what would you do? You would practice. It is just the same with being a positive thinker—practice every day, looking for positives and thinking positive thoughts.

It's a little thing that makes a big difference . . . ATTITUDE!

Value a positive attitude, and it will be a lot easier to maintain one.

Everything that happens (good and bad) is a learning experience. And if you have that attitude, then even those tough lessons in life won't seem as bad.

## My Tips

__________________________________________________________________

__________________________________________________________________

__________________________________________________________________

__________________________________________________________________

# Strategy Match

**TOPIC** Anxiety

**RATIONALE** Adolescents often get overwhelmed by their anxiety, which becomes one more thing they worry about. This simple matching activity is designed to give clients several useful strategies they can put in their pockets and use as needed.

**MATERIALS** Two sets of Strategy Match Cards

A sheet of paper

A pen or pencil

**PREPARATIONS** Copy and glue the Strategy Match Cards to sheets of tagboard, then cut apart.

**PROCEDURE**

1. When the client begins to describe things she is anxious about, have her write down her anxious thoughts and encourage her to talk more about how she experiences anxiety, including how frequent and intense it is. Invite her to play a card game with you that will help her identify strategies for dealing more effectively with it.
2. Lay two copies of the Strategy Match Cards facedown in four rows of four cards each. Explain that the cards describe eight strategies for handling anxiety. To play the game, you will take turns. On each turn, the player turns over two cards. If the cards match, then the player reads the strategy and discusses how it can be applied to one of the anxieties written on her list (see step 1). The player making the match keeps the cards. If the cards do not match, they are turned facedown again (in their original spot), and the other player takes a turn. Throughout the game, encourage the client to talk about the strategies. For example, it may be that a strategy that is matched later in the game might be more effective with an anxious thought that was discussed previously. Continually engage the client in conversation about which

strategies she thinks would be most effective for addressing her concerns and suggest that she add others that come to mind.

3. If possible, play until all cards have been matched. Give a copy of each strategy to the client so that she has a visual reminder of different ways to deal with her anxiety.

# Strategy Match Cards

### Success Journal

Keep a success journal. When you have had anxieties about a certain issue and have overcome the anxiety, write down the thoughts or activities that helped you. The next time you have a worry episode, take out your success journal to remind yourself of your successes and also to see whether there is something in it that might help you now.

### Journaling

Journaling is an option when you are worried and have no access to anyone to talk with. Sometimes, once you "empty" a worry from your brain, it goes away! If you write in a journal, you have the advantage of looking back at it the next time you are worried and seeing how many things that you worried about never happened or weren't as bad as you thought they would be.

### Physical Activity

Anxiety can cause changes in the body. Sometimes your heart will race, you might break out in a sweat, you might get a stomachache. Likewise, sometimes you can work through your body for the solution—to feel better. Try these ideas: go for a run, shoot some hoops, take a warm bath, do some yoga, go for a bike ride, or just take a leisurely walk.

### Relaxation and Breathing

Find a quiet place you can occupy for the next 5 minutes. Sit (or lie down) with your eyes closed and shoulders relaxed, and focus on your breathing. Take a slow, deep breath in to the count of 4 (stomach should go out, but shoulders should not rise). Hold that breath for 5 counts. Slowly blow out that breath for 7 or 8 counts. Repeat at least 10 times.

### Get a Second Opinion

Remind yourself, when you are having anxious thoughts, that anxiety tends to cloud your judgment. When this happens, it might be wiser to seek the opinion of someone else whom you trust rather than relying on your own opinion.

### Schedule It

Schedule worry time each day. Literally write it on your schedule. Be sure that you do it for 15 minutes each day. But when you have done your worrying for the day, you are done, and you may NOT worry again until tomorrow.

| | |
|---|---|
| **Be Your Own Best Friend**<br><br>Counteract your anxious thoughts by thinking what a supportive friend or parent might say to you to help you be less anxious. | **Artistic Release**<br><br>Plan ahead by finding relaxing music, as well as other artistic outlets that you find relaxing—drawing or painting, for example. |

# Who Knew? Me and You!

**TOPIC** Peer relationships

**RATIONALE** From the time they begin associating with peers, children notice differences between themselves and others. At times they can become fixated on differences and fail to see similarities, which can cause problems to develop in relationships. This activity encourages students to focus on their similarities in order to foster greater acceptance of others.

**MATERIALS** Two to six beanbags (Begin with two and then add others to increase the complexity, as described in step 4.)

A developmentally appropriate music CD

A CD player

**PROCEDURE**

1. Ask for two volunteers (a boy and a girl) to help you. Have them stand in front of the group and then ask the group, "What are the differences between these two students?" Elicit several responses.
2. Now ask if there is there anything the same about them. If they respond in the negative, give some examples, such as they both have eyes, ears, hair. Also include examples that are not readily visible, such as they both like to play, they both live in this city, they both go to school, and they both have several people in their families.
3. Explain that we all have many things about us that are the same as others, as well as things that are different from others. That is what makes us special. Tell students that they are going to be playing a game that celebrates their similarities.
4. Instruct students to sit in a circle and give a beanbag to two students who are sitting on opposite sides of the circle. Explain that when the music starts the two students with the beanbags will begin to pass them around the circle. When the music stops, the two students who are holding the beanbags will be asked to stand up next to each other and find two things that are the same about them. Repeat this procedure when the music starts again. As the

game progresses, you may add more beanbags, which increases the challenge of finding similarities. If four or more beanbags are used, students pair up with a person with a beanbag who is sitting closest to them, then each pair states their similarities before starting the next round.

5. When the game is finished, discuss what they learned about similarities and differences and how looking at similarities will help them make friends.

**NOTE** To adapt this activity for more developmentally advanced students, ask them to find similarities that are not visible: interests, desires, and talents, for example.

# Treasured Hunting

**TOPIC** Peer relationships

**RATIONALE** It is not uncommon for young adolescents to stay within a small group of friends for fear of being ridiculed, judged, or rejected by peers they do not know well. This activity focuses on developing social skills and giving them tools for building relationships. This should increase their level of confidence in their social skills so that they might be better able to reach out to others and make new friends.

**MATERIALS** A set of four Treasured Hunting Clues for each team of four to six

A copy of the Treasured Hunting Invitation for each student

**PREPARATIONS** Print as many copies of the set of clues as there are teams, each set on a different color of paper, such as red, blue, green, yellow, etc. (you may need more or fewer colors depending on the number of participating teams). Then cut the clues apart so there will be red clues 1 through 4, blue clues 1 through 4, and so forth. Be sure to read the clues first so you can place a clue for each team in the appropriate locations. Clue 2 refers to a clock, so these clue cards can be placed in different parts of the building for each team (i.e., on clocks in different locations), whereas the other clues will all be in the same place (e.g., clue 4 might send all teams to the library).

Fill out a Treasured Hunt Invitation for each student.

**PROCEDURE**

1. Start the session by asking: "How many of you would like to discover a buried treasure?" Wait for a show of hands, then add, "What if that buried treasure came with the requirement that you must sacrifice all your friendships in order to get access to the treasure? Would you still want the treasure?" Gather various responses, then suggest that many people would not accept the treasure if they could not keep their friends because friends are one of life's greatest treasures!

2. Tell the group that they will be going on a treasure hunt and the clues that will lead them to the treasure will also teach them some important skills for making and keeping treasured friendships. At this time, have them number off so that they form teams of four to six and ask them to pick a color for their team (give them choices that match the cards and make sure there are no duplications).
3. Explain that each team will retrieve the clues that match the color of their team. When they find the clue, they should follow the instructions on the clue. Specify that after receiving each clue, they should return to their starting point (i.e., the classroom, the counselor's office, or wherever the activity is being conducted) to complete the activity described.
4. Ask for questions, and when everyone is ready, give each team a copy of clue 1 and tell them to begin the hunt.
5. When they have finished the hunt, give each student a copy of the Treasured Hunt Invitation. (Roll it up and tie it with a piece of ribbon if you wish.)

## Treasured Hunting Clues

# CLUE 1

### Activity

Find a quiet place for your group to sit and talk. Have each member of your group tell about one quality that is important for a good friend to have. List each of the qualities your group brings up (only one per group member), then go on to the next clue (see the hint below).

Our group's friendship qualities

1. ______________________ 2. ______________________

3. ______________________ 4. ______________________

5. ______________________ 6. ______________________

### Where to find CLUE 2

"I have a face but no head, hands but no arms. I run but cannot walk. I can tell you something, but cannot talk. I am in lots of different places in the building, and when you find me, you will find CLUE 2."

> *Reminder: Upon retrieval of the clue, return to the classroom or counselor's office or wherever the activity is being conducted to follow the instructions on the clue card.*

# CLUE 2

## Activity

One thing that can cause problems between friends is conflict. Discuss the following situation in your group and practice how you could handle it with a friend by role-playing it. A good rule of thumb to keep in mind when dealing with conflict is "Attack the problem, not the person." "I-statements" are a great tool to help with this.

### Situation

You (friend A) decided to audition for the play. You heard that your buddy (friend B) said that he thinks you should have gone out for basketball instead because now everyone is going to call you a wimp. Good friends work out conflicts and disagreements by talking to each other directly. Using the "I-statement" formula below, practice discussing this fictional conflict (or a conflict of your choice) with a fellow group member. Friend A should start:

"I feel (or felt) ______________________________

*(insert a feelings word)*

when ______________________________,

*(insert what has happened that caused the feeling; try to describe an event and not blame a person),*

and I would really like it if ______________________________.

*(describe what you would like to happen instead)."*

Friend B may respond to the above, and then, if need be, repeat the process to work out any additional concerns. Time to move on to the next clue.

## Where to find CLUE 3

We love our school, this of course is true,
but without these people, whatever would we do?
They answer the phone, to take calls from our home.
They do all sorts of typing, make copies, listen to griping!
They cover it all, substitute mom and nurse, too,
And they are waiting, where you go for the very next clue!

> *Reminder: Upon retrieval of the clue, return to the classroom or counselor's office or wherever the activity is being conducted to follow the instructions on the clue card.*

# CLUE 3

If you want to be a good friend, you need to remember that we have TWO ears and only ONE mouth for a reason! Try to listen twice as much as you talk. This is not as easy as it sounds.

## Activity

To practice being a good listener, take turns in pairs, having one person talk briefly (approximately a minute) about one of the topics below, while the other person listens. When the person is done talking, the listener should tell the speaker in a sentence or two in his or her own words what the message was. This is a very helpful listening technique called *paraphrasing.*

**Possible topics:**

My favorite vacation ever was . . .

The most fun I had last summer was . . .

If I could have one wish, I would wish for . . .

I can't wait to be a grown-up because . . .

(Or you can talk about something of interest to you! Just keep it to a minute.)

## Where to find CLUE 4

You may go to this place for all sorts of reasons,
For some folks it's a necessary evil, for others it's pleasin'!
It all depends on what you like to do,
Though it's not a place where you are allowed to chew!
But if fantasy is your thing, it is a great place to be!
You are limited only by your imagination, you see!
Well, actually, I guess THAT's not really true!
'Cuz it's a place where you can borrow someone ELSE'S imagination if you want to!
Well, if you are into fiction, that is, nonfiction's another story!
Those kind of books aren't imagined, they're in the "facts" category!
But it's the best place you can go to look for a good book,
AND today it's where for CLUE 4 you should look!

*Reminder: Upon retrieval of the clue, return to the classroom or counselor's office or wherever the activity is being conducted to follow the instructions on the clue card.*

# CLUE 4

Sometimes, before we have gotten to know someone, it is easy to notice the differences instead of the similarities, especially if the person looks, dresses, or acts differently from you. For example, if you met a new student from another country, such as Japan or Nigeria, you might notice physical differences or perhaps differences in the way he or she dresses or eats. And you might not be able to understand him or her if he or she does not speak your language. It could be easy to focus on these differences instead of remembering that you have many things in common: You both probably like to laugh, you might both have families you love, he or she is probably nervous in a new school just as you would be, and he or she may like music or sports as you do, for example. One of the best ways to find out what you have in common is to be interested in him or her and ask questions about his or her family and interests or how he or she likes to spend time. This activity will give you practice in looking for commonalities.

## Activity

Pair up with the person you know least well in this group. When the leader says go, you will have two minutes to list as many of the things you have in common as you can. The team with the longest list wins.

## Where to find the treasure

The hidden treasure, worth more than gold,
Has been sought by millions, but can't be bought or sold!
Just like Dorothy in the *Wizard of Oz,*
Who realized in the end, within her the power always was!
This treasure so rich, has always been within your reach,
You didn't need a special key, or to hear some magic speech.
The treasure is friendship, and the magic is this:
To have a friend, you must be a friend.

*Return to the leader to collect your treasure, my friend.*

## Treasured Hunting Invitation

Dear ______________________________,

Thank you so much for participating in the Treasured Hunting activities today! I hope that you feel more confident in your ability to make friends, as well as your capacity to be a better friend.

I would like to invite you to use these new skills in the next few weeks while they are still fresh in your mind! If there is someone that you would like to get to know better, please see me to schedule a time for you and your new friend to come and hang out in my office. If you like, we can plan some structured "get to know you" activities and games, or you can choose other activities, such as playing cards or just talking together.

Once again, thank you for participating today, and good luck with all your treasured friendships!

Sincerely,

______________________________

# Shift

**TOPIC** Overcoming negativity

**RATIONALE** Some adolescents seem to focus more naturally on the negative aspects of life rather than the positive. The more they can learn to develop a positive attitude, the happier they will be. This board game is designed to help them become aware of their negative thinking patterns and to teach them a process for developing more positive ways of thinking. Players work their way around the board and encounter various obstacles that require them to shift their thinking and develop a more a positive attitude. This intervention is best suited for a small group rather than a classroom.

**MATERIALS**

Shift Game Board

A set of Shift Cards

A set of Moving On! Cards

A game marker for each player

A die

**PREPARATIONS** Copy the Shift Game Board and glue it to a sheet of tagboard. (Reproduce the game board in a larger format if you wish.) Copy the Moving On! Cards, fold vertically and cut, then glue to tagboard. (The Move On! Steps will be on one side of each card, and a situation will be on the other.) Copy, cut, and glue the Shift Cards the same way you did the Moving On! Cards.

**PROCEDURE**

1. Introduce this lesson by explaining that the group will be playing a game called Shift, which is designed to help them shift the way they look at problems. Instead of concentrating primarily on the negative aspects of situations, they will learn to focus on the positives, which will help make their lives happier.
2. To begin, ask each player to select a game marker and place it on the START space of the Shift Game Board. They will begin by each rolling the die to determine the order of play. In this game, the player who rolls the lowest number goes first, the player with

the next lowest number goes next, and so forth. Explain that when it is their turn, they should roll the die, move their marker the designated number of spaces, and follow the directions for what to do. Describe the three types of spaces:

- A space with a positive message: These cards give you practice using positive language. If the space says, "Repeat three times," then repeat the message three times.
- A space that says to draw a Moving On! Card. These cards pose a problem for you to deal with using the moving on process, described on the front of each card. The problems on these cards are in the past, and the outcome can't be changed. However, the process will help participants frame these problems in a more positive light.
- A space that says to move back two spaces, draw a Shift Card, and follow the directions: The Shift Cards are similar to the Moving On! Cards, except that you still have some power to change something about the problem if you can shift your attitude and are willing to work on it.

3. Initiate the game, instructing players to put the cards they draw back into the appropriate pile (at the bottom) when they have finished following the instructions on the card. Point out that the shift and moving on processes are written on the front side of the cards and the problem to react to and instructions about what to do are on the back.
4. Play the game until all players have reached the finish. Engage players in a discussion about what they learned about negative versus positive thinking and how they think they could apply the shift and moving on processes in their lives.

## Shift Game Board

| | | | | |
|---|---|---|---|---|
| START HERE | Repeat this three times: "I deserve to be HAPPY!" | Draw a **Moving On! Card.** | Move back two squares. Then draw a **Shift Card** and follow the directions. | Repeat three times: "Using positive language will help me be happy!" |
| THE BIG FINISH | | **MOVING ON! CARDS** | | Draw a **Moving On! Card.** |
| Move back two squares. Then draw a **Shift Card** and follow the directions. | | | | Move back two squares. Then draw a **Shift Card** and follow the directions. |
| Read aloud three times: "Stop being afraid of what could go wrong and start being positive about what could go right!" | | | | Repeat this phrase: "Positive people are happy people. I can choose to be positive. I can choose to be happy." |
| Move back two squares. Then draw a **Shift Card** and follow the directions. | | **SHIFT CARDS** | | Draw a **Moving On! Card.** |
| Draw a **Moving On! Card.** | Repeat:<br>"I am kind."<br>"I am smart."<br>"I am important." | Read aloud:<br>"It is adversity that helps me to grow and beome a stronger, more caring and well-rounded individual." | Move back two squares. Then draw a **Shift Card** and follow the directions. | Having something go "wrong" can be a blessing. For example: You miss your flight, and then it crashes! See if you can think of another example. |

## Moving On! Cards

| | |
|---|---|
| **Moving On! Steps**<br>1. Express and accept your feelings.<br>2. Check your attitude/check your language (keep it positive).<br>3. Evaluate: What can you change or improve?<br>4. Leave the past in the past, look to the future, and stay focused on positives! | **Situation 1**<br>Your class picnic was canceled due to rain. You cannot change the fact that it rained, so you change your focus to something else more positive. Give an example that applies in this situation and then move ahead two spaces. |
| **Moving On! Steps**<br>1. Express and accept your feelings.<br>2. Check your attitude/check your language (keep it positive).<br>3. Evaluate: What can you change or improve?<br>4. Leave the past in the past, look to the future, and stay focused on positives! | **Situation 2**<br>You just found out that you did not get the grade you wanted on your test. You cannot improve your grade or retake the test. Obviously, continuing to dwell on it will only make you feel worse. Explain what you could do to fulfill Moving On! step 3 next time, then move ahed one space, or explain how you would fulfill step 4 and move ahead three spaces. |
| **Moving On! Steps**<br>1. Express and accept your feelings.<br>2. Check your attitude/check your language (keep it positive).<br>3. Evaluate: What can you change or improve?<br>4. Leave the past in the past, look to the future, and stay focused on positives! | **Situation 3**<br>You auditioned for the play and did not get the role that you wanted. However, you did get a smaller part. Because you cannot change the past, what is something positive you can do (step 3) to improve your situation now? Move ahead one space. |

**Moving On! Steps**

1. Express and accept your feelings.
2. Check your attitude/check your language (keep it positive).
3. Evaluate: What can you change or improve?
4. Leave the past in the past, look to the future, and stay focused on positives!

**Situation 4**

You had overnight plans with your best friend tonight, but they were canceled due to a family emergency. Explain how you feel (move ahead one space), and say something positive about this incident (move ahead another space).

**Moving On! Steps**

1. Express and accept your feelings.
2. Check your attitude/check your language (keep it positive).
3. Evaluate: What can you change or improve?
4. Leave the past in the past, look to the future, and stay focused on positives!

**Situation 5**

You told a friend about who your "secret crush" is in your class. Your friend told everyone! Using the Moving On! steps, explain how you will work through this and keep a positive attitude. (Move ahead two spaces.)

**Moving On! Steps**

1. Express and accept your feelings.
2. Check your attitude/check your language (keep it positive).
3. Evaluate: What can you change or improve?
4. Leave the past in the past, look to the future, and stay focused on positives!

**Situation 6**

You sprained your ankle right before the track meet and won't be able to run. You were in three events, and it was the qualifying meet for the state. How can the Moving On! steps help you? Move ahead one space for each step you use.

# Shift Cards

| | |
|---|---|
| **S**HIFT into positive thinking!<br>**H**unt for the hidden opportunity!<br>**I**dentify the first step!<br>**F**ormulate the rest of the plan!<br>**T**ake positive action as soon as possible! | **Situation 1**<br>You went out for basketball but did not make the "A team." Your first reaction is to quit the team. Then you think about SHIFT. If you can apply SHIFT to help yourself develop and keep a positive attitude, you can move forward two spaces. |
| **S**HIFT into positive thinking!<br>**H**unt for the hidden opportunity!<br>**I**dentify the first step!<br>**F**ormulate the rest of the plan!<br>**T**ake positive action as soon as possible! | **Situation 2**<br>You really want your own cell phone, but your parents say that you and your sister have to share one. You think it is really unfair that you are expected to share! Use the SHIFT process to help you change your focus from the negatives to the positives. Use all five letters and one space for each "hidden opportunity" you can name (limit three total). If you can do this, move forward three spaces. |
| **S**HIFT into positive thinking!<br>**H**unt for the hidden opportunity!<br>**I**dentify the first step!<br>**F**ormulate the rest of the plan!<br>**T**ake positive action as soon as possible! | **Situation 3**<br>It's your birthday and your parents are taking you and your three best friends out to dinner and then to a movie. Right before you leave, one of your friends calls to cancel. You are ready to cancel the whole party! Use the SHIFT process to work through your disappointment. Move forward three spaces. |

| | |
|---|---|
| SHIFT into positive thinking!<br>**H**unt for the hidden opportunity!<br>**I**dentify the first step!<br>**F**ormulate the rest of the plan!<br>**T**ake positive action as soon as possible! | **Situation 4**<br>Your teacher wants you to enter your poem in a poetry contest. You don't think it is good enough. Use the SHIFT process to convince yourself to go for it! Move ahead three spaces. |
| SHIFT into positive thinking!<br>**H**unt for the hidden opportunity!<br>**I**dentify the first step!<br>**F**ormulate the rest of the plan!<br>**T**ake positive action as soon as possible! | **Situation 5**<br>You have always wanted to try out for a solo in the variety show. However, you do not feel you sing well enough. Using the SHIFT process, convince yourself that auditioning is the right thing to do. Move ahead two spaces. |
| SHIFT into positive thinking!<br>**H**unt for the hidden opportunity!<br>**I**dentify the first step!<br>**F**ormulate the rest of the plan!<br>**T**ake positive action as soon as possible! | **Situation 6**<br>Your parents tell you that your negativity is becoming more and more of a problem, so they want you to start working with a counselor. Use the SHIFT process to go into this experience with a positive outlook. Move ahead three spaces. |
| SHIFT into positive thinking!<br>**H**unt for the hidden opportunity!<br>**I**dentify the first step!<br>**F**ormulate the rest of the plan!<br>**T**ake positive action as soon as possible! | **Situation 7**<br>It seems to you that every time you ask your best friend to do something, she has always made plans with someone else or is already busy. It seems like she is avoiding you. Use SHIFT to focus your thinking in a positive direction and develop a plan. Move ahead three spaces. |

## CHAPTER 2

# Counseling Through Music

Just as Bob Seger sang some time ago, referring to rock and roll, "that kind of music just soothes the soul" ("Old Time Rock and Roll"). Music also helps people reminisce about the "days of old," as Seger pointed out, and can alter moods, communicate feelings, and "elicit a wide range of mental, emotional, physical, and spiritual responses" (Gladding, 2011, p. 23).

Music is a powerful medium. Just think about the number of times you have listened to tunes on the radio or your iPod and heard an "oldies" song start playing; it immediately transports you back in time. Not only do you flash back to where you were when you heard the song, but you might very well remember who you were with, what you were wearing, or what you were doing. That happens to me quite often, and the memories are usually very vivid. In fact, just recently I heard "Moon River," by Andy Williams. Instantly, I was at a junior high dance at the country club, wearing a dark blue sundress and holding hands with my first boyfriend! In addition to eliciting long-forgotten memories, music facilitates growth and development, increases self-awareness, and promotes social skills.

There is little doubt that music plays an important role in healing, and it has been used therapeutically over time (Thaut, 2009). Forinash (2005) describes how hospitalized World War II veterans suffering physically and emotionally responded to music as opposed to other forms of treatment, and Gladding (2011) notes that people from ancient cultures relied on music as a powerful source of healing. He stresses that music transcends boundaries; it is a universal, multicultural experience that can be used with people of all ages, cultures, and abilities.

Eckhardt and Dinsmore (2012) discuss how mindful music listening can be used in treating depression. They posit that listening to music arouses emotions and can serve as a springboard to help clients express feelings that might otherwise have been difficult to explain. These authors also suggest that music can help clients reframe problems and improve physical changes in heart rate and blood pressure, as well as lead to holistic healing.

Kane (2012) has developed a collaborative drumming program with a classroom teacher to help disengaged at-risk students with academic and behavioral problems become more involved in school and increase their resiliency. He discovered that the musical concepts involved in the drumming program were important life lessons that had a positive impact on elementary-age students.

## ADVANTAGES OF USING MUSIC IN COUNSELING

Think back to when you were first exposed to music and what role it played in your childhood and adolescence. When I was young, my mother bought records that also encouraged us to incorporate movement. I still remember walking around the house like an elephant as my sister and I sang along to "Train to the Zoo." As an adolescent I was hooked on my transistor radio and spent hours in my room listening to music. To this day, music is a significant part of my life; it's energizing, uplifting, entertaining, engaging, and relieves stress, among other things. The advantages of incorporating music into counseling are numerous, including the following:

- Music can reduce depression (Eckhardt & Dinsmore, 2012) and anxiety (Bradley et al., 2009).
- Music increases awareness of feelings and promotes emotional expression (Jensen, 2001).
- Music promotes self-confidence (Gladding, 2011), reduces negative self-talk, and helps clients reprogram negative messages (Jensen, 2001).
- Music increases verbal self-disclosure (Jensen, 2001).
- Music promotes catharsis and healing (Eckhardt & Dinsmore, 2012; Newsome, 2003).
- Music can help people recall past events and work through painful memories (Duffey, 2007).
- Music encourages resilience and coping (Duffey, 2007).
- Music can promote closeness and understanding (Vernon & Clemente, 2005).
- Music can increase attention and concentration (Thaut, 2009), as well as listening skills and teamwork (Kane, 2012).
- Music helps extend the client's experience in the counseling office to the rest of his or her world (Vernon, 2013).
- Music can promote development of a healthy self-identity, leading to positive self-esteem (Hendricks, 2000).
- Music can help clients deconstruct disempowering beliefs about themselves (Duffey, 2007).

## TYPES OF PROBLEMS AND POPULATIONS THAT BENEFIT FROM MUSIC INTERVENTIONS

Music has been used throughout the ages for a wide variety of problems with many different client populations. Several examples are subsequently listed.

- Music can bring about changes in children who are developmentally delayed (Forinash, 2005).
- Music can enhance athletes' performance (Gladding, 2011).
- Music can promote social interaction and self-expression in the elderly (Rio, 2002).
- Music helps terminally ill clients reflect, refocus, and share their feelings (Duffey, 2007).
- Music helps children deal with the trauma associated with abuse (Ostertag, 2002).
- Music has been used to help geriatric Alzheimer's patients (Forinash, 2005).
- Music has been used with clients with physical delays (Wigram, Pedersen, & Bonde, 2002).
- Music can be effective with socially maladjusted children and adolescents, as well as those with behavioral disturbances (Kane, 2012; Peters, 2000).
- Music is effective with clients who have chronic illnesses (Gladding, 2011).
- Music can help adolescents deal with grief (Slyter, 2012).
- Music can be used effectively with trauma victims to reduce the common PTSD symptom of hyperarousal and help the client to self-soothe.
- Of all the creative arts interventions, music has the most research to back its effectiveness in reducing blood pressure, heart rate, and respiration (Malchiodi, 2005).
- Music can facilitate treatment of delinquent behavior and drug addiction, as well as other psychological disorders (Davis, Geller, & Thaut, 1999).

## MUSIC IN COUNSELING VERSUS MUSIC THERAPY

There is an important distinction between using music in counseling and music therapy. According to Peters (2000), music therapy is described as

> a planned, goal-directed process of interaction and intervention, based on assessment and evaluation of

> individual clients' specific needs, strengths, and weaknesses, in which music or music-based experiences are specifically prescribed to be used by specially trained personnel to influence positive changes in an individual's condition, skills, thoughts, feelings, or behaviors. (p. 2)

The American Music Therapy Association has defined music therapy as "the clinical and evidence-based use of music interventions to accomplish individualized goals within a therapeutic relationship by a credentialed professional who has completed an approved music therapy program" (as cited in Gladding, 2011, p. 26). Music therapists must have technical skills, such as playing various musical instruments and being able to sing and compose music. They also assess clients' cognitive, physical, emotional, and social functioning, as well as develop specific treatment plans and evaluate outcomes. According to Gladding (2005, 2011), music therapy must be used by therapists who are specialists in music and human behavior.

In contrast, using music in counseling is a different process that includes listening, composing, singing, and improvising. These methods are therapeutic but are not as encompassing as music therapy. Counselors who use music in counseling should be flexible and creative and should understand the multiple ways music can have an impact on young clients. It is helpful if they have some musical ability, but that is not a requirement because children and adolescents have a natural affinity for music and can engage in this approach without a skilled musician to guide them.

## EXAMPLES OF MUSIC INTERVENTIONS

As previously noted, music in counseling can assume various forms, including listening, composing, improvising, and performing. As is true with any intervention, practitioners need to know which musical modalities might be most effective with a particular client and adapt accordingly. Several general strategies are subsequently described, and more specific and detailed musical interventions for children in elementary, middle school, and high school and interventions for use in classrooms and with small groups are then presented.

### Rapport Building

Music can effectively establish rapport, particularly with teenagers, who may be more resistant about being in counseling. After researching which radio stations are most appealing to adolescents, tune into these channels before the client comes into the office to facilitate communication and relaxation. It is generally most effective for the counselor to wait for the client to initiate conversation about the music, but if she or he doesn't, the counselor might comment on it, asking whether or not the client likes to listen to music, or this type of music in particular, and then ease into the traditional get-acquainted phase of the session.

### Using Counselor-Composed Songs

Just as you intentionally select a type of intervention to implement with a client, you can also compose a specific song to address a given problem. Suppose that you are working with an unmotivated student who falls asleep in class. One way to initiate some discussion about this behavior is to compose a song such as the following, sung to the tune of "Are You Sleeping?" ("Frère Jacques"):

*Are you sleeping, are you sleeping?*
*Not in class, not in class.*
*Stay awake and concentrate*
*Do your work and do it great.*
*No more sleeping, no more sleeping.*

Although this is a children's song, even middle school–age students respond positively to something of this nature when you sing it to them. It gets the message across with a bit of humor and can serve as a springboard to discussing the problem. Follow up by inviting the client to compose his or her own songs to generate other coping strategies.

### Music Homework

Music can be a useful homework assignment that helps reinforce concepts between counseling appointments. At the end of the session, the counselor can invite clients to bring songs that portray how they were thinking or feeling that week to the next session. They might also select songs that express who they are, their conflicts or problems, or their hopes and fears. This intervention is most effective with middle school and high school clients.

### Music Monitoring

An extension of music as homework is to have clients monitor their moods through music. Rather than keeping a feelings chart (Vernon, 2002) that requires them to designate a number that represents the degree of intensity of a selected emotion, such as depression or anger, music monitoring involves selecting a song or songs to represent their mood each day or for select periods of time. They can either print the lyrics from an Internet source or bring the actual music to the following session. Adolescents in particular have found this to be quite eye-opening, as they note how their moods shift from day to day or throughout the day.

### Music Collage

Invite clients to make a CD of several songs that serve a specific purpose, such as a collage of relaxing music, energizing music, music that makes them laugh, or music that increases their attention span and helps them concentrate.

### Make It with Music

Nonverbal clients in particular respond well to making music. Gather together drums or empty metal waste cans, drumsticks, harmonicas, a keyboard if available, bells, whistles, and so forth and invite the client to make music that lets you know he or she is sad, mad, angry, scared, excited, and so on.

## OTHER EXAMPLES OF MUSIC INTERVENTIONS

Bradley and colleagues (2009) describe using music to help children and adolescents reframe problematic experiences. For example, with an adolescent client who fails to see a reason for a curfew, these authors suggest helping the client reframe the issue by finding a song that conveys why parents might be acting out of care and concern for them. Newsome (2003) suggests using the song "Change Your Mind" by Sister Hazel, which describes how important it is to be able to change your thoughts when you are tired of battling with yourself. After playing the song and discussing the lyrics, the counselor and client can identify maladaptive thoughts and how to change them.

Gladding (1995) developed an intervention called "Line Spacers," which involves asking clients to find examples of songs that inspire hope or provide suggestions about how to deal with difficult circumstances. He suggests that clients write out the lyrics and then make a list of words or phrases that are encouraging and helpful so they can refer to their lists when they need support or are feeling overwhelmed by their circumstances.

Finally, Vernon (2002) has developed the concept of "silly songs" to use with elementary or middle school students. For this intervention, the counselor asks the client to select a favorite childhood tune, and together they write a silly song that they can sing whenever they are feeling bad and need some cheering up. An example, sung to the tune of "Twinkle, Twinkle, Little Star," is as follows:

*Mom said I couldn't go out to play*
*I was mad and cried all day.*
*Then I thought of things to do*
*I didn't have to be so blue.*
*I got up and danced around*
*Now I'm acting like a clown!*

## INCORPORATING MUSIC WITH OTHER CREATIVE ARTS TECHNIQUES

Music can not only be used as a stand-alone intervention, it can also be incorporated with other creative arts techniques. A natural combination is music and movement. I remember working with Nicky, a six-year-old who had the attention span of a hummingbird; he was always fluttering around mentally as well as physically. To help settle him down, I always played a selection from a personalized Kids' Juke Box CD, "Express to Song City," at the beginning of the session. These are energizing songs that invite movement, and after Nicky had jumped up and down and moved around some to expend some energy, he was ready to transition into another intervention that dealt more specifically with his temper.

Gladding (2011) suggests combining music with poetry, drama, and storytelling. He indicates that music, particularly classical music, serves as a good background for stories that are told to young children. I adapted this approach and used it with an adolescent who was struggling with an eating disorder. I had encouraged her to write her story so that others her age who were going down that same path might benefit from her insights about her serious battle with anorexia. She first recorded some solo piano music and then spoke over the music as she read her story. Doing it in this way made for a much more dramatic delivery than simply having others read her story.

Another way of integrating music into creative arts interventions is through play. I used this approach with a small group of second graders who needed to develop better anger management skills. I first asked them to make "mad music," using empty waste cans, brooms, silverware, and pots and pans. Following this, they were given a beanbag. As I read various ways to handle anger (such as punching someone, yelling mean things about a friend, holding your breath and counting to 10, walking away, etc.), group members had to take turns tossing their beanbag either into a hula hoop labeled "Bad Ways to Let Your Anger Out" or "Good Ways to Let Your Anger Out."

Music can also be incorporated with photography. I used this technique with an adolescent who was engaging in some risky behaviors. Although she was a good student, her grades were getting worse as a result of not doing her homework. She had been late to work several nights in a row because she was hanging out with her boyfriend and his friends, who were known to be using alcohol and other drugs. She wouldn't adhere to her curfew, and she was very defiant at home. It was obvious that she saw nothing wrong with her behavior and had no interest in changing. Rather than try and help her "see the light," I simply suggested that she might think about what her life would be like in six to eight months if she didn't change her risky behaviors or perhaps even increased them, and I asked her to take several photos that would depict how things might be. Then I asked her to find some music that would convey the essence of the photos. This proved to be a powerful intervention. The pictures and music portrayed themes related to being a failure, addicted to substances, and floundering. I followed up by asking her to take photos and find music depicting how her life might be if she decided to change. These photos and musical selections were in sharp contrast to the first ones, conveying much more hope and success.

There are countless combinations that incorporate music into other creative arts therapies. As you read the following chapters, think about how you could integrate music with other approaches.

## CLASSROOM OR SMALL-GROUP APPLICATIONS

Some readers may recall that one of the very first emotional education curricula was DUSO (Developing Understanding of Self), developed by Dinkmeyer and Dinkmeyer (1982). This program utilized a dolphin puppet named Duso, as well as several other puppet characters. Each time Duso came to classroom guidance, he sang the Duso song, which was followed by a story about a variety of typical developmental problems experienced by young children. Since then, counselors have routinely incorporated music into small-group and classroom guidance lessons, and as Gladding (2011) notes, "Music is often a primary ingredient in teaching guidance lessons" (p. 30).

In both small-group and classroom guidance sessions, children can be introduced to music that helps them remember main ideas of the lessons. I wrote the following song, sung to the tune of "Twinkle, Twinkle Little Star," for a fourth-grade friendship group, and we sang it at the beginning of each group session:

*Finding friends can be hard to do*
*So if you don't have a clue,*
*Try being friendly*
*A smile can't hurt*
*Don't try to push them down in the dirt.*
*Offer to help or play with them*
*Before you know it you'll have a friend.*

I followed this with a game called "Finding Friends" (Vernon, 2009, pp. 288–290). In essence, this game involves hiding note cards around the room. Each card contains either a helpful or an unhelpful way to find and make friends. Group members are divided into two teams of three, and each team chooses a leader. Their instructions are to stay silent as they hunt throughout the room for the friendship cards. When a team member finds a card, he or she motions to the group leader, who picks up the card and puts it in a paper bag. When all the cards have been located, they regroup into their respective teams, and the leader reads the cards, one by one. The team members decide whether what the leader reads is a helpful or an unhelpful friendship behavior. Debriefing with the class focuses on the distinction between helpful and unhelpful friendship behaviors.

Music can be used in small groups to address a specific topic, such as divorce. DeLucia-Waack and Gellman (2007) have developed a program that, through music, teaches children how to handle feelings associated with divorce and how to develop healthy ways of coping. Peter Yarrow (2000) released the CD *Don't Laugh at Me,* which includes songs to help children learn how to deal with teasing and bullying, and Dan Conley (1994) developed a series of songs to help children deal with typical developmental problems. Counselors can work in conjunction with music teachers or take the initiative themselves and develop experiences that involve music for students in classroom guidance and small-group counseling.

In the classroom, music can be used to introduce classroom guidance lessons or units. For example, middle school students' interest in a drug and alcohol unit was piqued when they learned a rap tune about saying no to drugs. The counselor (K.L.B.) used a generic rap track (included on the CD) as a background, then wrote some fun antidrug rap lyrics introducing students to a drug prevention unit. The song touched on some of the key topics that would be covered and raised awareness about the importance of becoming educated on this topic. Finally, it served as a tremendous motivational tool. The students begged to start and end each class with the rap, even after the unit was completed!

**Drug-Free Rap**

*Listen up friends, 'cause you just got to see,*
*The only way to go is living' drug free!*
*Say "no!" to alcohol, tobacco, crack, and marijuana, too!*
*Livin' drug-free is the thing to do!*

*Just say "no!" Just say "no!" Just say "no!" now!*
*There's nothing' to it if you just know how!*
*Say, "no!" to alcohol, tobacco, crack, and marijuana, too!*
*Livin' drug-free is the thing to do!*

*Drugs are no good, they really mess up your life!*
*They bring you lots of problems, heartache, and strife!*
*If your friends try to tempt you, now don't be a fool!*
*Sayin' "no!" is the way to be cool!*

*Just say "no!" Just say "no!" Just say "no!" now!*
*There's nothin' to it if you just know how!*
*Say "no!" to alcohol, tobacco, crack, and marijuana, too!*
*Livin' drug-free is the thing to do!*

*Just say "no!" Just say "no!" Just say "no!" now!*
*There's nothin' to it if you just know how!*
*Say "no!" to alcohol, tobacco, crack, and marijuana, too!*
*Livin' drug-free is the thing to do!*

## SUMMARY

As previously described, music is very therapeutic, and it can be incorporated into individual, small-group, and classroom guidance in numerous ways, limited only by the creativity of the counselor. Music has been successfully employed with people of all ages for a wide array of presenting concerns. Not only does music "soothe the soul," it promotes bonding, spontaneity, healing, and learning. The interventions on the following pages address teasing and tattling, procrastination, relationships, perspective taking, self-awareness, rights and responsibilities, underachievement and goal setting, behavior awareness, coping with depression, and stress management. We hope they will be useful in your work with children and adolescents.

# Give 'em Five!

**TOPIC** Teasing and name calling

**RATIONALE** It is common for most children to experience teasing and name calling at some time during childhood. Although it might seem easier to have an adult intervene, the reality is that it is far more empowering for children to learn to handle teasing on their own, which is the purpose of this intervention.

**MATERIALS** A copy of the Give 'em Five! Song lyrics (song appears on the CD)

**PROCEDURE**

1. When a client tells you about problems she has when others tease her, tell her that the next time this happens, she should "give 'em five!"
2. Discuss the usual meaning of the phrase "give 'em five," or what it means to "high five" someone, helping her understand that it's called this because when you slap all five of your fingers (i.e., your palm) against another person's palm, it is a gesture of friendship or means that the person has done something well.
3. Tell her that you are going to be teaching her a different way to give a high five by figuring out five ways to solve problems when others tease her. When she uses her five fingers as people do when they high five someone, it will help her remember the five ways to solve the teasing problem. She will also learn a song to help her remember what to do.
4. Take out the Give 'em Five! Song and have the the client lay one hand on the blank part of the paper, while tracing around it with her other hand. Then number each finger, starting with the pinky.
5. Walk the client through the steps of the song, discussing how she might carry out each step of the process relative to teasing. For example:

   **Solution 1—Ignore them:** Try to pretend that you don't even hear what the teasers are saying. They are trying to upset you, so if you act like you can't hear them or that you are not upset, they might quit. If that doesn't work, move on to solution 2.

**Solution 2—State your feelings:** Tell them how it feels when they call you names. If you feel sad or embarrassed, say so. They may feel bad if they realize how you feel, which might make them stop. However, if this doesn't work, move on to solution 3.

**Solution 3—Move away:** If solutions 1 and 2 don't work, try moving away from them to another part of the classroom or playground. Or stand beside an adult or another group of children. If this doesn't stop them, move on to solution 4.

**Solution 4—Ask adults for help:** This is different from tattling. Don't tell the adult who is teasing or causing you problems; just tell them what the person is doing, how you are feeling, and ask for suggestions about what you can do to stop the problem. If you have tried all of the other solutions and they don't work, move on to solution 5.

**Solution 5—Hold a peace meeting:** This does involve an adult, but it's not tattling either. It's sitting down with the children who are teasing you, along with a teacher or the counselor, and working out a peaceful solution together!

6. Teach the client the Give 'em Five! Song, sung to the tune of "Alouette," as another way to remember the options for handling teasing.

## Give 'em Five Song

*Sing to the tune of "Alouette."*

One: Is ignore them,

Two: You state your feelings,

Three: Move away,

Four: Ask adults for help.

Then if you have done all four, don't you worry anymore!

Please don't shout! Work it out! At a PEACE MEETING.

So remember, fighting's not the answer!

Winning together is what it's all about!

*Trace your hand in the space below.*

# Music Makes the Medicine Go Down

**TOPIC** Procrastination

**RATIONALE** When children are anticipating what they consider to be unpleasant tasks, they will sometimes focus entirely on the negative aspects of the job. These thoughts reinforce their negative feelings about the chore, often causing them to procrastinate. The purpose of this intervention is to encourage children to look for things they might enjoy about the assignment, thereby thinking more positively so they will procrastinate less, enjoy the task more, and develop an overall optimistic attitude about things they think they might not like to do.

**MATERIALS**

Several sheets of paper

A pen or pencil

CDs/song(s) client listens to when happy

The movie *Mary Poppins* (available for purchase, rental, or authorized download)

**PROCEDURE**

1. When your client presents with problems related to procrastination, ask him to think about the last time he had to do chores at home and whether there was anything at all about one or more of the chores that was enjoyable. If so, ask him to make a list of these enjoyable qualities.
2. Next inquire as to whether he has seen the movie *Mary Poppins* and tell him that the two of you will be watching part of the movie. Explain that in the scene you will show him, a brother and his sister are supposed to clean up their messy bedroom, but they really don't want to do it. Mary Poppins is their nanny (babysitter), and she is teaching them, through a song, how to make cleaning their room fun.
3. Play a clip from *Mary Poppins* that starts at approximately 31 minutes and 50 second into the movie and stops at about 36 minutes

and 20 seconds. Then discuss with your client how the children made it fun to clean the room, eliciting such things as using magic, singing, working together, making a game of it, and just looking for ways to have fun instead of thinking about how much they didn't want to do it.

4. Give the client a piece of paper and ask him to think about a task he has been avoiding and write it at the top of the page. Ask him to use the ideas from the video clip and list as many ways as possible that he could make his task more pleasant, positive, and enjoyable.
5. If he did not put music on his list, have the following discussion. Ask if he thinks the song in the video affected the way the children performed their chores, and if so, how? Does he think that playing an upbeat song or songs during the task is something that could influence how pleasant or unpleasant the task would be?
6. Invite your client to make up a song that would make the task he has been avoiding more enjoyable to do. Work with him to develop a simple song that he could sing while he is performing the chore, such as the following, to the tune of "Jingle Bells":

*Dashing through my chores*
*With a lot of speed*
*Best to get them done today*
*So I can go out to play.*
*I use a broom to clean my room*
*And put all my toys away,*
*Before you know it I'm all done*
*And now can have some fun!*

# Think It Through

**TOPIC** Tattling

**RATIONALE** Tattling on classmates is often the reason a child is rejected by peers and labeled a tattletale. However, there are times when it is appropriate for children to report things to adults. The purpose of this intervention is to help children know when it is appropriate to report another child's actions to an adult and when it is best to handle it themselves.

**MATERIALS** Puppet with a long tail (for example, a monkey)

A copy of the Think It Through Song lyrics (song appears on the CD)

**PROCEDURE**

1. When a client comes to you complaining that she has been called a tattletale, introduce her to Marco the Monkey and suggest that she might want to discuss this with Marco because he has had the same problem. Playing the role of Marco, share with the client that others have called him a tattletale and it hurt his feelings.
2. Have a brief discussion with your client and Marco regarding why she thinks the kids are calling her a tattletale. Marco thinks it is because he has a long tail, and he thinks that all the guilty parties should have to stay in during recess. Marco asks your client if she thinks kids are calling him this because he has a long tail or if there is some other explanation. You want to elicit the idea that tattling to an adult about what other kids did wrong and wanting to get them in trouble was probably what the kids were upset about.
3. Briefly discuss the idea that there are times when you should tell (when someone is in danger or needs adult help) and times when you should not tell (when your feelings are hurt or you are just angry and want to get others in trouble). A good way to tell the difference is to ask yourself, "What would I want if I were them?" or "If I told, would I be helping them or hurting them?"

4. Teach the client the Think It Through Song, sung to the tune of "My Pony Boy." Afterward, discuss with the client what the lyrics meant to her and what she needs to think about when making the decision regarding whether or not to tell an adult about a peer's behavior.

## Think It Through Song

*Sing to the tune of "My Pony Boy."*

Tattletale, tattletale,
Please don't be a tattletale.
Before you do, ask yourself,
"Will it help, or hurt?"
Treat a friend, like you would,
Want them to treat you!
Stop and think,
Don't forget,
Stop and think, when . . .
You want to tell!

# Relationship Rationality

**TOPIC** Relationship problems

**RATIONALE** Many issues adolescents present in counseling center around relationships with peers, parents, teachers, and others. Adolescents frequently become irrational about these problems, believing that they must be 100 percent successful in all relationships or they will be rejected or disapproved of or be a total failure as a person. The purpose of this intervention is to equip them with a process they can apply in various situations to overcome their irrational thinking about themselves and their relationships.

**MATERIALS** A copy of the Relationship Rationality Song lyrics (song appears on the CD)

**PROCEDURE**

1. When your client tells you about his latest relationship issue, such as not being invited to a classmate's party or not being included in other activities, explain that you would like to teach him a process that he will be able to use in the future whenever he is having problems with others.
2. Explain that you will be teaching him the "ABCs" as a way to think more carefully about relationship problems. Then you will teach him a song that will make it easier to remember rational ways to handle relationship problems.
3. Give your client the Relationship Rationality Song sheet, which has the verse on the left side. Ask the client to fold the right side of the paper over and crease it, making sure to not cover up the words. Then, on this blank side, have him write the letter A, explaining that it stands for the activating event, or what happened. Ask your client to write down the relationship issue that brought him to counseling (his issue) beside the A.
4. Next have him write the letter C under the A, explaining that this is the consequence, which is how he felt and how he behaved. Ask him to write how he behaved and how he felt when this happened next to the C. For example, did he get angry and yell? Did he cry and feel depressed? Was he just disappointed?

5. Next ask him to write the letter B under the C, explaining that this refers to what he was thinking (beliefs) regarding this relationship problem. Assume, for example, that his issue was not being invited to go to the movies with friends. If he was angry or depressed or experiencing other negative emotions, you might ask if he had thoughts such as "This isn't fair; I should have been invited" or "Because I didn't get invited I must be a loser and I won't ever get invited to things or have friends." The beliefs should correspond to the feelings and behaviors, so, if he was depressed and upset, the beliefs would relate to his thinking that he was a loser and would never have friends. If the feeling was anger, he would be thinking that this wasn't fair and that he should have been invited.
6. Discuss the difference between rational and irrational thinking. Help him to see that if he was merely disappointed instead of depressed, he might have been thinking that he wished he had been invited but that it's not the end of the world and that it doesn't mean he is a loser just because he didn't get invited to the movie. Or if he was a little angry, he might think that it would have been fun to go, but that there isn't a law that said he should have been invited.
7. Now comes the fun part! Ask your client if there is anyone he enjoys arguing with. Have him write the letter D under the C and have him pretend he is arguing with himself about why he didn't get invited to the movie, referring to the beliefs he wrote under the B. For example, if he wrote that he is a loser because he didn't get invited, have him write arguments to himself, such as "Why would I be a loser just because I didn't get invited? Where is the proof that I'll never be invited to a movie?"
8. Have him write the letter E under the B and invite him to list one or more of these new beliefs that will help him remember to think rationally about problems.
9. Teach him the Relationship Rationality Song, sung to the tune of "The Marine's Hymn," to review and reinforce rational thinking as a way of handling relationship problems.

# Me Music

**TOPIC** Self-awareness

**RATIONALE** Music is very important to adolescents as they listen to lyrics and try to piece together their identities based on themes and concepts that have some meaning for them. In addition, they may identify with the songwriter and connect with the things the songwriter seems to value. This intervention utilizes music to help adolescents develop greater self-awareness.

**MATERIALS** A computer with Internet service

**PROCEDURE**

1. Have your client describe the music he listens to and ask him if there is any particular type of music he most identifies with. Discuss some of the songs he likes and why they appeal to him.
2. Have him choose a song on iTunes or YouTube that he feels conveys something about him that he considers important: a particular lifestyle, beliefs about friends and family, values such as independence and uniqueness, and so forth. Listen to the song together, and when it is finished, ask the client to talk about why he chose that song to represent what is important to him, focusing on the following:
   - What is it about this song that you relate to?
   - When you listen to certain songs, do you identify more with the lyrics or the music?
   - What is it that is appealing to you about this song or other favorites?
3. Suggest to your client that during the coming week he set aside time to listen to music that he connects with and journal about the experience afterward by writing about what he identified with, how the music represents what he thinks are important values and beliefs, lyrics that do or do not define who he is, and so forth. The following questions may also stimulate his thinking relative to what he listened to:

- Is this a song you find yourself wanting or not wanting to share with others?
- Does this song help you understand yourself better? If so, in what ways?
- Is it possible that this song might help another person understand you better?

4. Invite your client to bring some of his journal entries to the next counseling session, informing him that he does not have to share anything he isn't comfortable sharing.

# Rights, Privileges, and Responsibilities

**TOPIC** Rights and responsibilities

**RATIONALE** Adolescents are frequently in a hurry to grow up and enjoy the rights and privileges of young adulthood, such as the right to drive a car when they are old enough or the privilege of owning a car if they have enough money. However, they sometimes want the privileges and rights before they are willing to accept some of the responsibilities associated with them. The purpose of this intervention is to help adolescents recognize and accept that rights, privileges, and responsibilities gradually increase as they grow up.

**MATERIALS** A copy of the Rights and Responsibilities Song lyrics (song appears on the CD)

A pen or pencil

Several blank sheets of paper

**PROCEDURE**

1. When your client expresses her impatience with growing up because she wants to drive a car, get a job, or achieve similar rites of passage, ask if she has considered the other changes in her life that will come along with these rights and privileges. Explain that although people are granted more rights and privileges as they mature, they also need to recognize that there are responsibilities associated with them.
2. Ask her to think of privileges that she has already acquired but was not permitted to enjoy when she was younger, such as walking to school alone, picking out her own clothes, going places with friends unsupervised, or staying home alone. Discuss why she is allowed these privileges now but not when she was younger.
3. Next talk about responsibilities that she has also gradually gained as she has matured, such as making her own lunch for school, helping with chores at home, or babysitting for a younger sibling.

4. Discuss the fact that many privileges and rights come with being an adult and that it is normal to look forward to them. Ask your client what privileges she is looking forward to the most. Have her record these in list form, down the left side of a sheet of paper, and label it "Rights-Privileges."
5. Teach her the Rights and Responsibilities Song (to the tune of "Deck the Halls"). When the song is over, discuss what the song conveys about rights and responsibilities (for every right there is at least one responsibility; you only get to enjoy the privileges if you take care of the responsibilities).
6. Invite the client to look at the privileges or rights that she listed on the paper as those she is looking forward to. Ask her form a new list to the right of the privileges, labeling it "Responsibilities." Have her identify a responsibility that will come with each privilege and write it across from the corresponding privilege. For example, with the right of driving a car comes the responsibility of following the traffic laws and the responsibility for the lives and safety of everyone who rides with you or who is also on the road while you are driving. Discuss what she thinks might determine when these privileges and responsibilities are given to her.
7. A possible homework assignment could be to write another verse for the song, using the client's list of rights and privileges.

## Rights and Responsibilities Song

*Sing to the tune of "Deck the Halls."*

I can't wait to drive a car.
But then you'll be responsible for all those lives!
Can't wait to grow up and do what I please.
You'll pay for your food, car, gas, and house!
I'll make great money as a doctor or a lawyer.
You'll need to get excellent grades in school!
And go to college for 1 to 10 years!
Rights always come with responsibilities!

# Re-Solution Revolution

**TOPIC** Underachievement and goal setting

**RATIONALE** Adolescent underachievers often choose to put little effort into improving their performance. The reason may be that they tried one solution and did not get the results they were hoping for, so they don't want to try again and be disappointed; or they simply may not want to put energy into the task because it is too hard, too frustrating, or unimportant to them. The purpose of this intervention is to show them that it often takes more than one try to find the "right" solution.

**MATERIALS** A copy of the Re-Solution Revolution Song lyrics and Re-Solution Goal Worksheet

A pen or pencil

**PROCEDURE**

1. When a client presents with concerns about underachieving, ask him to imagine that he can "wave a magic wand" and have his wish come true relative to his school performance. Where would he like to be in terms of progress toward a goal by the end of the month?
2. Talk with him to determine where he is now in relation to his goal and what steps he has taken thus far to reach this goal.
3. Next, ask if there were any steps he had planned to take to work toward the goal that he didn't complete. Discuss in detail what might have gotten in the way and how he felt about it. Next explain that goals sometimes don't get completed but that this doesn't mean that he cannot eventually achieve the goal. A good example of this would be New Year's resolutions—it is more common for these resolutions to be broken or not completed because most people don't really consider the meaning of the word *resolution.* But resolution means resolving the problem, which is a process that might help him resolve his problems relative to achievement.

# Time and Place

**TOPIC** Behavior awareness

**RATIONALE** Very young children can often get confused as to why some behaviors are appropriate in one situation but not in another. The purpose of this intervention is to clarify this confusion and give them practice making appropriate choices in various settings.

**MATERIALS** Six Action Sticks and Six Time and Place Sticks

Copies of the Time and Place Song lyrics (song appears on the CD)

A puppet

**PREPARATIONS** Create the Action Sticks by writing various actions on craft sticks—for example, hugging, running, jumping, taking turns, singing, and laughing. Create the Time and Place Sticks by writing various times and places—for instance, lunchroom, recess, hallway, music class, dinner table, and friend's house.

**PROCEDURE**

1. To begin, introduce Mr. Chuckles (the puppet) to the group and ask them to be respectful listeners as he sings his favorite song for them. Sing only verse 1 of the Time and Place Song, and at the end comment on any good listening behaviors you noticed (eye contact, quiet hands, etc.). Then ask if it is always appropriate to be a good listener. Give an example of when it is not appropriate to be a good listener, such as listening to another person's private conversation. Discuss other examples.
2. Have Mr. Chuckles share that he got his name because he likes to be silly and make people laugh. However, he has learned that it is not always the right time to joke and be silly. He knows a song about this that he would like to teach them.
3. Sing the entire song to the students and then discuss the meaning of the italicized lyrics in the song, asking them how they can tell whether something they do is done at the "best time" or not.
   - How can they tell whether they are doing it in the "best place" or not?

- How can they tell whether their behavior helps them or others do their jobs?
- How do they know whether their behavior is kind and safe for themselves and others?

4. Divide the class into four groups and assign each group a verse for which they are responsible. Have Mr. Chuckles draw an Action Stick and a Time and Place Stick and then go to each group and sing the question for their group's verse. For example, if someone draws *jumping* (Action Stick) *at the dinner table* (Time and Place Stick), you would ask each group the following:

   **Group for verse 1:** Is it the best time and place to jump at the dinner table?

   **Group for verse 2:** Does it help you and others do your job at dinner, when you jump at the table?

   **Group for verse 3:** Are you being kind to others and to yourself when you jump at the dinner table?

   **Group for verse 4:** Is it safe for yourself and others when you jump at the dinner table?

5. Encourage each group to sing a response, such as "Yes, it is" or "No, it's not." Briefly discuss their answers, ascertaining that they understand why it would or would not be a good response.
6. Continue drawing sticks as time permits and then discuss what they learned about appropriate times and places for certain behaviors. End the lesson by singing the song again.

that they usually perform well; they try to do too many things at one time without prioritizing them; and so forth.

6. Talk about the fact that stress is part of life but it can be managed. Emphasize that one stress management technique is to slow down periodically and think about what you are doing. Just as in the game, which went so fast that they didn't realize that the only action that was actually important in order to keep the game going was the passing at the end, in real life it can help to slow down and think things through so as to have a more realistic handle on stressors.
7. Invite more discussion about stress management techniques that have been or could be helpful to them.

## Chapter 3

# Counseling Through the Visual Arts

We've all heard the expressions "a picture is worth a thousand words" and "picture that." Whether we are looking at photographs, drawings, paintings, sculpture, or other art forms, pictures can be a mirror to the soul. Visual images help us reminisce about people, places, and significant events in our lives and conjure up memories that evoke a wide range of emotions.

Art has been used since the beginning of history as a means of communication, as exemplified by cave drawings and hieroglyphics, for example. However, not until the mid-20th century was it used as a definable method of practice in assessment as well as treatment, according to Malchiodi (2005). Today the visual arts, which encompass more than just painting and drawing, are widely used in work with adults and children in groups and individually. Couples and families also benefit from this approach, which is used in school and mental health settings, as well as in hospitals and rehabilitation centers. Gladding (2011) defines the visual arts as "those processes within the realm of art that focus on visually representing reality symbolically or otherwise" (p. 80).

Think back to your early experiences with visual arts. You might have enjoyed finger painting, drawing or coloring, or using watercolors. As you got older, your artistic creations became more sophisticated, and you may have discovered that you had some artistic talent . . . or not, which was my experience. I took art lessons when I was 10 and to this day will never forget my teacher telling me that I didn't draw the tree branches the right way. What a way to stifle creativity and put a damper on the desire to draw! Despite that experience, I have an appreciation for works of art and frequently use various visual arts techniques with clients because it is often the most effective way for them to convey what they are feeling or experiencing. In fact, their pictures don't have to be perfect or "right" in order for them to communicate. The invitation to visually represent what they need to share comes with no requirements as to shape or form.

One of the lessons I learned in using the visual arts is to be cautious about reading too much into a picture, especially if one is not a certified art therapist. I recall working with a young boy whose parents were going through a divorce, and although Ryan hadn't verbalized anything about conflict at home, I assumed it was quite prevalent based on things his mother had shared with me. During one of our sessions I asked him to draw a picture about how things were going at home, and because he finished it just as our time ran out, I hadn't had a chance to process it with him. When I looked at it a few hours later, I was alarmed because there were people in the picture shooting each other. I immediately went to Ryan's classroom and asked him to come to my office so that we could talk about his picture. When I told him that I was concerned about the guns, Ryan's immediate response was "Oh, that's the show I watched on TV last night. My mom and dad yell, but they don't hurt each other." I was relieved and guessed that Ryan had rather liberally interpreted my invitation to make a drawing about how things were at home. Nevertheless, I did call his mother to verify that he had watched this show and that the violence depicted in the picture wasn't a portrayal of what was happening at home.

This chapter presents a variety of visual arts interventions that can be used effectively in counseling children and adolescents, although the visual arts are highly applicable to clients of all ages in multiple settings. We begin by describing the advantages of using this approach with young clients in school, as well as in mental health settings.

## ADVANTAGES OF USING THE VISUAL ARTS IN COUNSELING

Various types of visual arts interventions can be used in a developmental, preventive, or remedial context to help engage clients in a process that helps them clarify and rectify problems. As Brems (2002) notes, the visual arts can be cathartic in that clients freely express their feelings and needs as they deal with current or past issues. In addition, visual arts techniques facilitate growth, as clients explore problem-solving alternatives, skill development, and increased goal directedness. Furthermore, because art transcends cultural boundaries, it is especially effective with diverse populations (Gladding, 2011).

Following are some advantages of using the visual arts in counseling children and adolescents:

- Multiple modalities are used in conjunction with the visual arts, including kinesthetic and perceptual experiences. The hands-on experience is often more engaging than verbal approaches (Malchiodi, 2005).
- Through the visual arts, clients are able to picture themselves or their situations more concretely (Nichols, 2010).

into a scrapbook or on poster paper, and passive phototherapy, in which they make a scrapbook of or put photos on poster paper that have already been taken by others. Discussion about the themes and what the photos represent increases clients' understanding and perceptions. Stevens and Spears (2009) suggest that taking photos can increase clients' sense of mastery, which can result in higher self-esteem.

In my experience, using photos in counseling can be a very enlightening experience that can have an impact on clients on multiple levels. I recall working with a young adolescent who was extremely upset that her parents were sending her to summer camp for two weeks. Prior to leaving, she assured me that she would not make any friends, she would have a terrible time, and she would definitely be bored to death. I suggested that she take pictures of her time there so that if it really was horrible she would have tangible proof that might help convince her parents not to send her there again. After her return, she brought the pictures to share with me at our next counseling session. Interestingly enough, as I looked at them, I saw her laughing, associating with others, and engaging in lots of different activities. Yet she still insisted that she had had a terrible time. "I'm puzzled," I said. "You look like you are having fun in almost all of these pictures . . . but is this just someone who looks like you?" "No, that's me. Once I started making friends, I guess I did have a pretty good time." This was a perfect example of how pictures told the true story.

I also used photos when working with children and adolescents who were having issues with their parents, feeling as if they weren't loved or cared about or that their parents never did things with them or for them. I encouraged them to look through scrapbooks and find evidence for or against their argument that their parents cared very little about them. In almost all cases, this was an excellent reframing technique, a visual reminder of good family times and caring relationships.

Newsome (2003) describes a visual arts activity called "The Bridge," which helps clients deal with problem solving and goal setting. First, clients are given a sheet of paper and instructed to divide it into three panels or sections. They are instructed to draw a picture of a specific problem in the first panel and a picture of what it would look like if the problem were solved on the third panel. In the second panel, they are asked to draw symbols of what is preventing them from reaching the solution. Following this, they are asked to draw a bridge connecting the problem in the first panel to the solution in the third panel, drawing symbols on the bridge to signify various solutions that bridge the gap between the problem and the solution.

Vernon and Clemente (2005) suggest having clients make "artifacts"—that is, create something tangible to serve as a reminder to practice new behaviors or learn a new skill. For example, an angry client can make an alarm clock out of cardboard and draw pictures of things around the clock face that trigger anger. On the back side of the clock he or she can draw a symbol that represents setting the alarm, indicating that it is time to let go of the anger. Ways to do that could be drawn on that side of the clock face.

"The Volcano" is an intervention developed by White and described by Newsome (2003). As the title suggests, this is a good visual arts strategy to help clients deal with anger. First, counselor and client talk about the concept of a volcano erupting, likening this to what people do when they get very angry. The client is invited to draw a volcano with steam and lava coming from it. Next the client is asked to write words on the lava stream that describe hurtful ways that people express their anger when they explode, such as yelling, hitting, and so forth. Finally, the counselor asks the client to think of an event in his or her life that might result in a blowup like an erupting volcano, to draw vents leading from the pressure sources to the outside of the volcano, and to draw symbols representing healthier ways to express anger.

## INCORPORATING THE VISUAL ARTS WITH OTHER CREATIVE ARTS TECHNIQUES

The visual arts can readily be combined with other creative arts techniques. For example, clients may be invited to write about issues they are dealing with and then draw illustrations, compiling them to make a book. This can be a very powerful intervention, particularly for children and adolescents experiencing any type of loss.

Incorporating bibliotherapy with the visual arts is particularly effective. After clients read or listen to a book, poem, or short story, they can paint or draw pictures that represent what the written words mean to them. I used this technique with a teenager who was struggling with body image and eating issues. I had shared a true short story with her titled "I Have to Be Thin" (Vernon, 1998b, pp. 105–109) that was written by another client with an eating disorder. After reading the story aloud, I invited the client to draw a picture of how that story affected her. In this case, the picture she drew was worth a thousand words in motivating her toward healthier goals.

The visual arts and music are another effective combination. Clients can listen to a song or series of songs and make a collage illustrating what feelings are evoked or what images came to mind. Or they can draw a picture about something they are feeling or experiencing that is troublesome and then find music that emphasizes the themes in the picture.

Gladding (2011) describes combining phototherapy with words in a technique used by Goessling and Doyle (2009) in which at-risk adolescents took pictures that represented their lives and communities and then discussed the following questions: S (What do you see happening in this photo?); H (What is really *happening?*); O (How does it relate to *our* lives?); W (*Why* do these issues exist?); and D (What do we *do* to address these issues?).

## CLASSROOM OR SMALL-GROUP APPLICATIONS

There are numerous ways to incorporate the visual arts into small-group and classroom guidance lessons. For example, in a small-group setting, group members can be provided with a large sheet of poster paper, as well as fabric scraps, crayons and markers, glue and glitter, and construction and tissue paper. As a group, their task is to create something that represents who they are as individuals and who they are as a group. This activity is best suited to older elementary children or middle school adolescents. Younger children can use the same materials but create a collage around a specific topic, such as what to look for in a friend or how to get along with others.

Another small-group activity to use as an icebreaker is a group drawing: One child in the group draws something and, after 30 seconds, passes the paper to the next person, who adds to the first drawing, and so on. Discussion can focus on what it felt like to add to someone's drawing, what group members think the drawing represents, and how the activity might have been different if they were doing it alone.

A classroom intervention that helps children learn how people are alike and different involves giving the class magazines, four sheets of mural paper, scissors, and glue and asking them to cut pictures out of the magazines and make a collection of eight to ten different kinds of people. They could represent different ages or ethnic groups, or the people could be doing different activities or live in different places or different types of houses, for example. The counselor divides each sheet of the mural paper into four columns and writes the words "Age"; "Skin, Eye, or Hair Color"; "Activities"; and "Homes and Place" across the top. The counselor then divides the class into four groups and gives each group one of the mural papers. Each individual in the group glues his or her pictures in the appropriate categories on the mural paper. After everyone has finished, the counselor hangs the murals and has children move silently in a line, looking at each mural and noting the types of pictures in the various categories. Discussion focuses on how people are different and alike and how to appreciate all types of people.

A classroom visual arts intervention that is well suited for middle school and high school adolescents is to divide the class into smaller groups of five or six and give each group a roll of masking tape, scissors, magazines, newspapers, colored construction paper and markers, wrapping paper scraps, and yarn. They are instructed to create "an object of beauty" using the materials they have been given. This object can hang on the wall or be modeled by one of the group members. Groups are given 25 minutes to complete this activity but can talk only during the initial 10 minutes, during which time they come up with a plan. At the end of the time, they share their creation with the rest of the class. Processing focuses on how they decided what was beautiful, how they worked together, and who assumed what roles in the group.

## SUMMARY

Using the visual arts can be an exceptionally therapeutic approach to address a wide array of problems that children and adolescents present in counseling. Visual arts interventions promote creativity, help build a sense of community if used in small-group and classroom settings, and facilitate healing and growth. Through the visual arts, clients can communicate joys and concerns that they might not be able to share verbally. The interventions next described are intended to provide you with practical strategies to use individually, as well as in small groups and classroom guidance lessons. They address self-awareness, perfectionism, feelings, perspective taking, peer relationships, career decision making, transitions, depression, and problem solving.

# Look at Me

**TOPIC** Self-awareness

**RATIONALE** This intervention promotes self-awareness of personal abilities and preferences, which is beneficial to younger clients who are just developing greater awareness of self.

**MATERIALS**

One large sheet of butcher paper

Several magazines

Crayons or markers

A glue stick

Yarn

**PROCEDURE**

1. To help promote self-awareness, engage the client in this activity. First, invite her to lie down on the sheet of butcher paper and draw around her body. Then ask if she would like to draw her face on the outline and glue some yarn on the head for hair.
2. Next discuss the fact that she is learning new things often—things she likes to do and things she is good at. Ask her to look at the drawing of her body and think about something she can do or likes to do with her hands and her feet. Suggest that she look through the magazines to find pictures that represent these things and paste them on the body outline—or she can draw pictures if she prefers or is unable to find things in the magazines. After she finishes with her hands and feet, move to her ears, her head (for thinking and remembering), her mouth, and so forth.
3. Discuss what she has pasted or drawn and invite her to describe in more detail what she is able to do with her body. Because children at this age are continually learning to do new things, suggest that she keep the body poster and add to it over time.

# Picture Perfect

**TOPIC** Perfectionism

**RATIONALE** Children can readily adopt perfectionistic standards for themselves or others, which can become problematic in many ways. This intervention addresses the issue by focusing on the importance of learning to differentiate between demanding perfection and doing a good job.

**MATERIALS** A copy of the Picture Perfect Sentence Stems and Picture Perfect Ribbon

A pen or pencil

A can of Play-Doh

Several pipe cleaners

Crayons or markers

A pair of scissors

**PROCEDURE**

1. When working with a young client with issues related to perfectionism, first discuss what it means to be perfect, eliciting ideas such as never making mistakes, always doing things exactly the right way, and being excellent. Then give him a copy of the Picture Perfect Sentence Completion Stems and ask him to write a response for each one.
2. Discuss his responses to the Picture Perfect Sentence Stems and engage him in a discussion about why he thinks he needs to be perfect, how he feels when he demands this of himself, and what it might be like if he didn't always do things perfectly.
3. Next give him the Play-Doh and pipe cleaners. Ask him to create something "perfect," giving him 10 minutes to do this. If he asks for direction as to what he should make or how to do it, tell him that it can be anything he wants it to be, just as long as it is perfect.
4. When the time is up, give him the Picture Perfect Ribbon and ask him to color it any way he likes and then cut it out. Then ask him to pretend that he is entering his "perfect creation" in an art show

and that he is going to be one of the judges. As a judge, he needs to evaluate the creation on a 1 to 5 scale, with 1 being terrible and 5 being excellent, and write that number on the ribbon he made.

5. Discuss his rating and how he arrived at it. If he didn't rate it a 5, ask how he feels about that and what it says about him if he thinks it wasn't perfect. Focus on helping him understand that he doesn't have to rate himself on everything he does and ask him if it is reasonable to think that judges at an art show would always rate everything 5, excellent. Continue to discuss issues related to perfectionism, emphasizing that, realistically, nobody does everything perfectly all the time.

## Picture Perfect Sentence Stems

*Directions: Read the sentence stems below and complete as many as you can.*

I think I should be perfect because ________________________________.

Someone who expects me to be perfect is ________________________________.

When I make a mistake I think ________________________________.

It's hard to be perfect because ________________________________.

If I try to do something perfect but can't I feel ________________________________.

The best thing about not being perfect is ________________________________.

If I do my best but it's not perfect, I think ________________________________.

If I'm not perfect I'm afraid others will think ________________________________.

## Picture Perfect Ribbon

# Show Me How You Feel

**TOPIC** Identifying and expressing feelings

**RATIONALE** Developmentally, children may have difficulty identifying and expressing feelings, yet this is a very crucial skill to learn. This intervention focuses primarily on negative feelings, which are often associated with typical developmental issues as well as with more serious situational factors.

**MATERIALS**

Two hula hoops

A set of Show Me How You Feel Cards

Six paper plates

Markers or crayons

Other art supplies, such as yarn, cotton balls, pipe cleaners and so forth

A pair of scissors

**PREPARATIONS** Copy the Show Me How You Feel Cards page, glue it to tagboard, then cut apart.

**PROCEDURE**

1. When working with a young client who has difficulty identifying and expressing negative feelings, help her develop this skill by implementing this intervention. First, point out the two hula hoops and designate one for feelings you like to have (positive feelings) and the other for feelings you don't like to have (negative feelings). Then explain that you will show some feelings words to her, one at a time. After identifying the feeling and discussing the meaning, she can decide whether the feelings word is one that she likes to have or one that she doesn't and then jump into either the positive or negative hula hoop.
2. After she has identified each of the words and jumped into the hula hoops, discuss how she determined which feelings were positive versus negative and which ones she has experienced. Then tell her that you will be reading some situations to her and that after she thinks about how she would feel, she can draw that

feeling on a paper plate and use the other art supplies to further illustrate the feeling.

3. Proceed to read the following scenarios, allowing adequate time for her to draw the feelings face. After discussing what she has illustrated, move to the next scenario. Proceed in this fashion as time permits.
   - Your little brother grabs a favorite toy that you have been playing with. Show me how you feel.
   - Your new friend sits by someone else at lunch. Show me how you feel.
   - Your mother puts you in time-out because you didn't pick up your room. Show me how you feel.
   - Your teacher won't let you take home the book that you have been reading. Show me how you feel.
   - You lost some parts to your favorite Playmobil set. Show me how you feel.
   - Your older sister locks you out of her room. Show me how you feel.
4. Debrief by discussing which negative feelings she experiences most frequently, how she lets others know how she is feeling, and what she typically does to start feeling better.

## Show Me How You Feel Cards

| | |
|---|---|
| Excited | Disappointed |
| Surprised | Confused |
| Scared | Nervous |
| Mad | Proud |
| Worried | Furious |
| Happy | Jealous |

# That's How I See It

**TOPIC** Perspective taking and problem solving

**RATIONALE** Given their egocentric nature, young adolescents often have difficulty seeing things from others' perspectives, which makes it more difficult for them to get along with peers and adults. This intervention is designed to increase their ability to look at other perspectives, which in turn can enhance their problem-solving abilities and relationships with others.

**MATERIALS**

A half-filled glass of water

A worn-looking baseball cap

Several sheets of drawing paper

Markers

Several magazines

Yarn or string

Buttons, glitter, straws, wrapping paper scraps, and other art supplies

Glue stick

**PROCEDURE**

1. When working with a client who has difficulty seeing things from other perspectives, hand him a half-filled glass of water and ask him what he sees. Then ask him if there is another way to look at it—in other words, if he sees it as half full of water, others might see it as half empty. Then hand him the cap and have him examine it carefully before putting it on. Ask him how he sees the cap, discussing the fact that he might see the cap as old, whereas others might see it as a special cap because it obviously has been worn a lot.
2. Engage the client in a discussion about how there are usually multiple ways of looking at situations and that it is fairly common for people to have different perspectives on the same issue. Ask him if he can think of examples from his own life—situations with his friends, parents, or teachers.

3. Next hand the client a sheet of paper and markers and invite him to make a poster representing, from his perspective, a current problem he is having with peers or adults. Encourage use of magazine pictures, yarn or string, buttons or straws, or other art supplies. Invite him to share his illustration with you, discussing the problem situation in more detail.
4. Give him another sheet of paper. Ask him to imagine that he is the other person in the problem or conflict and suggest that he make a poster that illustrates how he thinks this person would portray the problem—would it be the same, or would it be different?
5. Discuss what he created relative to the two perspectives, focusing on similarities and differences and how each person's perspective may influence possible problem-solving strategies. Suggest that in the future he can apply this strategy of drawing other perspectives to help him gain insight into how others might see a situation, thus facilitating problem solving.

# Who Do You See?

**TOPIC** Self-awareness and identity development

**RATIONALE** A major task of young adolescence is developing greater self-awareness and formulating a more stable self-image as adolescents learn to define who they are and what is important to them.

**MATERIALS**

A mirror

A sheet of drawing paper

Colored pencils

Yarn, material scraps, and several buttons

Glue stick

Copies of the Who Do You See? Attributes page

A pen or pencil

**PREPARATIONS** Locate clip art or magazine pictures representing the following: music, books, sports, and academics. Glue each symbol on a separate sheet of paper.

**PROCEDURE**

1. When an adolescent client presents with issues relating to self-identity, hand her a mirror and ask her to make a picture representing what she sees in the mirror, using the paper and other art supplies.
2. After she has finished and you have discussed how she sees herself, tell her that what she drew is the observable part, but that she is much more than that, so together you will be looking at who she is on the inside—her interests and personal characteristics.
3. Place the separate sheets of paper with the pictures or symbols representing music, books, sports, and academics in front of the client and have her either write or draw something on these sheets that identifies the type of music she likes or performs, what types of books she likes to read, what sports activities she participates in and/or likes to observe, and what academic subjects she likes best or achieves well in. After she has completed this part of the

intervention, discuss what she has written or drawn, encouraging her to elaborate on these categories representing her interests.

4. Next give her a copy of the Who Do You See? Attributes page and invite her to complete it to learn more about herself. After she has finished, invite discussion about how she sees herself, whether there are attributes she wishes were more or less like her, and what she learned about herself from this intervention.

## Who Do You See? Attributes

*Directions: Think about who you are and put a checkmark in the box that best describes you.*

| | A Lot Like Me | Somewhat Like Me | Not at All Like Me |
|---|---|---|---|
| 1. A risk taker | ☐ | ☐ | ☐ |
| 2. Fun to be with | ☐ | ☐ | ☐ |
| 3. Shy | ☐ | ☐ | ☐ |
| 4. A leader | ☐ | ☐ | ☐ |
| 5. A follower | ☐ | ☐ | ☐ |
| 6. Insecure | ☐ | ☐ | ☐ |
| 7. Talented | ☐ | ☐ | ☐ |
| 8. Smart | ☐ | ☐ | ☐ |
| 9. Caring | ☐ | ☐ | ☐ |
| 10. Truthful | ☐ | ☐ | ☐ |
| 11. Rebellious | ☐ | ☐ | ☐ |
| 12. Loyal | ☐ | ☐ | ☐ |
| 13. Outgoing | ☐ | ☐ | ☐ |
| 14. Popular | ☐ | ☐ | ☐ |

# Picture Your Peers

**TOPIC** Peer relationships

**RATIONALE** Friendships are all-consuming at this age and can be a positive as well as a negative influence. Seeing peers in a realistic light helps young adolescents avoid assuming negative behaviors just to fit in.

**MATERIALS**

A copy of the client's school yearbook (ask client to provide)

Six copies of the Picture Your Peers Outline

A pen or pencil

**PROCEDURE**

1. When a client is referred or presents with friendship issues, discuss the nature of the problem, how it is affecting him, and how often problems of this nature occur. To have a better picture of the situation, invite the client to bring his school yearbook to the next session.
2. Invite the client to share pictures from the yearbook of the friends he is having problems with, as well as those he gets along well with. After discussing the problems and the peers, talk about the facts that friendships can be quite complex and that people aren't always who they appear to be on the outside. For example, some friends may be fickle—a good friend one day and a not-so-good friend another day. Or some friends may have different values or interests and may not always be a good influence. Ask the client to reflect on these ideas relative to his own relationships.
3. Give the client one of the Picture Your Peers Outlines and then ask him to select one classmate from the yearbook pictures he previously shared with you. Explain that you would like him to take a closer look at this person, identifying positive traits as well as any negative realities that characterize this classmate. After he has completed this exercise, discuss what he wrote and focus on helping him look at this person in a realistic light, noting any negative influences and also strong positive traits.
4. Proceed in a similar manner with the other classmates he identified through the yearbook pictures, providing an outline sheet

for each one. When he has finished and you have discussed how he sees each, ask him to lay the outline sheets side by side and underline any similarities in terms of positive traits and circle any similarities relative to negative traits. Invite him to reflect on what he has learned about these classmates now that he is seeing them in a realistic light. Encourage him to talk about how he is like and unlike his peers and whether there are some who are better influences on him than others.

5. Finally, ask the client if he thinks that some of the relationship problems he is having relate to the negative realities he identified in one or more of his peers. If so, what message does that send to him about these relationships?

## Picture Your Peers Outline

What I like about this person

What I admire about this person

What I might have in common with this person

What I dislike about this person

What I don't admire about this person

What I don't have in common with this person

# As I See It

**TOPIC** Career decision making

**RATIONALE** Adolescents are often confused about what career paths to pursue after high school. This visual activity is designed to help them clarify career aspirations.

**MATERIALS** Six to eight sheets of paper

Colored pencils, crayons, or markers

Several magazines

A glue stick

A pair of scissors

A pencil or pen

**PROCEDURE**

1. When a client presents with confusion about what to do after high school, give her six to eight sheets of paper and invite her to draw pictures or symbols or cut and paste pictures from magazines of several different options that she has been considering, one option per sheet. Suggest that she use no more than the top half of the page.
2. Next have the client take one page at a time and draw a line across the page under the picture. Then ask her to make three columns underneath this line and label them "What I already know about this option," "What else I need to know about this option," and "Why this is one of the options I am considering."
3. Engage the client in a discussion about what she has drawn and written (this will take more than one session), working with her to clarify facts and beliefs about each possible choice. Suggest that she do further research on each possibility to address what else she needs to know about the options. This could involve visiting colleges or technical schools, doing research on the computer, interviewing people in the field, job shadowing, and so forth.
4. In subsequent sessions, continue discussing what else she has learned about each option. Then, when she feels as though she

has adequate information, ask her to rank order the pictures, starting with the most appealing option.

5. Then have her take two more sheets of paper and divide each into six to eight columns, depending on how many choices she has identified. Ask her to label one page "Advantages" and the other page "Disadvantages" and at the top of each page, write each of the options identified, one per column. Next, have her identify advantages of each choice on the corresponding sheet of paper and do the same for the disadvantages.
6. Discuss the advantages and disadvantages of each option according to their rank order, inviting her to rank them again them if anything new emerges during the listing of the advantages and disadvantages.
7. Continue discussion over subsequent sessions, helping her clarify career goals and viable options.

# Photo Friends

**TOPIC** Friends and transitions

**RATIONALE** As the high school years come to a close and adolescents transition to the next stage of their lives, they will undoubtedly be saying goodbye to some long-time friends. Preserving memories can be an important part of the transitioning process.

**MATERIALS**

A disposable camera

Various colors of construction paper (10–12 sheets)

A glue stick

Fine-point markers

A pen

Wrapping paper scraps, glitter, buttons, yarn, or other art supplies

Several brass fasteners or a stapler

**PROCEDURE**

1. When adolescents are transitioning away from high school, it is quite likely that relationships with friends will be affected. For example, friends might be moving away from their hometowns to work or attend college or join the military. For many adolescents, this can be painful, especially if they have known these friends for many years. Encourage your client to talk about what the transition means to him relative to his relationships with his friends and discuss the fact that it is important to have some sort of closure in order to successfully complete this part of the transition.
2. Suggest to the client that it might be helpful for him to make a short book that includes photos of his closest friends. Give him a disposable camera and request that he take pictures and bring them to the next session. (This project will most likely span several sessions.)
3. When he brings his photos, invite him to talk about the pictures, elaborating on the importance of the relationship, how long he has known the friends in the pictures, and what he will miss most when he doesn't see them as frequently. Give him the construc-

tion paper and the art supplies and invite him to glue the photos on separate sheets on construction paper and decorate the sheets, either by adding a frame or drawing symbols or pictures that best characterize the relationship.

4. Either as he works or after he has completed one page, encourage discussion about what he values most about the relationship, struggles he may have had with the person, special memories, and so forth. Invite him to write short messages on each page. When all pages have been completed, fasten them together with brass fasteners or staples, making a short book that will help him preserve the memories.
5. Debrief by discussing what it was like for him to make the book and anything else about these special friendships he would like to share.

# "Snap" Out of It

**TOPIC** Depression

**RATIONALE** Adolescents are no strangers to depression, so it is imperative that they learn how to cope successfully with it. Because depression can be very serious and many adolescents are frequently overwhelmed by their depression and think things will never get better, it is critical to introduce them to concrete strategies that can empower them and help decrease the frequency and intensity of this negative emotion.

**MATERIALS**

A copy of the "Snap" Out of It Feelings Chart

A disposable camera

10–12 sheets of paper

A pen or pencil

A glue stick

**PROCEDURE**

1. When a client presents with depression, encourage her to talk about what the depression is like for her in terms of frequency and intensity, how it affects her relationships and school performance, and how she deals with it. Give her a copy of the Snap Out of It Feelings Chart and ask her to keep track of her depression during the coming week, explaining that the chart is a good visual representation of the frequency and intensity of the depression and can be a helpful assessment. She should use a 1 to 5 rating, with 1 being "very depressed" and 5 being "not depressed."
2. At the next session, review the ratings on the chart, discussing any patterns: Were there particular days or times of the day that were especially good or bad? Was every hour of every day very low, or were there also some highs? Discuss in greater detail how the depression affects her ability to function as she normally would. Then give her a disposable camera and ask her if she could snap some pictures during the week that would show what her life would be like if she weren't so depressed: What would she be

doing, who would she be with, and how might she look? (Another person would need to take the last picture.)

3. As she shares her pictures, encourage her to talk about what she depicted and what would need to happen for her to be able to act as if she weren't so depressed. Next give her blank sheets of paper and ask her to glue each picture to a sheet. When she is finished, suggest that she think about what she might be able to do to deal more effectively with her depression in order to make this "picture" her new reality and then write these suggestions on the appropriate page. As she does this, help her identify various options if she needs help. As a homework assignment prior to the next session, encourage her to act "as if" she isn't depressed and to follow some of the suggestions she identified.
4. At the next session, discuss how things are going and whether any of her pictures are becoming her new reality.

# "Snap" Out of It Feelings Chart

| | Sunday | Monday | Tuesday | Wednesday | Thursday | Friday | Saturday |
|---|---|---|---|---|---|---|---|
| 6:00 a.m. | | | | | | | |
| 7:00 a.m. | | | | | | | |
| 8:00 a.m. | | | | | | | |
| 9:00 a.m. | | | | | | | |
| 10:00 a.m. | | | | | | | |
| 11:00 a.m. | | | | | | | |
| 12:00 p.m. | | | | | | | |
| 1:00 p.m. | | | | | | | |
| 2:00 p.m. | | | | | | | |
| 3:00 p.m. | | | | | | | |
| 4:00 p.m. | | | | | | | |
| 5:00 p.m. | | | | | | | |
| 6:00 p.m. | | | | | | | |
| 7:00 p.m. | | | | | | | |
| 8:00 p.m. | | | | | | | |
| 9:00 p.m. | | | | | | | |
| 10:00 p.m. | | | | | | | |
| 11:00 p.m. | | | | | | | |
| 12:00 a.m. | | | | | | | |

# The Me We See

**TOPIC** Self- and other awareness

**RATIONALE** Middle childhood is an important formative period with regard to awareness of oneself and others. This intervention, best suited for a small group, is intended to help children learn more about themselves and others.

**MATERIALS** Two butcher paper cutouts of a T-shirt for each child (one for the front and one for the back), which will be stapled together at the shoulders once children have completed the activity

Crayons or markers for each child

**PROCEDURE**

1. Distribute the materials to each child and indicate that they are each going to be making a T-shirt about themselves. Ask them to think about how they would describe themselves: things they do well, things they are learning to do, and things they like to do with their friends and family.
2. Then have them draw pictures on their T-shirts (both front and back) to represent how they see themselves. Have them put their names on the front and, when finished, staple the shirts together at the shoulders so that the pictures are on the outside.
3. Next invite one child at a time to circulate among the other group members so that they can see what he or she has drawn. Then have them sit down and verbally share some of the things that they have drawn that represent them.
4. Finally, have the children take turns introducing another child to the rest of the group members by pointing out some of the other child's skills and interests. Close the session by asking the group what they learned about themselves and others, discussing similarities and differences among group members.

# See the Options

**TOPIC** Problem solving and group cooperation/collaboration

**RATIONALE** During this stage of development, many adolescents have difficulty identifying multiple solutions to problems, but it is much easier if they collaborate with others. Learning to work effectively with others is an important skill that will benefit them in school and in future employment.

**MATERIALS**

A four-inch stack of newspapers per group of four

A roll of masking tape for each group

A pair of scissors for each group

Fabric scraps, wrapping paper scraps, colored ribbons, and buttons for each group

Markers and glue stick for each group

A copy of the See the Options Group Process Form for each small-group observer

A pen or pencil for each small-group observer

**PROCEDURE**

1. Introduce this lesson by explaining that students will be working together in small groups to design an item of clothing that could be modeled in a fashion show. They may use only the materials given to them, and they will have a limited time to complete the task.
2. Divide them into groups of five, asking them to select one person per group to be the observer. Give each of the observers a copy of the See the Options Group Process Form and ask him or her to carefully observe the process so as to be able to respond to the items on the form. The observer will not participate in the design project but instead will focus on the various options that the group discussed regarding what to design and on how group members worked together to complete the task.
3. Allow 20 minutes for the groups to complete their designs. When they are finished, have them model their design for the other

groups as if in a fashion show. Then have each of the group observers report on the options their group generated. During these reports, ask students to focus on how many options were identified and initiate discussion about how they came up with the various alternatives. Also ask them whether they think their project was better because they worked together as a group or whether they could have done a better job if they had worked alone.

4. Next ask the group observers to give feedback to their group about how well the group worked together to complete the task. After they have done this, direct discussion to the total group and ask everyone to reflect on the items on the process form, focusing on why they think it is important to learn how to collaborate in a group.

## See the Options Group Process Form

*Directions: Carefully observe the group so that you can record the options the group identifies and how well they work together to complete the task. Complete this form as outlined below.*

How many different options did the group come up with for their design? List them.

_______________________________________________

_______________________________________________

_______________________________________________

_______________________________________________

_______________________________________________

Which group member(s) assumed leadership roles in the group, getting the group started, suggesting what to do, and directing the group to complete the task?

_______________________________________________

_______________________________________________

_______________________________________________

Which group member(s) shared the most ideas?

_______________________________________________

_______________________________________________

_______________________________________________

Which group members complimented others' ideas and were the most cooperative?

_______________________________________________

_______________________________________________

_______________________________________________

| | | |
|---|---|---|
| Did all group members take an active part in the project? | ☐ Yes | ☐ No |
| Were there any group members who blocked the process by goofing off, arguing, or not listening? | ☐ Yes | ☐ No |
| Did group members cooperate with one another? | ☐ Yes | ☐ No |
| Were group members willing to compromise in order to get the task completed? | ☐ Yes | ☐ No |

# Mask It

**TOPIC** Self-identity

**RATIONALE** As they struggle to identify who they are, adolescents try on many new ways of thinking, feeling, and behaving. And because friends are such an important influence on them, they often resort to "hiding behind a mask," not revealing their true identities for fear they may be rejected by peers. This intervention focuses on helping them see who is behind the mask in order to further their self-understanding.

**MATERIALS**

A large sheet of card stock per person, at least 12 by 18 inches

Tissue paper, glitter, wrapping paper scraps, markers, watercolor paints, and other art supplies

Several glue sticks

Scissors for each person

A ball of string

**PROCEDURE**

1. To introduce this intervention, engage students in a discussion about how it is typical for adolescents to "hide behind a mask," unsure whether they should reveal who they are for fear of being rejected by peers. In addition, they may not even have a good understanding of their own identities. Read the following quote to them from *Alice in Wonderland,* by Lewis Carroll:

   **Caterpillar:** And who are you?

   **Alice:** I hardly know, Sir, just at present—at least I know who I was when I got up this morning, but I think I must have changed several times since then.

2. Invite some discussion about what this dialogue means and how it might apply to their own lives as adolescents.
3. Next give all students a large sheet of card stock and explain that they will be making masks. They can decorate them any way they choose, using the materials provided. When they have finished decorating the masks, they should poke a hole in each side

of the mask and thread string through the holes so that they can actually tie the masks around their heads. Then they should turn their masks over and write 10 to 15 words or phrases describing the person who is behind the mask.

4. Divide students into small groups of four to five and invite them to put their masks on for a few minutes, then take the masks off and take turns sharing about the person behind the mask. Invite discussion about how they decided what to write; whether they think they "wear a mask" with peers, parents, or teachers; and what they learned about themselves by doing this.

# Chapter 4

# Counseling Through Expressive Writing

You have probably heard the expression "the handwriting's on the wall," meaning that something is obvious or perhaps inevitable. The use of expressive writing in counseling does make things more obvious because writing records thoughts, feelings, and experiences that are significant at a particular point in time. By committing things to writing, we have a concrete way of monitoring where we have been and, on reflection, where we want to go, metaphorically speaking. Writing helps clarify our dreams, desires, thoughts, and feelings. Depending on the form of writing, it can be cathartic, tap our creativity, and give us greater insight.

Using expressive writing in a therapeutic way is often referred to as scriptotherapy (Gladding, 2011; Newsome, 2003; Wright & Chung, 2001). Simply put, *scriptotherapy* refers to the various forms of writing used in counseling and is a very effective self-help approach. As Newsome (2003) points out, writing has been used since the 1940s, when counselors began incorporating journaling, stories, poems, and autobiographies into their work with clients.

Writing helps clients develop perspective, and although it can be a very powerful adjunct to the counseling process, it may not be the best approach for clients who find writing too laborious, for younger clients who have a limited vocabulary, or for non-native speakers of English. However, non-native speakers can write in their native language, especially if they are journaling or writing poetry, which is more personal and intended to be cathartic, and counselors can serve as scribes for younger children. Some clients find certain forms of writing more helpful than others, and therefore it is important to gear the intervention to what seems most appropriate for achieving the desired goal.

When I was an adolescent, I found writing letters to be the most effective way for my mother and me to communicate about typical teenage issues that might have resulted in conflict if we hadn't used this medium. When we were having problems, I usually initiated the process by putting my thoughts and feelings in writing and leaving a letter in my mother's drawer. Somehow I must have let her know it was there, and she would then write a response. There usually was some back-and-forth exchange, and clearly it was a helpful process for us. Several years ago, I shared one of these letters with an adolescent client who was struggling with her parents because she wanted to be more independent and, in her mind, they were curtailing her freedom. Because she was quite shy and had been referred by her mother—who thought that her daughter was the one with the problem—my client really wasn't very willing to talk about their relationship. However, after she read my letter, which described similar conflicts, she immediately said that that was exactly how she felt and proceeded to share her frustration and anger about her parents not trusting her or letting her do things her friends were allowed to do. During the next session, she wrote a letter to her parents that she subsequently shared with them. This proved to be an effective way of initiating dialogue and resulted in better communication and understanding for both client and parents.

There are many different ways to use writing in counseling. Although we may think of writing as a creative endeavor, which it certainly can be, therapeutic writing may be more structured—for example, taking the form of activity sheets that help clients clarify thoughts, articulate feelings, and develop skills. Examples of these are presented in this chapter, along with numerous other ways to incorporate writing into the counseling process.

## ADVANTAGES OF USING EXPRESSIVE WRITING IN COUNSELING

Various types of expressive writing interventions—stories, poems, journals, letters, open-ended sentences, and so forth—can be used in a developmental, preventive, or remedial context to help clients gain perspective about their lives. As Bradley and colleagues (2009) note, writing enhances awareness by helping clients organize their thoughts and feelings. In addition to being beneficial in many diverse settings (Baikie & Wilhelm, 2005), the approach has many other advantages:

- Writing provides cathartic release of emotions (Bradley et al., 2009).
- Writing helps clients resolve problems (Bradley et al., 2009).
- Writing can be an effective self-help approach (Gladding, 2011).
- Writing contributes to self-integration and validation (Bradley et al., 2009).
- Writing facilitates healing and coping (Degges-White & Davis, 2011).
- Writing can improve physical and emotional well-being (Pennebaker, 2004).

- Writing can help clients with goal setting (Cook, 2011a).
- Writing is effective with clients from diverse backgrounds (Vernon & Clemente, 2005).
- Writing can serve as a starting point for discussion during counseling sessions (Vernon, 2009).
- Writing helps clients clarify thoughts and concerns, as well as increase self-awareness (Vernon, 2009).
- Writing can stimulate self-exploration and creativity (White & Murray, 2002).
- Through writing, clients can articulate thoughts and feelings that they might not be able to express verbally (Vernon & Clemente, 2005).

## TYPES OF PROBLEMS AND POPULATIONS THAT BENEFIT FROM EXPRESSIVE WRITING

Different forms of writing can be effective with many problems and populations:

- Expressive writing has been shown to be effective with clients who have experienced trauma (Degges-White & Davis, 2011).
- Writing has been used to help clients experiencing major life transitions establish goals (Cook, 2011b).
- Poetry can be used to facilitate healing for clients dealing with depression (Vernon, 2009).
- Writing can decrease psychological distress in male college students relative to emotional connectedness (Lepore & Smyth, 2003, as cited in Gladding, 2011).
- Writing can empower sexual abuse survivors and help them gain personal control (Kress, Hoffman, & Thomas, 2008).
- Letter writing has been used effectively with clients dealing with loss (Thompson, 2003).
- Letter writing is helpful for clients dealing with anger or other strong emotions (Newsome, 2003).
- Writing can help clients clarify career aspirations (Vernon, 2002).
- Poetry therapy has been used with clients who have HIV/AIDS (Malchiodi, 2005).
- Writing has been effective with clients suffering from life-threatening illnesses, such as cancer or Crohn's disease (Vernon, 2009).
- Writing has been beneficial for adolescents experiencing anxiety about transitions (Vernon, 2009).
- Writing has been used with counselors to help prevent stress and burnout (Gladding, 1987).

## WRITING THERAPY VERSUS EXPRESSIVE WRITING IN COUNSELING

As with other expressive arts approaches, a distinction exists between using writing in counseling and being a trained scriptotherapist. For example, poetry therapy is the use of poetry in counseling, and it is important to differentiate between trained poetry therapists and counselors who use poetry as a therapeutic tool (Gladding, 2005). Professionals trained in a particular style of writing generally approach the writing in a different manner than do counselors who are incorporating various writing interventions into the counseling process. This chapter addresses specific applications for counselors who are not trained in the specific discipline of writing.

## EXAMPLES OF EXPRESSIVE WRITING INTERVENTIONS

As previously noted, writing can be an excellent self-help approach, or the counselor may prescribe different forms of writing. In the prescriptive approach, the counselor directs the client to write a poem, a personal story, or an autobiography, for example, but what the client writes is his or her own creative endeavor. Even with more structured types of writing, such as in activity sheets, the outcome represents the client's own perceptions, stimulated by such devices as open-ended questions or decision-making dilemmas. Several general writing strategies are subsequently described.

### Journal It

Chances are that many of us have kept a journal at some point during our lives. Journaling is a form of expressive writing that helps clients reflect on their personal experiences. Through journaling, clients gain insight, and because journaling is often a cathartic experience, it is a nonthreatening way of expressing feelings. Journaling is an especially effective intervention to use with adolescents to increase self-awareness, clarify values, and facilitate decision making. With nonverbal clients, journaling is particularly helpful because it heightens awareness of issues and motivates them to discuss these with the counselor. It is also an appropriate multicultural approach: In some cultures, people are not openly encouraged to share their feelings verbally but may do so in writing.

There are several different forms of journaling. Unstructured journaling, a popular self-help approach, simply involves the counselor's inviting the client, either in session or as a homework assignment, to record thoughts and feelings for a specified time period. If the journaling is more structured, the counselor invites the client to reflect specifically on topics that might stimulate reflection, such as the high point of the week, the low point of the week, challenges during the week, things the client was proud about, and so forth. Although journaling can be therapeutic in and of itself, it is generally more effective if the clients are willing to share parts of their journal with the counselor so that additional interventions can be developed for issues that emerge during the journaling process. During each session, the counselor can invite clients to share anything from the journal that they feel is significant or would like to talk more about.

Other forms of journaling include the period log, in which clients are encouraged to reflect on a specific period of their lives, and the daily log, which is more like a diary of one's experiences (Gladding, 2011). Gladding also describes a type of journaling called "stepping stones," in which clients write about significant points of movement in their lives, helping them clarify patterns and goals. Clients can also keep journals of their dreams, desires, or dilemmas. Clients who are reluctant to express themselves in writing can be encouraged to keep journals in the form of audiorecordings.

## Personal Stories

An effective strategy to help clients with personal dilemmas and decision making is writing personal stories with different endings. In using this strategy, the client is first invited to write about a personal dilemma and then encouraged to write several different endings to the same story. This technique was effective with Simona, a high school senior who was debating whether to attend the local community college and live at home or to apply for a scholarship to go to a four-year college several hours from home. After she wrote her stories and shared them with her counselor, dialogue between counselor and client focused on the advantages and disadvantages of each ending, as well as consequences. The process helped Simona make the decision that she would move away from home if she was able to get a scholarship.

A variation of the personal story is to write a story from the perspective of another person. This is an effective intervention for both children and adolescents, whose egocentric tendencies make it difficult for them to see another person's point of view. To implement this intervention, the counselor invites the client to write a story involving a dilemma with another person. The client first writes from his or her point of view and then writes about the same dilemma from the other person's perspective. For example, this strategy was helpful with a brother and sister who had problems getting along. By writing stories from their sibling's point of view, the brother and sister were able to look more objectively at the problem, which in turn facilitated conflict resolution. This technique is also good to use with parent-child relationship problems.

## Letters

Letter writing has been shown to have positive effects (Oliver, Nelson, Cade, & Cueva, 2007) and can be a very powerful form of writing. It may be used in several different ways. First, a client can write a letter to another person for the purpose of sharing thoughts and feelings to improve communication or resolve conflicts. Although clients may not actually send the letters, the act of putting something on paper can be very therapeutic. Another way that letter writing can be incorporated into counseling is to have clients write letters to an abstract concept—such as anger, grief, or depression—or to their disease or disability. I used this approach with an adolescent who was severely depressed. Her "Dear Depression" letter was a viable way for her to express her anger and powerlessness over this disorder, and it actually motivated her to work harder at combating it.

Letter writing also helped a young child who had leukemia. It was very difficult for him to express how he felt about being hospitalized for long periods of time and having to battle the disease, which made him feel different from his peers. As soon as he started writing the letter, his anger and fear poured onto the page, and I was able to develop other effective interventions because I had a better idea of what he was experiencing.

Writing letters is especially effective in helping clients deal with various forms of loss—relationships, transitions such as moving or parental divorce or remarriage, and death. Clients may find that writing a series of letters is necessary for them to work through the issues.

## Personal Poems

Sloan (2003) notes that poetry helps clients "sift through the layers of their lives in search of their own truths" (p. 35). According to Gorelick (2005), who describes poetry as "the language of the heart" (p. 118), this form of healing began many years ago with shamans' incantations and today is used either as an in-session intervention or as a homework assignment. Poetry helps clients understand themselves and others, increases sensitivity, and promotes change and healing.

Writing poetry encourages emotional soul searching and can be very helpful for clients because, in addition to being a cathartic experience, poetry written over time allows them to monitor their progress in counseling. This intervention proved to be very beneficial for one of my clients, who suffered from severe depression. In the beginning, Laurie's poems were very dark, with frequent references to depression and hopelessness. Over time, she expressed these themes less frequently, and it became obvious that she felt more optimistic about her life. Two poems, reprinted with her permission, illustrate the change. The first is an example of an early poem:

### So Much Pain

*So much pain,*
*Tearing, ripping, scorching your heart,*
*That brings you down to nothing.*
*The pain is so intense*
*That everything else is nonexistent.*
*The slice of that razor*
*And the jab of that knife*
*Do not hurt,*
*But just bring hope.*
*Hope of a day that my heart won't feel pain*
*And the scars on my arms will be gone,*
*Lying in my coffin,*
*Deep down into the ground*
*With nothing remaining but my rotting bones.*

After many months of counseling, Laurie expressed her thoughts and feelings in a much more optimistic manner:

### A Finalizing Day

*Every day the same obstacles.*
*But now we can overcome.*
*The shadow upon me is slowly drifting away*
*To where I can actually see myself and all that lies around me*
*So this will all end and I will finally get my wish,*
*Of happiness—now and forever.*

Some clients feel intimidated about writing poetry and may do better with sentence stems to get them started, such as "Sometimes I'm . . . but other times I . . ." With clients who feel uncertain about writing poetry, the counselor can try asking them some specific questions about a troublesome event; as the client talks, the counselor writes down what is shared, and together they can try to put these thoughts into verse form.

## Limericks

Limericks are a form of poetry written with a specific meter and rhyme scheme, according to Sloan (2003). This form of writing is engaging, especially for younger children, and as they develop limericks to address specific problems, they also generate coping skills and problem-solving strategies. The following example was developed with a 10-year-old client, who misbehaved in class:

*There once was a girl named Lil*
*Who had a very hard time sitting still,*
*So her teacher got mad,*
*Which made Lil very sad,*
*So she calmed herself down by pretending she was ill.*

Clients generally have fun writing limericks. Posting them in a locker or on a desktop helps to reinforce the intended message.

### Autobiographies

More suitable for older adolescents, an autobiography reflects the client's life and helps him or her clarify what has been important up to this point in time. Writing an autobiography helps clients recall meaningful relationships, successes and failures, and dreams and disappointments. Through this medium, they can develop insight. According to Bradley and colleagues (2009), autobiographies can cover the life span or can address a specific time period or aspect of one's life, such as relationships with friends or family over the last several years. The counselor interacts with the client to encourage clarification, probe for feelings, identify specific concerns, or establish goals for change.

## OTHER EXAMPLES OF EXPRESSIVE WRITING INTERVENTIONS

Newsome (2003) describes the "Life Review" exercise, which is similar to an autobiography, in which clients reflect on past experiences and future possibilities. In doing a life review, clients are asked to write descriptions of significant events in their lives, as well as feelings they associate with these events. These events are written on separate pages and do not necessarily have to be in chronological order. The pages can be compiled into a book or folder, and as the counselor and client review it, the counselor helps the client identify themes and patterns.

Uninterrupted, sustained, silent writing is a technique described by Bradley and colleagues (2009). For this intervention, the counselor invites the client to write down everything related to feelings that occurs to him or her in a three- to five-minute time period. The counselor and client discuss what has been written and explore ways to change negative feelings and maintain positive feelings.

Newsome (2003) describes another writing intervention, developed by Hobday and Olliver, called "Past, Present, and Future." The intervention is more appropriate for adolescents than for younger children. In implementing this technique, the counselor asks the client to divide a large sheet of paper into four columns. In the first column, the client writes several significant things about his or her life, including friends, fun, family, school, and so forth. He or she then labels the second column "Past," selects one or more topics from the first column, and writes about what happened concerning the topics in the past. In the next column, labeled "Present," the client describes something about how selected topics are manifested in the present. The last column is "Future," in which the client writes about what he or she hopes for in the future relative to the selected topics.

The counselor can encourage the client to reflect on what has been written and to look for positive changes as he or she moves from past to present and then to future.

Another intervention, described by Gladding (2011), is the "Therapeutic Fairy Tale," in which clients use the typical fairy tale opening "Once upon a time." They then imagine a scene far away from the present in terms of space and time. Next they describe a problem within this setting, as well as a solution, and complete the fairy tale in six to ten minutes. This strategy is effective with adolescents, who gain insight into themselves as they analyze the characters, how the story unfolds, and what contributes to the solution.

## INCORPORATING EXPRESSIVE WRITING INTO OTHER CREATIVE ARTS TECHNIQUES

Writing can readily be incorporated into other creative arts techniques. Clients can illustrate their personal stories and make books, or they can draw pictures to accompany the "Life Review" exercise (Newsome, 2003). Counselors can also suggest that adolescents find photographs to incorporate into their autobiographies; the visual images, combined with the written chronology, will have more impact.

Music can be a powerful adjunct to writing, especially poetry. The counselor can encourage clients to find music that conveys the themes in their poems or music that can be used as background music as they read a personal story or poem.

Another suggestion is to use drama in conjunction with limericks. I did this with a young girl with AD/HD. During one of our sessions, we wrote a limerick, and she then acted it out. Doing so actually helped her remember the concept because she could "see herself" implementing the solution. Here is Clair's limerick, reproduced with her permission:

*There once was a girl named Clair*
*Who couldn't sit still in her chair.*
*Her teacher got very mad,*
*And Clair felt very bad,*
*So she made a sign: "Don't you dare get out of your chair."*

Drama can also be used with letter writing. I recall working with a client whose parents were alcoholics. The situation was getting much worse, and Angela had a hard time coping not only with their drinking but also with parenting her siblings and trying to keep up with her schoolwork. Angela was afraid to tell her parents how she felt because she didn't know how the message would come across. She decided that writing a letter might be a better way for her to express her feelings about how alcohol was ruining her life and their family.

However, she was afraid that her parents wouldn't read the letter and was confused about what to do. I suggested that she first write the letter. I would then role-play her mother or father, and she could practice telling them the essence of what she had written in the letter. The role-playing enabled her to rehearse so that she came across assertively as opposed to aggressively, and it lowered her anxiety about confronting her parents.

## CLASSROOM OR SMALL-GROUP APPLICATIONS

Writing interventions are highly applicable in small groups. Jacobs (1992) contends that group members are more involved if they have to put things in writing and that it is easier for them to share because they have thought about their responses. He suggests that incomplete sentences are an effective way to stimulate discussion in a group setting. The sentences can be related to the topic for the group, such as friendship:

Friends are important because . . .

The best thing about having friends is . . .

Friends should . . .

Something I like to do with friends is . . .

When I have a fight with a friend, I feel . . .

A good friend is . . .

Another small-group intervention for adolescents is to discuss the difference between assertive and aggressive messages and which behaviors go with which type of message. Group members may be provided with several situations and then write both assertive and aggressive responses to the situations. As an example, one of the situations could read "You got a bad grade on a test, and you think the teacher was unfair. You decide to talk to him about it. Write an assertive and an aggressive response." As they each share their responses, group members can give feedback about the content of the message and what effect it might have on the person receiving it. Role-playing can also be incorporated into this intervention so that group members have an opportunity to practice the responses.

A writing intervention for the classroom involves considering consequences before making a decision. In "Consider the Consequences" (Vernon, 1998b, pp. 79–80), sixth graders are given several index cards containing situations such as cheating on a test, lying to parents, not studying for a test, coming home an hour late, and so forth. Students are subdivided into groups of four, and, after discussing the meaning of the word *consequence,* they are given a situation card. After reading it, they discuss short- and long-term consequences and record these on the back of the index cards. After the groups have identified the consequences, they make up skits to illustrate them.

Another classroom intervention for high school students, involving brainstorming, can be geared to many different topics. For example, adolescents often find themselves in unhealthy relationships characterized by too much dependence, control, and so forth. A technique to address this is to divide the class in half and ask one group to brainstorm characteristics associated with healthy relationships and the other half to brainstorm words associated with unhealthy relationships. One person in each group acts as a recorder and writes their responses on poster paper. After the two lists of characteristics have been read and discussed, students who were in the "healthy" group are subdivided into smaller groups and asked to write a story about teenagers in a relationship (either a friendship or a romantic relationship) characterized by the words they generated in their brainstorming. The same procedure applies for the "unhealthy" group. After the stories are completed and read aloud, further discussion focuses on how to maintain healthy relationships.

## SUMMARY

Incorporating writing interventions into the counseling process is very effective with most clients. An exception is young children, who have not yet developed the skills to express themselves effectively in this manner, although the counselor can act as their recorder. Several interventions have been described in this chapter. More activities are described in detail in the following pages, targeting topics of self-awareness, decision making, expression of feelings, and relationships. Many include activity sheets that require writing, excellent for use in individual counseling, as well as in small-group and classroom settings.

# Write About Me

**TOPIC** Self-awareness and self-acceptance

**RATIONALE** Developing greater self-awareness is very important for children because being more aware of individual characteristics helps them develop their unique personalities. Furthermore, it is important for them to learn to accept themselves as individuals with strengths and weaknesses and to avoid rating themselves as good or bad based on performance.

**MATERIALS** A copy of the Write About Me Activity Sheet

A pen or pencil

**PREPARATIONS** Fold the activity sheet in half and place it inside a small box under a mirror

**PROCEDURE**

1. When a young client presents in counseling with issues related to self-acceptance and lack of self-awareness, give her the box and tell her that there is something very special inside. Invite her to open it and tell you what she sees.
2. After some discussion about what she sees in the mirror, ask her to look underneath the mirror and open up the sheet of paper. On it she will see some unfinished sentences. Depending on the age of the client, you can read these to her and write down her responses, or she can do this herself.
3. After she has completed this task, encourage her to share what she has written and engage her in discussion about what she learned about herself from completing this activity.

# Write About Me Activity Sheet

*Directions: In order to learn more about yourself, read each of the following sentences and write a response that you think best describes you.*

Something that I think is special about me is ______________________________

______________________________________________.

Something that I do well is ______________________________

______________________________________________.

Something I would like to do better is ______________________________

______________________________________________.

Something I like about the way I look is ______________________________

______________________________________________.

Something I don't know how to do is ______________________________

______________________________________________.

Something I am proud about is ______________________________

______________________________________________.

Something I can do now that I couldn't do last year is ______________________________

______________________________________________.

Something I do to make others happy is ______________________________

______________________________________________.

Something I do that sometimes gets me in trouble is ______________________________

______________________________________________.

Three words I would use to describe myself are ______________________________

______________________________________________.

# "Write" Choices

**TOPIC** Decision making

**RATIONALE** As the world becomes more complex, it becomes increasingly important to teach children about the decision-making process because of the significant impact it will have throughout their lifetimes. This intervention uses writing as a way to help them learn a decision-making process.

**MATERIALS** A copy of the "Write" Choices Activity Sheet

A pen or pencil

A coin

**PROCEDURE**

1. When working with a client who has difficulty making good decisions, hand him a coin and tell him that he has a choice to make: Before flipping the coin, he has to decide whether it will land on heads or tails. Let him make the call and flip the coin.
2. Discuss what was involved in making this decision—that it basically was just a guess, but that most decisions aren't that easy. Invite him to discuss some decisions he has made recently, how he decided what to do, and whether or not he considered his decision to be a good one.
3. Next introduce the intervention by giving him the "Write" Choices Activity Sheet and a pencil. Then explain the decision-making process, which involves understanding the decision to be made, identifying alternatives and consequences, evaluating the alternatives and consequences, and making a decision. Invite him to read each of the decision-making dilemmas and write a response.
4. When he has completed this, engage him in a discussion about each of the dilemmas and what he had to consider before making a decision. Focus on the process: understanding the dilemma, identifying alternatives and consequences, evaluating the alternatives and consequences, and making a decision.
5. Discuss how he can apply what he learned from this intervention to decisions he needs to make in his own life.

# "Write" Choices Activity Sheet

*Directions: Read and answer the questions about each of the following decision-making dilemmas.*

1. Your mother has to go to the grocery store, and you will be home alone for about 30 minutes. She tells you to do your homework, but you don't feel like doing it and would rather play a game on the computer.

   What is the decision to be made? ______________________________

   What are the alternatives (choices)? ______________________________

   What might be the consequences of doing what you want rather than what your mother told you to do?

   ______________________________

   ______________________________

   What do you think is the best decision and why? ______________________________

   What do you think you would actually do? ______________________________

2. You aren't a very good student in math, but your friend is. One day after school, the two of you are doing your homework, and your friend says that you can copy his problems so that you will get them right.

   What is the decision to be made? ______________________________

   What are the alternatives (choices)? ______________________________

   What might be the consequences of copying his homework?

   ______________________________

   ______________________________

   What do you think is the best decision and why? ______________________________

   What do you think you would actually do? ______________________________

3. You are on the playground, and another kid comes up to you and starts calling you names and threatening to beat you up. Other kids who are watching yell at you to fight back.

   What is the decision to be made?______________________________

   What are the alternatives (choices)? ______________________________

   What might the consequences be if you do what they say?

   ______________________________

   ______________________________

   What do you think is the best decision and why? ______________________________

   What do you think you would actually do? ______________________________

4. The teacher puts you in charge while he goes to the principal's office. He tells you to make sure everybody works quietly and finishes the spelling test. Just after he leaves, you see two kids in the back of the room looking at each other's papers.

   What is the decision to be made? ______________________________

   What are the alternatives? ______________________________

   What might the consequences be of telling or not telling the teacher what happened?

   ______________________________

   ______________________________

   What do you think is the best decision and why? ______________________________

   What do you think you would actually do? ______________________________

5. A good friend invites you to go camping with her and her family. You have never been camping, and you think you would be afraid to sleep in a tent in the woods. You don't want your friend to think you're scared.

   What is the decision to be made? ______________________________

   What are the alternatives? ______________________________

   What might the consequences be if you go or don't go?

   ______________________________

   ______________________________

   What do you think would be the best decision and why? ______________________________

   ______________________________

   What do you think you would actually do? ______________________________

6. You have a social studies test today, but you forgot to bring your book home to study. You think that you could pretend to be sick so you could stay home and take the test later.

   What is the decision to be made? ______________________________

   What are the alternatives (choices)? ______________________________

   What might be the consequences if you do pretend to be sick?

   ______________________________

   ______________________________

   What do you think is the best decision and why? ______________________________

   What do you think you would actually do? ______________________________

# Write All About It

**TOPIC** Expression of feelings

**RATIONALE** During this developmental period, children have many "firsts" that may cause some degree of anxiety, such as staying overnight away from home, starting school, going to camp, or participating in a new activity. This structured writing intervention is designed to help them identify feelings and coping strategies.

**MATERIALS** A copy of the Write All About It Activity Sheet

A pen or pencil

Two puppets (optional)

**PROCEDURE**

1. When a client appears to be experiencing some anxiety about a first-time experience, invite her to tell you more about what she is feeling or act it out with puppets.
2. Explain that writing about her feelings can be helpful. Give her a copy of the Write All About It Activity Sheet and explain the process of writing a story about this first-time experience. All she needs to do is to fill in the blanks. (If she is too young to write, you can act as the recorder).
3. After she has finished writing, engage her in discussion about whether writing the story helped her feel different or better about this upcoming experience and whether she has some ideas about how she will deal with it.

## Write All About It Activity Sheet

*Directions: Think about a "first time" experience you are about to have and write a story about it, filling in the blanks on this activity sheet.*

Once upon a time, there was a ______ (boy or girl) named ________ (your name) who was

____ years old. Now _________ (your name) had never ________________________

______________________________________________, and ________ (he or she)

was feeling ____________ about this experience because ______________________

___________________________________________________________.

The reason that ________ (he or she) was feeling so ____________ was that ________

(he or she) kept thinking that ____________________________________________

___________________________________________________________.

_________ (your name) thought about things ________ (he or she) could do so ________

(he or she) would not feel quite as ________ about ______________________, and here

are some ideas that ________ (he or she) had about it.

________ (He or she) could __________________________________________,

and ________ (he or she) could also ____________________________________.

Something else ________ (he or she) could do is to ___________________________.

After thinking about different things to do, _______________ (your name) was feeling

____________ and thought ________ (he or she) would ______________________

___________________________________________________________.

# Personal Prose

**TOPIC** Expression of feelings

**RATIONALE** Many young adolescents experience a myriad of intense negative emotions, which can be confusing and troublesome. Writing has proven to be an effective intervention for catharsis, as well as for insight and coping.

**MATERIALS**

A pen or pencil

A sheet of paper

A copy of the Personal Prose Activity Sheet

**PROCEDURE**

1. When a client presents with issues related to intense negative emotions, work with him to identify the specific emotions, such as anger, anxiety, depression, and so forth. Give him a sheet of paper and ask him to write each emotion on the paper. Then ask him to draw two lines next to each feelings word and label one "Intensity" and the other "Frequency." Have him put a 1 on the left side of each line and a 10 on the right side and then rate each emotion on both the intensity and frequency scales, 1 signifying a low level of intensity of frequency and 10 signifying a high level. Have him do this for all the emotions he has identified.
2. Next give him a copy of the Personal Prose Activity Sheet and invite him to follow the directions and write about the most troublesome emotion. This can be done with other emotions as well.
3. Invite him to share what he has written, focusing on how to reduce the intensity of the emotion and helping him identify effective coping strategies.

## Personal Prose Activity Sheet

*Directions: Follow the prompts as you write about your emotions.*

When I am ___________ (identify an emotion), I also feel ______________________________

____________________________________________________________, and I

think ____________________________________________________________

____________________________________________________________.

I ________ (do or don't) like feeling this way because ______________________________

____________________________________________________________

____________________________________________________________.

When I feel this way, I don't feel like doing ______________________________

____________________________________________________________.

When I feel this way, I wish ______________________________________

____________________________________________________________.

When I feel this way, I wish others would ______________________________

____________________________________________________________.

If I were talking to this feeling, I would like to say ______________________

____________________________________________________________.

When I feel this way, I just want ______________________________________

____________________________________________________________.

I try to deal with this feeling by ______________________________________

____________________________________________________________.

What hasn't worked for me is ______________________________________

____________________________________________________________.

What has worked best for me is ______________________________________

____________________________________________________________.

Some advice I would give myself about dealing with this feeling is ______________

____________________________________________________________.

# "Write" Through It

**TOPIC** Friendship conflicts

**RATIONALE** At this age, friendships are essential to an adolescent's existence. However, these relationships can be a source of both pain and pleasure. This intervention can help young teens work through these relationship conflicts and think about the issues from different perspectives.

**MATERIALS** A copy of the "Write" Through It Activity Sheet

A pen or pencil

**PROCEDURE**

1. When a client presents with friendship conflicts, first discuss her feelings and her perspective relative to the problem.
2. Next explain that it is often helpful to write about the problem to gain insights and also to express feelings. Give her the "Write" Through It Activity Sheet and a pen or pencil and discuss the directions with her, giving her adequate time to write her responses.
3. After she has finished writing, invite her to discuss what this was like for her and whether it provided any clarification or direction relative to her friendship conflicts. Encourage her to make an action plan to address the current friendship problem.

## "Write" Through It Activity Sheet

*Directions: Describe a recent conflict with your friend by answering the following questions.*

What happened? ______________________________________________

______________________________________________

______________________________________________

Who was involved? ______________________________________________

______________________________________________

When and where did it happen? ______________________________________________

______________________________________________

How did you feel at the time? ______________________________________________

How do you feel now? ______________________________________________

If your friend were here, what do you think he or she would have to say about what happened?

______________________________________________

______________________________________________

______________________________________________

______________________________________________

What would you like to see happen? ______________________________________________

______________________________________________

______________________________________________

What do you think you could do to solve the problem? ______________________________________________

______________________________________________

What are you willing to do? ______________________________________________

______________________________________________

# Put It in Writing

**TOPIC** Decision making

**RATIONALE** As they get older and more independent, young adolescents have more opportunities to make decisions that affect their lives in various ways. This intervention is intended to provide some perspective on the decision-making process.

**MATERIALS** A copy of the Put It in Writing Activity Sheet

A pen or pencil

**PROCEDURE**

1. When working with a client who has difficulty making good decisions, help him learn to think through decisions by using the following expressive writing intervention.
2. First, ask him to describe an example of a decision he has recently made that he felt had a good outcome, as well as an example of a decision that did not have good outcome. Encourage him to talk about what differentiated the good outcome from the not-so-good outcome.
3. Next give him a pen or pencil and a copy of the Put It in Writing Activity Sheet, asking him to read the instructions and complete the process.
4. When he has finished, invite him to share what he wrote, what he learned, and how he can apply this information to future decision-making situations.

# Put It in Writing Activity Sheet

*Directions: Think about a decision you need to make and write about it, using the following structure.*

A decision I need to make: ______________________________

Possible choices regarding this decision are:

(a) ______________________________

(b) ______________________________

(c) ______________________________

If I select choice (a), possible consequences could be:

______________________________

______________________________

______________________________

If I select choice (b), possible consequences could be:

______________________________

______________________________

______________________________

If I select choice (c), possible consequences could be:

______________________________

______________________________

______________________________

Which choice makes the least sense and why?

______________________________

Which choice makes the most sense and why?

______________________________

What do you think you will do after considering other alternatives?

______________________________

# J Is for Journaling

**TOPIC** Self-awareness

**RATIONALE** Adolescence is a critical period for self-exploration and identity formation. As adolescents gradually become less dependent on peers and concentrate more on clarifying their own values and learning more about what is important to them as individuals, they can benefit from a process that helps them in their search for self.

**MATERIALS** A pen or pencil

A copy of the J Is for Journaling Activity Sheet

**PROCEDURE**

1. When working with a client who is struggling to define herself, invite her to participate in a structured journaling experience to help her reflect on who she is and what is important to her. Tell her that she has the option of sharing the journal with you or not, but that the process should be helpful to her regardless. Also tell her that she may initially use this structured form of journaling but after a while may not need the stimulus questions to help her think about herself and her life.
2. Give her the J is for Journaling Activity Sheet and a pen or pencil and invite her to start the journaling process.
3. If she chooses to share the journal with you, discuss what she learned about herself through this process and encourage her to continue to address these questions, to write her own and respond to them, or to journal in a less structured manner. If she doesn't wish to share, you can invite her to summarize her journaling by writing down three things she learned about herself from this process.

## J Is for Journaling Activity Sheet

*Directions: Use the questions in this structured journaling format to help you think about yourself and what is important to you. You can elaborate as much as you wish or deviate from these "starters" if something else comes to mind.*

When I think about who I am, I would describe myself as ______________________________

______________________________________________________________________.

Others might describe me as ______________________________________________.

I think my greatest strengths are ___________________________________________.

Something that is different about me this year from last year is _______________________.

What I see myself doing as a result of these strengths could be _______________________

______________________________________________________________________.

Some goals I have for myself are ___________________________________________.

What I don't think I would be very good at is _________________________________.

What I really have no interest in doing is ____________________________________.

Where I see myself five years from now is ____________________________________.

A dream I have for my future is ____________________________________________.

# A Personal Story

**TOPIC** Decision making

**RATIONALE** During this period of development, adolescents are faced with numerous decision-making challenges, such as postsecondary planning, romantic relationships, friendship issues, and moral decisions related to sex, drugs, and alcohol. Writing a personal story can help them clarify issues and enhance their decision-making abilities.

**MATERIALS** A pen or pencil

Several sheets of paper

**PROCEDURE**

1. When working with an adolescent who is confused about a decision he needs to make, discuss the idea of writing a personal story with different endings as a way to help him clarify the issue and make a well-thought-through decision.
2. Give him several sheets of paper and a pen or pencil and invite him to write about a personal dilemma. He could begin the story as "Once upon a time there was . . ." or use first person: "I have a decision to make about _______, and I don't know what to do." Suggest that he first describe the dilemma and write about his thoughts and feelings relative to this issue. Then encourage him to write several different endings to the story that would essentially be the various alternatives. With each ending, he should include positive and negative aspects.
3. After he has finished, invite him to read his story with the different endings. Engage him in a discussion about what he has written, focusing on how he would feel about each alternative and what, if anything, has become clearer to him as a result of writing his personal story.
4. Encourage him to make an action plan based on the ending that he thinks is best for him at this time.

# Writing Remedies

**TOPIC** Relationships with peers or parents

**RATIONALE** It is not uncommon during mid-adolescence for teens to have conflicts with parents, often centering around issues involving establishing themselves as more independent beings and relying less on parental guidance. As peers replace parents as a major source of influence, those relationships may also be conflicted, particularly those of a romantic nature. Using letter writing to address these issues can be very effective.

**MATERIALS** Several sheets of paper

A pen or pencil

**PROCEDURE**

1. When an adolescent presents with relationship issues that are troubling or conflicted, invite her to talk more about her feelings and thoughts relative to the issue.
2. Suggest that it can be very helpful to write a letter to the other person because she can express her thoughts and feelings and also clarify other aspects of the problem. If she is angry, it might be best for her to write two versions of the letter: one to express the anger and the other to address the issues in a less angry tone.
3. Explain to the client that the letter should include her thoughts and feelings about the problem, how she sees things from her perspective, what she thinks the perspective of the parent or peer might be, and what she would like to see happen.
4. The letter can be written either in session or as homework, but either way, it is important to stress several things: (a) that she should read the letter out loud and preferably record it and play it back so that she can really "hear" what she is saying to the other person; (b) that she should think about the impact the letter may have on the other person and consider editing or rewriting it if it sounds too accusatory or hostile; and (c) that, if she does revise an angry letter, she should destroy the first one and send the revised version.

5. Invite the client to read her letter to you, if she desires, to get feedback. Encourage her to discuss how she felt and what she learned from writing the letter.

# What's "Write"?

**TOPIC** Decision making

**RATIONALE** Children need to work continually on developing good decision-making skills, which involves identifying alternatives and consequences. This intervention can be done in a classroom or small group and can be readily adapted for middle school students as well.

**MATERIALS**

A bag of candy

A copy of the What's "Write"? Activity Sheet for each person

A pen or pencil for each group

**PROCEDURE**

1. To introduce this intervention, ask for a volunteer. Give the volunteer a bag of candy and ask him or her to make a decision about what to do with it. After a decision has been made, ask how the decision was made, what alternatives were considered, what possible consequences might be, and so forth.
2. Next tell students that they will be given an activity sheet that describes several different situations that require a decision. Divide them into groups of four to six and distribute an activity sheet to each person.
3. Instruct them to read each of the situations and follow the directions listed at the top of the activity sheet.
4. When they have finished, engage them in a discussion about how they decided what to do, what alternatives and consequences they considered, and what they think is important to remember about making decisions.

# What's "Write"? Activity Sheet

*Directions: Read each of the following situations and, as a group, discuss alternatives and consequences suggested by the questions listed after each situation. One person in the group should be the recorder, who writes the responses on this sheet.*

1. You are waiting outside the school building for your mother to pick you up. The buses have left, and so have most kids. You are getting worried, but just then a car pulls up and a woman rolls down the window and tells you that she is your mom's coworker and that she is supposed to pick you up because your mother has to work late. What do you think you should you do?

   (a) What are the alternatives (choices)?

   ______________________________________________

   ______________________________________________

   (b) What do you need to think about before making your decision?

   ______________________________________________

   ______________________________________________

   (c) What are some possible consequences of the alternatives you identified?

   ______________________________________________

   ______________________________________________

   (d) What do you think you should do?

   ______________________________________________

2. Your older sister is taking care of you while your parents are at a meeting. You are doing your homework when you smell smoke coming out of her room. When you peek in the door, you see that she is smoking a cigarette. You have heard your parents say that she is never supposed to smoke because it is bad for her. What do you think you should do?

   (a) What are the alternatives (choices)?

   ______________________________________________

   ______________________________________________

   (b) What do you need to think about before making your decision?

   ______________________________________________

   ______________________________________________

   (c) What are some possible consequences of the alternatives you identified?

   ______________________________________________

   ______________________________________________

(d) What do you think you should do?

____________________________________________

3. Your good friend asks you to spend the night, but you don't really want to because his house is really old and kind of spooky. You don't want him to think you are a chicken. What do you think you should do?

   (a) What are the alternatives (choices)?

   ____________________________________________

   ____________________________________________

   (b) What do you need to think about before making your decision?

   ____________________________________________

   ____________________________________________

   (c) What are some possible consequences of the alternatives you identified?

   ____________________________________________

   ____________________________________________

   (d) What do you think you should do?

   ____________________________________________

4. Your dad has to run to the grocery store, and you don't want to go. He says you can stay home alone as long as you don't leave the yard. A few minutes after he leaves, you are in the front yard playing basketball when some of your friends ride by on their bikes. They stop and ask you to go with them. What do you think you should do?

   (a) What are the alternatives (choices)?

   ____________________________________________

   ____________________________________________

   (b) What do you need to think about before making your decision?

   ____________________________________________

   ____________________________________________

   (c) What are some possible consequences of the alternatives you identified?

   ____________________________________________

   ____________________________________________

   (d) What do you think you should do?

   ____________________________________________

   ____________________________________________

5. Your parents are getting divorced, and your dad wants you to move in with him. Your mom works two jobs, so she isn't home much, but you don't know if you want to leave your neighborhood. What do you think you should do?

(a) What are the alternatives (choices)?

______________________________________________

______________________________________________

(b) What do you need to think about before making your decision?

______________________________________________

______________________________________________

(c) What are some possible consequences of the alternatives you identified?

______________________________________________

______________________________________________

(d) What do you think you should do?

______________________________________________

______________________________________________

6. Your friend wants to borrow your brand new bike. You are afraid he will fall and scratch it up. He says he'll give you three baseball cards of your favorite players, which you have been wanting for a long time. What do you think you should do?

(a) What are the alternatives (choices)?

______________________________________________

______________________________________________

(b) What do you need to think about before making your decision?

______________________________________________

______________________________________________

(c) What are some possible consequences of the alternatives you identified?

______________________________________________

______________________________________________

(d) What do you think you should do?

______________________________________________

______________________________________________

# Write Around

**TOPIC** Self- and other awareness

**RATIONALE** This intervention is best suited for small groups with middle school or high school students. It is a simple strategy designed to promote awareness of self as well as of others, and the procedure can be used with any topic.

**MATERIALS** Several sheets of paper

A pen or pencil for each person

A watch with a minute hand or a timer

**PROCEDURE**

1. To begin, have students sit in a circle. Give each one a pen or pencil. Next explain that you are inviting them to participate in a "write around," in which one member of the group will write a short response (one minute) to a question about being an adolescent, then fold the paper so his or her response isn't showing and pass it to the person to his or her left. The second person writes a response and does the same, passing the paper until everyone in the group has responded.
2. At the top of the first sheet of paper, write the following, and then give it to one of the group members to start the process: "What I like most about being an adolescent is . . ."
3. After that paper has been passed to all participants, start a second sheet with the following topic: "One of the most challenging things about being an adolescent is . . ."
4. As time permits, introduce the following additional topics and follow the same procedure:

   During this period in my life, I hope . . .

   Being an adolescent is fun because . . .

   Something I don't like about being an adolescent is . . .
5. It is important to leave adequate time for sharing and discussion. Begin the sharing process by giving the folded paper with the responses to a person in the group—but not to the one who

started the process. (It might be easier if there is some degree of anonymity.) Invite him or her to read the response and then pass it to the next person and so forth until all responses have been read out loud. When finished, discuss the similarities and differences in the responses and whether there is anything they are more aware of as a result of hearing what their peers wrote. Repeat this process for each completed sheet.

# Express It

**TOPIC** Self-awareness and values clarification

**RATIONALE** An important task for adolescents is to clarify what is important to them. Because peer influence is so prevalent, it is especially critical for adolescents to clarify their own values and beliefs so that they can live their lives according to what is important to them.

**MATERIALS** A copy of the Express It Activity Sheet for each person

A pen or pencil per person

**PROCEDURE**

1. To introduce this intervention, ask students to take something out of their desks, purses or wallets, or backpacks that is important to them. Engage them in a discussion about why their particular object was important to them and how it represents their beliefs or values. Encourage discussion about the importance of clarifying what matters to them as they continue developing an awareness of self.
2. Make sure everyone has a pen or pencil. Give each student a copy of the Express It Activity Sheet and invite them to complete it according to the directions at the top of the page.
3. When everyone has finished, divide them into groups of four to six and invite them to discuss their categorizations, how they determined what was important to them, how they act on their values, and how they might change as they get older.

# Express It Activity Sheet

*Directions: Read the list below and think about what is important to you—what your values are and what matters to you. Next refer to the three columns: what is very important, not at all important, and somewhat important. Rate each of the values according to how important it is you by to putting a checkmark it in the appropriate column.*

| | Very Important | Somewhat Important | Not at All Important |
|---|---|---|---|
| 1. Having a good relationship with parents | ☐ | ☐ | ☐ |
| 2. Having a good reputation | ☐ | ☐ | ☐ |
| 3. Doing well in school | ☐ | ☐ | ☐ |
| 4. Being successful | ☐ | ☐ | ☐ |
| 5. Being popular | ☐ | ☐ | ☐ |
| 6. Having lots of friends | ☐ | ☐ | ☐ |
| 7. Having a lot of freedom | ☐ | ☐ | ☐ |
| 8. Having a lot of money | ☐ | ☐ | ☐ |
| 9. Being religious | ☐ | ☐ | ☐ |
| 10. Being honest and loyal | ☐ | ☐ | ☐ |
| 11. Being drug and alcohol free | ☐ | ☐ | ☐ |
| 12. Fighting for this country | ☐ | ☐ | ☐ |
| 13. Having equal rights for women and minorities | ☐ | ☐ | ☐ |
| 14. Getting a good job | ☐ | ☐ | ☐ |

# Chapter 5

# Counseling Through Literature

How many times have you lost yourself in a good book? You might have been so engrossed in it that you didn't want to put it down or were disappointed when you finished it. As an English major, I remember taking adolescent literature during a summer school session. I read voraciously and felt as though I had catapulted back into my own adolescence as I immersed myself in some of the classic books for young readers. For many people of all ages, literature is almost as essential as breathing. It can be an escape, as well as entertaining, enlightening, informative, and cathartic. When literature is used to help clients find solutions to their problems, it is referred to as bibliotherapy or bibliocounseling or poetry therapy, although *bibliotherapy* is the most commonly used term (Gladding, 2011). Doll and Doll (1997) stress that, although bibliotherapy as it is most simply defined means helping with books, some experts specify that this term be used only when other activities such as discussion, role-playing, and other creative efforts are used in conjunction with the reading.

Bibliotherapy is an interactive process that helps individuals gain control over their lives as they develop greater self-awareness, learn new skills, practice new behaviors, and solve problems (Jackson, 2001). Bibliotherapy can be used individually, as well as in small groups or classroom settings, and although it is often used in a remedial sense to help clients cope with problems, it can also be used for personal growth and problem prevention when the focus is on helping children cope with developmental needs and typical problems. Pardeck (1998) has identified the following five goals of bibliotherapy: (a) to provide information and insight, (b) to communicate values and attitudes, (c) to stimulate discussion about problems, (d) to create awareness of how others have dealt with similar problems, and (e) to provide solutions to problems.

Bibliotherapy has a longstanding history of application in many different counseling settings and has been used to educate clients, as well as to help them explore their lifestyles, deal with unfinished business, and achieve self-understanding (Bradley et al., 2009). In addition, bibliotherapy can help clients explore new ways of interacting with others to promote more effective relationships (Doll & Doll, 1997). Several different types of literature can be used for bibliotherapy, including nonfiction, fiction, poetry, storytelling, autobiographies, self-help books, and fairy tales (Vernon & Clemente, 2005). In addition, films can be considered a form of bibliotherapy (Caron, 2005), otherwise known as cinematherapy (Dollarhide, 2003; Shallcross, 2011a). As with books, *cinematherapy* involves selecting a film or film clip that parallels issues the client is struggling with, requesting that he or she watch it, and then engaging the client in a guided discussion about what he or she has experienced to promote insight and a deeper perspective on personal issues. According to Shallcross, films are very effective because clients are "not processing it in their head; they're processing it in their heart" (p. 37), referring to how clients react to the ways the characters in the film handle issues similar to their own. Dollarhide stresses that this type of vicarious learning helps clients cope with their own life challenges.

Regardless of which form of bibliotherapy is used, materials need to be developmentally appropriate and carefully selected to match the client's reading or comprehension level. They should pertain to the presenting problem and reflect the client's culture, age, gender, and family values (Dollarhide, 2003). It is also critical to select books or films that have believable characters and situations. Selections should offer realistic hope, as opposed to magical endings that promote false hope, and solutions should not be simplistic. This can be a delicate balance because if a child or adolescent is unsuccessful in an attempt to apply a simple solution to his or her own problem, the client may become discouraged and give up. On the other hand, if too many complex problems are portrayed, the client may become overwhelmed and think that problems such as these are too difficult to deal with (Doll & Doll, 1997). The counselor needs to have a good relationship with the client and know him or her well in order to match the book or film to the child or adolescent. As Orton (1997) has noted, having a good match helps the client identify with the content and characters and facilitates catharsis and insight, which are necessary for problem resolution, change, and growth.

Bibliotherapy, as well as cinematherapy, is a directed process used to help clients find solutions to their problems as opposed to reading or watching something for pleasure (Gladding, 2011), even though many will find this approach very enjoyable. This process helps clients explore their own personal uniqueness, concerns, and feelings (Degges-White & Davis, 2011), identify ways to cope with changes in their lives, and learn new ways of behaving. Pehrsson and McMillen (2007) note that bibliotherapy also strengthens clients' understanding of their worldview and cultural self-identity, and Ballard (2012) stresses that using films in counseling can build empathy, which is especially critical for adolescents.

Another form of bibiotherapy that helps increase empathy and understanding of others involves poetry, also considered to be an excellent way to express and explore oneself (Ingram, 2003). Ingram states, "The real poetry is hearing the reason in the rhythm" (p. 23). Just as with other forms of bibliotherapy, the most important consideration is that the client be able to relate to the poem, the goal being to "build a resonance" (p. 20) with the characters. Analyzing and discussing the key aspects of the poem and getting clients to talk about what they felt and learned are essential to the process.

## ADVANTAGES OF USING BIBLIOTHERAPY IN COUNSELING

One of the major advantages of using bibliotherapy (or cinematherapy) with clients is that, through reading or watching, they learn that they are not alone. Many readers have no doubt experienced the relief that comes from knowing that there are others who share their circumstances. This promotes a connectedness that can occur with people across culture, time, and gender (Lerner, 1994, as cited in Gladding, 2011). Other advantages of using this approach as an adjunct to counseling include the following:

- Bibliotherapy helps clients explore personally relevant thoughts and feelings (Vernon & Clemente, 2005).
- Bibliotherapy can be used in multiple settings: hospitals, outpatient clinics, schools, and treatment centers (Gladding, 2011).
- Bibliotherapy can be used to help clients deal with a wide range of problems (Vernon & Clemente, 2005).
- Bibliotherapy helps clients release emotions (Ingram, 2003; Vernon, 1998c).
- Ethnically diverse clients feel empowered after reading about others from their culture who have overcome difficulties and succeeded in life (Vernon & Clemente, 2005).
- Bibliotherapy is especially effective for clients who process things visually as opposed to auditorily (Vernon, 2013).
- Many different creative and experiential strategies can be used in conjunction with bibliotherapy (Pehrsson, 2006; Pehrsson & McMillen, 2007):
- Bibliotherapy in the form of self-help books can reduce isolation when clients think they are the only ones who have problems (Joshua & DiMenna, 2000).
- Bibliotherapy, and poetry in particular, promotes understanding of others (Ingram, 2003).
- Cinematherapy helps clients externalize the issues they are struggling with, allowing them to look at them from a more objective point of view (Shallcross, 2011a).

- Cinematherapy lowers clients' defensiveness, thus making it easier for them to open up and discuss their own issues (Shallcross, 2011a).
- Cinematherapy provides distance, which makes it easier for clients to understand problems others are having and ultimately recognize that they have similar issues (Shallcross, 2011a).

## TYPES OF PROBLEMS AND POPULATIONS THAT BENEFIT FROM BIBLEOTHERAPY

As noted previously, fiction, nonfiction, poetry, and other forms of literature, including films, can be used to address problems that clients of all ages and cultures present. Consequently, there is great versatility in this approach. Furthermore, a wide selection of excellent literature is available, which makes it easy for practitioners to find suitable materials. The many uses of bibliotherapy and cinematherapy are exemplified in the following list:

- Bibliotherapy has been used to help clients deal with grief (Slyter, 2012).
- Bibliotherapy has been used to help clients reduce compulsive behaviors (Black, 2007).
- Bibliotherapy has been used to help clients with perfectionism (Nugent, 2000).
- Bibliotherapy has been used to increase academic and emotional development with children having serious emotional disturbances (Bauer & Balius, 1995).
- Bibliotherapy has been used to help children cope with fears (Nicholson & Pearson, 2003).
- Bibliotherapy has been used to help assist adolescents in dealing with the transition from childhood to adulthood (Gladding, 2011).
- Bibliotherapy has been used to help adolescents experiencing parental divorce (Pehrsson, Allen, Folger, McMillen, & Lowe, 2007).
- Bibliotherapy has been helpful for clients with anger management problems (Joshua & DiMenna, 2000).
- Storytelling has been used to help adolescents increase self-confidence and deal with the challenges of puberty (Bartlett, 2003).
- Cinematherapy has been used with families to facilitate understanding and increase communication (Ballard, 2012).
- Cinematherapy has been advantageous for addicted youths (Shallcross, 2011a).

- Cinematherapy has proven helpful in facilitating emotional expression in adolescent males (Shallcross, 2011a).

## CLINICAL BIBLIOTHERAPY VERSUS DEVELOPMENTAL BIBLIOTHERAPY

There are many advantages to using bibliotherapy with clients, but it is important to note the distinction between clinical bibliotherapy, which Pehrsson and McMillen (2006) describe as an approach implemented by a qualified counselor or therapist, and developmental bibliotherapy, which is used by teachers and lay people to promote growth and development, as opposed to prescribing literature to remediate specific problems. School and mental health counselors working with children and adolescents using the clinical approach follow the treatment procedure subsequently described.

## EXAMPLES OF BIBLIOTHERAPY INTERVENTIONS

The bibliotherapy process entails more than just handing a book to a client to read. In fact, Gladding (2011) stresses that "at its best, bibliotherapy is interactive" (p. 111), and studies conducted on bibliotherapy emphasize the importance of accompanying the reading of the literature with discussion and/or counseling for it to be most effective (Pardeck & Pardeck, 1993). This interactive format stresses guided discussion between the counselor and client to help integrate the client's thoughts and feelings relative to the literature. This is in direct contrast to the reactive format, in which clients are asked to read a specific selection without subsequent discussion; in this format, the counselor assumes that the client will gain insight and release emotions through identifying with the literature (Gladding & Gladding, 1991). Clearly, this approach leaves too much to chance. The more current viewpoint is that bibliotherapy is an intervention that uses guided discussion to achieve therapeutic goals.

Pardeck and Pardeck (1993) note that there are four stages of bibliotherapy. The first is identification, in which the counselor builds rapport with the client in order to become sensitive to his or her needs. Selection of the specific form and piece of literature is the second step, which, as previously noted, is very important. Given that there are so many excellent examples of bibliotherapy resources, this is much easier than it used to be, but it is still critical to select books that match the client's gender, age, and culture for identification to occur. The next stage is the presentation of the book or other form of literature. Depending on the age of the client and the length of the selection, the counselor may read to the client, or the two of them can take turns reading together during the session. These approaches are frequently the practice with younger children. Because literature selections for adolescents are typically longer, they are generally read between sessions, with discussion occurring in session. This guided discussion is the follow-up stage, in which the client reflects on the book or other form of literature to gain insight into his or her problem.

Kelsch and Emry (2003) also outline four stages of the bibliotherapy process, differing slightly from what Pardeck and Pardeck (1993) describe: identification, in which clients identify on an intellectual level with the characters or plot of the story; catharsis, which occurs as they become emotionally involved in what they are reading and identify with the conflicts and feelings of the characters and/or situations described in the literature; insight, the point at which they can begin to apply the concepts to their own lives; and universality, the realization that their issues are similar to those of others.

Depending on the client's maturity level, intellectual ability, and willingness to verbalize, it may not be necessary to provide much structure during the discussion. However, based on my own experience, I generally find that clients need some guidance in order for them to get the most benefit from the intervention. Two levels of questions, content questions and personalization questions, result in a more focused discussion and are especially helpful with less verbal clients. Content questions relate to the content of the literature and are factual questions or opinion questions that help determine how well the client understands the concepts. Personalization questions are intended to help the client apply the messages from the literature or film to his or her own life; they are intended to elicit personal thoughts and feelings that can result in increased insight and problem resolution.

To illustrate this process, imagine that you are an eight-year-old who is very grouchy, especially with your sister. Your mother asked the school counselor to meet with you, which made you even grouchier! But the counselor was nice and read you a book called *The Grouchies* (Wagenbach, 2010). You really liked this book because it had silly pictures and the boy in the story got mad at his sister just like you did. At the end of the story the counselor asked you some content questions about the book: What were some of the things that the boy in the story was grouchy about? What did the "grouchies" keep saying to the boy? What did they tell him to do when he was asked to do something he didn't want to do? Did the "grouchies" plan work out for him? What did Mom and Dad tell him to do to get rid of the "grouchies"? After you and the counselor talked about these questions, she asked you if you ever felt like the boy in the story. She asked if you acted the same way he did when he was grouchy or if there were other things that you did. She wanted to know how you felt after you had been grumpy with your sister or your parents and if you wanted to get rid of the "grouchies" just like the boy in the story did. She asked if you would like to try some of the ideas for getting rid of the "grouchies" that the parents in the book suggested, and then she asked you to think of some other ideas that would help you. At the end of your time together, the counselor asked if you would like to come back next week so you could tell her how your ideas worked and asked if you would like to make your own "grouchy" book, which you thought would be fun.

When using cinematherapy, the same principles described for bibliotherapy are applicable, although films are more typically used between sessions rather than in sessions because of their length (Shallcross, 2011a). Because most people like watching films, clients may be more motivated to watch a film than read a book, although this will vary from client to client. Regardless of the medium, clients are often better able to talk about a book or film character's problems than they are their own, so discussing content questions first and gradually moving to personalization questions is an effective way to process the material with the client.

Several general bibliotherapy strategies are next described, and more specific and detailed interventions for children in elementary, middle school, and high school and interventions for use in classrooms and with small groups are subsequently presented.

### Rapport Building

Fiction is especially good to use with younger children to build rapport. Select books with eye-catching illustrations that will capture their attention and begin with something general, such as books about feelings. *The Way I Feel,* by Janan Cain (2000), is a fanciful book that appeals to young readers, as does *Sometimes I Feel Like a Storm Cloud,* by Lezlie Evans (2007), which introduces children to a variety of feelings and associated behaviors. Reading books such as these can put children at ease and invite discussion about their feelings. It is more difficult to find examples of short selections that can be used with adolescents. For that reason, I ask clients to write short stories about their experiences with topics such as anger, eating disorders, parental divorce, substance abuse, teen pregnancy, or mood swings (Vernon, 1998b, 1998c). When I have new clients presenting with similar issues, I share one of these stories with them, finding this to be effective in helping develop rapport, putting them at ease, and creating awareness that others have had similar issues. This is particularly important with adolescents because their egocentric nature prevents them from realizing that they are not alone in their struggles.

### Watch It

As previously noted, bibliotherapy includes not only various forms of print literature but also film. Caron (2005) describes the benefits of using film as a bibliotherapy tool, especially for adolescents who may be much more willing to watch a film than to read a book. For some clients, films generate more identification and catharsis than books, and they can also learn coping strategies as they see how the characters handle various problems. For a film to be therapeutically meaningful, it should depict events or emotions similar to the client's issues. Also, practitioners should preview the film to make certain that the content is relevant and appropriate for the client. As with literature, the film selections should be realistic and promote the client's emotional and behavioral adjustment. Films may be assigned as homework, with guided discussion in the following session, or counselor and client can view the film together in parts over a series of sessions, stopping in key places to discuss insights and feelings. Using cinematherapy is generally very appealing and motivating for reluctant clients. Furthermore, when clients watch films, they process the issues affectively. For suggestions of films on various counseling-related problems, consult *Rent Two Films and Let's Talk in the Morning* (Hesley & Hesley, 2001).

## True Stories

It is especially effective to have clients read true stories or poems that have been written by others their age, particularly if the stories are empowering and describe how to overcome difficult circumstances. Examples of stories written by my adolescent clients, who remain anonymous so they can share their experiences with others, include "Peer Pressure," a story about an adolescent male's experiences with peer pressure (Vernon, 1998b, pp. 141–142); "I Hate My Weight," a story about a young adolescent's struggle with anorexia (Vernon, 1998c, pp. 89–93); "Heartbreak and a Half," a story about the ending of a romantic relationship (Vernon, 1998c, pp. 121–122); "It's a Dilemma," a story about teenage pregnancy (Vernon, 1998c, pp. 261–262); and "Dangerous Decisions," a story about a teenager's experience with substance abuse (Vernon, 1998c, pp. 147–148). Most clients readily identify with these stories if they relate to a problem they are experiencing. In addition, the stories are very short and can be read in a few minutes, leaving plenty of time during the counseling session to discuss how the client reacts to the story, whether it relates to his or her own circumstance, how the person in the story coped with the problem, whether the client thinks those strategies might work, and so forth. Clients generally find these stories insightful and cathartic. *Kids Write Through It: Essays by Kids Who Have Triumphed Over Trouble* (1998) and *Teens Write Through It: Essays from Teens Who Have Triumphed Over Trouble* (1998) are useful collections of true stories written by youth who have overcome challenges relating to depression, drugs and alcohol, racism, and many other dilemmas. These essays are motivational and inspirational for children and adolescents who are contending with problems that negatively affect their lives.

## P Is for Poetry

Just as it is helpful for clients to read true stories, children and adolescents can also benefit from poems that others their age have written, such as "Love You, Love You Not," about a teenager's struggle to get out of a controlling relationship (Vernon, 1998c, p. 253) or "Living Up to an Image" (Vernon, 1998c, p. 97), a poem about trying to be true to oneself without letting others down. I recall working with an adolescent whose boyfriend had just broken up with her. She had done some journaling, which proved helpful, but she was having difficulty getting past the betrayal of her boyfriend, who left her for her best friend. Reading "It Hurts to Be in Love" (Vernon, 1998c, p. 233), written by another teen who had dealt with this same issue, was very cathartic for her and helped her clarify her thoughts and feelings about this painful experience. Counselors can also select published poems that address clients' problems. Poems are usually short but prompt good reflection and can be very effective for some clients, although others may find reading fiction or nonfiction to be more beneficial than poetry.

## Homework

Various types of literature can be assigned as homework, but it is important to know whether or not the client is motivated to read on his or her own. I remember one of my clients saying that she'd do anything if it didn't involve reading. So rather than prescribe something that may be ineffective, know your client's learning style and preferences before taking this step. I use bibliotherapy homework with adolescents more often than with children because the literature for adolescents is longer and more difficult to read in session. I also often use children's books with that age group, as well as with adults, explaining that the message is good, the book is short, and it will probably generate some things to think about. For example, when working with a 14-year-old who had high anxiety as a result of her perfectionism, I invited her to read *Being Bella: Discovering How to Be Proud of Your Best!* (Zuzo, 2008). Just as I had anticipated, after reading this short book, Amanda talked about seeing herself in Bella and asked me to make a copy of the last page of the book to help her remember that she didn't have to be perfect, she just needed to do her best.

## Comically Speaking

For those clients who don't like reading longer selections of literature, comic strips may be appealing. They are short, readily available, and make a point. Along the same line, suggesting that depressed or humorless clients read jokes can be an interesting intervention. I used this approach with a high school boy who didn't have many friends, in part because he appeared to have no sense of humor and couldn't take a joke. I am sure he thought I was a bit crazy when I gave him a joke book, but he took it and returned it the following week, saying that he had read it. I coupled the joke book with a homework assignment of watching a comedy film and writing a short reaction paper about what he thought was funny. I repeated these interventions several times, and he gradually developed a better sense of humor, which improved his status with his peer group.

## OTHER EXAMPLES OF BIBLIOTHERAPY INTERVENTIONS

Pehrsson (2006–2007) has developed a process called "co-story-ing," a five-step process that involves helping children put their own stories into written form. She feels that this approach is especially appropriate for young children who might not be good candidates for talk therapy. After the story is written, it can be read to the child and revised if desired. Insight comes after the story is written, read, and discussed.

Another form of literature that can be used effectively with some adolescents is inspirational readings in the form of short stories, sayings, or verses that serve as a reminder to be courageous and hopeful. I used this approach with a young woman who had chronic pain as a result of several health issues. I found several quotes that I thought she might relate to and shared them with her. She reprinted them in calligraphy and framed them, reporting that it was helpful to read these each day. The first quote was from a young girl who had a rare form of muscular dystrophy: "We all have life storms, and when we get through them or recover from them, we should celebrate that we got through them instead of just mourning and waiting for the next one to come along and wipe us out again." The other quotes were from a Dear Abby column: "Don't give up and don't give in," "Keep on trying no matter how hard it seems," and "Ignore those who try to discourage you." As a follow-up homework assignment, I encouraged her to write her own inspirational quotes.

Self-help literature in the form of nonfiction is a good medium with adolescents in that it is educational and skill oriented. Although most self-help books are geared to an adult audience, many are appropriate with adolescents. For example, I recall working with several young females who were very nonassertive and consequently were being controlled by peers or boyfriends. I assigned an old standby, *Your Perfect Right* (Alberti & Emmons, 1974), a short, easy-to-read book that explains the concept of personal rights. I coupled that with *The Assertive Option* (Jakubowski & Lange, 1978), which provides information about the emotional and behavioral consequences of assertion versus nonassertion and aggression, with specific examples of assertive responses. The self-help approach is also good for issues such as dealing with abusive or dependent relationships, healthy eating and exercise, and building self-confidence.

Yet another form of bibliotherapy that can be helpful for some clients, especially adolescents, involves the reading of biographies or autobiographies. Usually these forms of literature chronicle an individual's life, including events, challenges, major influences, and personal insights. I found this to be beneficial with a young male who wanted to be a basketball star but had no clue as to how much effort and self-discipline it would take. Reading *Salt in His Shoes,* a story of Michael Jordan's journey to success, written by his mother and sister (Jordan & Jordan, 2003), proved to be a good selection for my client. After he read the book, we discussed how Michael had to work hard to achieve his goals and what he had to do physically and academically in order to succeed. We then began to develop some realistic goals for Antonio, including studying and doing his homework so he could get good grades and be eligible for the basketball team, developing an exercise routine, and replacing junk food with healthier alternatives. Although Antonio still had high hopes, the book helped him realize that being a star doesn't occur magically—perseverance and persistence are needed, along with talent.

## INCORPORATING BIBLIOTHERAPY WITH OTHER CREATIVE ARTS INTERVENTIONS

There are numerous ways to incorporate bibliotherapy with other creative arts interventions, such as music, writing, art, and drama, all of which enhance the intervention by engaging the client on many different levels. Which other strategies are incorporated must, of course, depend on what will be most therapeutically beneficial for the client. For example, I was working with a high school senior who had been in a tragic swimming accident the previous summer and as a result was a paraplegic. In addition to feeling depressed and helpless because she was quite dependent on others, she felt hopeless about her future; she didn't see herself being successful in any career because of her disability. Because she had always been an avid reader, I invited her to read some nonfiction accounts about how others in similar circumstances had managed to succeed despite their disabilities. I combined this with writing, requesting that she write about the ways in which the people in the literature had been able to deal with their disabilities and find success and meaning in their lives and how those ideas might apply to her situation. I suggested also that she might consider doing a music collage in which she compiled words from songs that would be inspirational to her as she considered what her future might be like. Given the severity of her problem, she faced multiple adjustments and challenges, but the bibliotherapy, combined with other strategies, proved beneficial.

Various forms of the visual arts also can be incorporated with bibliotherapy. After reading a work of fiction, young children can convey their reactions and feelings by making their own books or simply drawing pictures to illustrate what the book means to them. They can create clay structures to represent something they took away from the book or express it through painting or felt figures. Clients can also act out their interpretation of what they read as it applies to their own lives.

Cinematherapy can also be incorporated with creative arts approaches. For example, after watching a film, clients can be asked to identify three or four of the most significant parts and incorporate art by making a poster or a banner, illustrating or cutting pictures from magazines to represent the key messages. I used writing in conjunction with cinematherapy when working with a young adolescent who was struggling with maturation issues. I suggested that she watch *Then and Now*, a coming of age film that chronicles how four friends mature at different rates during their early teen years. I invited my client to write about the characters with which she most and least identified, a task that was a good stimulus for talking about her issues.

Combining bibliotherapy with other expressive arts interventions is limited only by the counselor's creativity and the client's willingness to participate. There is much to be gained by thinking of new ways to make bibliotherapy more successful.

## CLASSROOM OR SMALL-GROUP APPLICATIONS

Bibliotherapy is a very popular approach to use in both small-group counseling and classroom guidance, particularly in the elementary level grades, at which level the books are shorter and can be more readily incorporated. As noted previously, *Developing Understanding of Self and Others,* by Dinkmeyer and Dinkmeyer (1982), was one early program that incorporated short stories, songs, and puppetry to help elementary school children learn about getting along with others, express their feelings, and learn more about their strengths and weaknesses. Since that time, counselors routinely incorporate books into small-group or classroom guidance sessions. For example, counselors conducting lessons about teasing and put-downs can read *Simon's Hook* (Burnett, 2000), discuss the story by using both content and personalization questions, and then have children work in small groups and put on skits to illustrate the ideas presented in the story about how to handle teasing.

An excellent book to help students in a small group learn to deal with anxiety is *What If It Never Stops Raining* (Carlson, 1992). After reading the story, group participants can discuss what the main character worried about, how many of his worries never materialized, and how others helped him learn to deal with his anxieties. A good follow-up activity is to have children write their own "what if" stories. Although this is a book written for elementary children, the simple but powerful message is very applicable for older children, including adolescents.

Adolescents in either classroom or small-group sessions benefit from seeing movies or movie clips that illustrate issues they are dealing with. For example, *The Breakfast Club* is an excellent film about cliques, and *Dying to Be Thin* is an informative film about the dangers of eating disorders. Both of these selections generate good discussion about issues teens face.

## SUMMARY

Incorporating bibliotherapy and cinematherapy into the counseling process is very effective for clients of all ages, especially if they are visual learners. Several different interventions involving fiction and nonfiction, poetry, and films have been described in this chapter, and others addressing specific topics of divorce, sadness, bullying, friendship, relationships with parents, self-acceptance, trust, expressing emotions, underachievement, and prejudice are described in detail on the following pages. We hope these practical strategies will be useful. Another helpful resource is *Read Two Books and Let's Talk Next Week: Using Bibliotherapy in Clinical Practice* (Joshua & DiMenna, 2000).

# What's the Story?

**TOPIC** Divorce and living in two homes

**RATIONALE** When a child's parents divorce, one of the more difficult challenges is going back and forth between two homes. The logistics are challenging enough, but there are also significant emotional aspects. This intervention will help the client focus on the positives in the situation, as well as providing some simple strategies for keeping the process as trouble free as possible.

**MATERIALS** The book *Charlie Anderson,* by Abercrombie and Graham (1990)

A beach ball

Permanent red and black markers

**PREPARATIONS** Write the What's the Story? Tips in permanent red marker on the beach ball.

**PROCEDURE**

1. When your client discusses her feelings of worry, sadness, or frustration because of having to go between her two parents' homes, invite her to read *Charlie Anderson* or read it to her. This is the story of a stray cat that appears on the doorstep one night and is taken in by two young girls and their mother. They name him Charlie and feed and care for him. The next morning he is gone, but he starts showing up at the same time each evening, staying overnight and then disappearing into the woods the next morning. One night during a storm he does not come to their home, and the girls go looking for him. They discover that he wasn't actually disappearing in the woods but that in fact he has another home where another family takes care of him during the day. They had named him Anderson. The girls could relate to Charlie even more because they also had two homes, living with their mom during the week and going to their dad and stepmom's house in the city each weekend. The two families share them, just as the two families share Charlie, now called Charlie Anderson.

2. Discuss the story with your client and ask her if she thinks there are mostly good things about Charlie having two homes or mostly bad things. Ask her to identify some of the good things and some things she thinks are not so good about his situation.
3. Invite your client to identify some of the positives and negatives of her situation of living in two homes. Introduce her to the idea that some things that go "back and forth" are actually even fun, such as playing Ping-Pong or volleyball or even catch.
4. At this time, take out the beach ball and marker and ask the client to write (or you write for her) on the beach ball in black marker the good things about being at Mom's house and also at Dad's house (there will also be tips for handling this back and forth transition that have already been written on the ball in red marker).
5. Now begin tossing the ball back and forth between the two of you. Each time either one of you catches the ball, that person either reads one of the positive statements that the client wrote or one of the prewritten suggestions in red taken from the What's the Story? Tips. Encourage discussion about these tips, as well as her feelings in general about going between two homes, as you toss the ball back and forth.
6. As the session is ending, ask her if she has learned anything from the story or the ball toss and encourage her to identify and try some of the tips she thinks might be helpful to her.

## What's the Story? Tips

- Keep a calendar at both homes (Mom's days/Dad's days).
- Keep pajamas, a toothbrush, and at least one set of clothes at both houses.
- Keep a picture of Mom in your room at Dad's house and a picture of Dad in your room at Mom's house.
- Create a space where you can do homework at both homes.
- Find a place to keep your book bag or backpack, shoes, and coat.
- Ask for a special place to keep your things where no one will bother them.
- Keep at least three things you enjoy doing at each place, such as books, games, and toys.
- Post Mom's phone number at Dad's house where you can always find it and talk to Dad about the rules for calling Mom.
- Post Dad's phone number at Mom's house where you can always find it and talk to Mom about the rules for calling Dad.
- Have a special bag that you always take to your parents' houses and have it packed and ready to go all the time.

# Story with a Happy Ending

**TOPIC** Sad feelings

**RATIONALE** Although middle childhood is generally a happy time as children master new skills, make friends, and participate in different types of activities, children this age are not immune to feeling sad. This intervention helps clients understand that there are different ways to feel and that happiness can be a choice.

**MATERIALS** A copy of the Story with a Happy Ending (adapted from Vernon, 2002, p. 123)

Three sheets of paper

A pen or pencil

A pair of scissors

**PROCEDURE**

1. When the client begins talking about feeling sad, give him paper and pencil and ask him to make a list of what he is sad about. Discuss his list in more detail.
2. Then read him (or have him read) the Story with a Happy Ending. After reading and discussing the story, ask him to turn his sheet of paper over and make a list of things that he enjoys doing, people he enjoys spending time with, and whatever else makes him feel happy. Help the client brainstorm to make this list as long as possible.
3. Next explain to the client that he is going to make his own book. Give him a sheet of paper and have him make a small book by folding the paper down the middle one way and then folding it down the middle in the other direction. Then cut the pages free on the short (4-inch) side of the booklet. This will result in a small (4- by 5½-inch) blank book.
4. Have the client draw a smiley face (or another symbol that represents happiness to him) on the front of the book. Ask him to open the book and copy his list of happy things into his book.

5. Now flip the book over to what you would think of as the back of the book, but turn it so that the binding of the book is on the left and the open part is on the right, as if it were the front of the book. Now have the client draw a sad face or some other symbol that represents sadness and copy the list of sad things he made at the beginning of the session.
6. Review with the client how, in the story, Simon finally realizes that he is thinking about things that he can't do anything about. Have the client look at his list and see how many of the things on the sad list are things that he can do something about, put a check mark beside them, and cross off the things he really can't change or control. Discuss what he checked and what he crossed out.
7. Then remind the client that Simon also took action and started making an effort to do things he could have some control over and think about things that helped him feel happier. Stress that Simon had a choice to be happy or sad, just as the client does. Invite the client to take his book and read the happy side when he wants to feel better.

# Story with a Happy Ending

Simon was very sad. It seemed like everything in his life was awful. His mom and dad were getting a divorce, and his dad was moving out soon; his best friend, Raul, had just moved to another city; and his dog was pretty sick. Simon felt like his whole world was falling apart. School was pretty terrible, too. Because he was so sad about everything, he couldn't concentrate very well, so he flunked his spelling and math tests. He had never flunked anything before in his life, and he felt even worse when his parents got mad about it and told him he had to try harder. At home he just moped around and yelled at his little sister for messing with his stuff. He didn't know how things could get much worse.

Days went by, and Simon's mother just kept dragging him out of bed each morning to go to school. Simon kept telling her he didn't feel good, but his mother felt his head and said he didn't have a fever, so staying home was not an option. At school he stopped going out for recess, and his grades went from bad to worse. At night he cried himself to sleep. Finally, one day his next best friend, Aidan, yelled at him for moping around and ignoring everybody. "You think you have it so bad? Sure, your parents are getting a divorce, but they're both still alive and you'll get to see your dad every week, won't you? Just think about Sal. His dad got killed in a car crash, so he can't ever see him. Sure, it's tough that your best friend moved, but don't you have other friends? You've got me, but you won't if you keep ignoring me and crying about how much you miss Raul. Get a grip . . . things might be bad, but are they as awful as they could be?" On that note, Aidan ran off to play with other friends and left Simon by himself to mope.

At first Simon was mad at Aidan for yelling at him, but then he started to think about what he had said. It was true that Simon would still get to see his dad every week; at least his dad wasn't dead. And he knew that even though his dog was pretty sick, the vet said she would probably get better. Although he missed Raul a lot, he did have other friends. The more he thought about it, the more Simon realized that things weren't totally awful, but he still wished he could make his parents get back together, his best friend move back to town, and his dog get better. He knew that those things wouldn't happen—except that maybe his dog would get better. So he figured that the only thing he could do was concentrate on what to do to make himself less sad. But what could he do?

Simon thought and thought. Finally, he realized that it had been a long time since he had watched cartoons, and they always made him laugh. He also remembered that it had been a while since he had listened to music, which usually cheered him up. Then he thought about visiting the old lady next door, who usually had a surprise for him and something sweet to eat. Finally, he thought it might help to just get his mind off all his troubles and go outside to play.

So Simon proceeded to try his strategies, and little by little he felt better. It did help to remember that things could be worse and that even though he felt sad now, he probably wouldn't stay this way forever unless he just continued to mope around and feel sorry for himself and keep dwelling on how awful his life was. So, even though nothing in Simon's life changed, once he put the problems in perspective and started doing something about his sad feelings, he didn't feel quite so sad.

# Bully Books

**TOPIC** Being bullied

**RATIONALE** Although it would be ideal if schools were bully free, the reality is that bullying goes on "under the radar" of the adults in charge. It is empowering for clients to learn to handle bullying successfully themselves when possible.

**MATERIALS** A copy of the Bully Books Story

**PROCEDURE**

1. When your client complains about a classmate who has been teasing and bullying her, encourage her to talk more about the specifics, including what happened, how she felt, and what she did. Encourage her to think of other options that might have been more effective in dealing with the bully if what she did hadn't been very successful.
2. Then read the Bully Books Story to her or have her read it herself. Ask her if she thinks any of the ideas she heard in the story might work for her.
3. Have the client decide on a plan to try and someone she will ask to help her with it. Encourage her to keep a journal of the ideas she tried that worked or didn't work for her and discuss these at the next session.

# Bully Books Story

Sophia was really frustrated! This was the third time this week that she had to walk away from a game she was playing at recess just to avoid getting into a fight with Amelia. She was so tired of being bullied by Amelia, and so were other kids in her class. Something had to be done about it, but Sophia didn't know what to do. She didn't want to be a tattletale and tell the teacher every time something happened, but she wanted to be able to play with her friends without being bullied.

Today during classroom guidance time, Ms. Garcia, the counselor, was talking about ways to handle bullies. She said that you don't have to get in their face and tell them to quit being mean because that might make matters worse. Ms. Garcia asked the class why it might make things worse, and Sophia's friend said that it might make the bully meaner and he or she might hit someone. Ms. Garcia then talked about the kids who are bystanders—they aren't in with the bullies, but they don't try to stop them, either. She said that if the bystanders didn't just stand by, but instead all got together and stood up to the bully, they could have a lot of power. Ms. Garcia asked if the class had any ideas about what the bystanders could do to help classmates who were being bullied.

Tony suggested that all the bystanders could stand around the bully so maybe he or she would back off. Serita thought they could all go together to tell the teacher, because if just one of them did that, the bully might come after that person next, but it would be harder to do that if all the bystanders were in it together. Freddie said that maybe all the bystanders could go over to where the bully was and shout, "Hey, let's all play something else," which might distract the bully so the victim could move away.

Suddenly Sophia had an idea! She raised her hand and said, "Maybe we could start an Anti-Bullying Club! The people in the club could look out for each other at recess and in the lunchroom or on the bus when the bully was most likely to try to hurt others." She noticed that other kids were nodding their heads, agreeing that this was a great idea. Serita said that she thought Sophia should be the club president. Everyone but Amelia got excited talking about the club, and Ms. Garcia said she thought if they put all their ideas to work they could have a lot of power to stop bullying.

# Parent Poem

**TOPIC** Relationship with parents

**RATIONALE** It is common for young adolescents to have conflicts with their parents. Developmentally, they are at the stage where they are beginning their quest for independence and autonomy, but they still need the support of the adults in their lives. They are often confused by the process of growing up and many of the messages they receive. This intervention will give adolescent clients the opportunity to express feelings, as well as help them see the issues from other perspectives.

**MATERIALS**

A copy of the Parent Poem

A sheet of paper

A pen or pencil

**PROCEDURE**

1. When a client complains about how his parents are never happy with what he does, are always nagging him about something, or don't understand him, give him a copy of the Parent Poem and ask him to read it.
2. Ask the client if he can relate to the poem, and, if so, what part of the poem in particular speaks to him the most. If he doesn't bring it up, be sure and point out the following dichotomies:
   - Always tell the truth, but white lies may be all right.
   - Always be kind to others, but don't be friends with "those kids."

   Ask the client if he gets mixed messages like these from his parents or others, and, if so, how he feels about it. Talk about the meaning of the word *dichotomy,* emphasizing that there are many dichotomies in life and asking him to give examples of what he has experienced.
3. Next have the client make a list of the frustrations he is currently experiencing with his parents. Then have him select one or two issues from his list to role-play. Have him play the role of the par-

ent, and you play the part of your client trying to get the parent to understand how he feels about the issue. The client's job is to do his best to think and respond as his parents would. Then reverse roles so that you play the parent and your client plays himself.

4. After the role-plays, discuss how the client felt in the role of parent. Did this give him any insight into how his parents might think or feel? Did he have any reactions to "himself" (played by you, the counselor) that surprised him? What reactions did he have when the roles were reversed and he was playing himself? What, if anything, did he learn from this exercise, and how can he apply this to his life?

## Parent Poem

Mixed messages! Confusion!
It spins around my head!
Just when they tell me one thing,
They seem to mean another instead!
Always be kind to others,
And treat them with respect!
But don't be friends with "those kids,"
They don't act the way good kids should act.

Mixed messages! Confusion!
It spins around my head!
Just when they tell me one thing,
They seem to mean another instead!
You're "too old" for this!
You're "too young" for that!
Do your homework right this minute!
But first be sure to feed the cat!

Mixed messages! Confusion!
It spins around my head!
Just when they tell me one thing,
They seem to mean another instead!
No you can't go out tonight,
You must babysit your sister.
Even though in their opinion,
I'm not as responsible as they expect.

Mixed messages! Confusion!
It spins around my head!
Just when they tell me one thing,
They seem to mean another instead!
Be a leader not a follower,
Stand up for your beliefs!
As long as I do what they say,
and give THEM zero grief!

Mixed messages! Confusion!
It spins around my head!
Just when they tell me one thing,
They seem to mean another instead!
Always tell the truth,
But white lies may be all right
'Cuz sometimes the truth hurts too much,
So being honest may be unkind.

Mixed messages! Confusion!
It spins around my head!
Just when they tell me one thing,
They seem to mean another instead!

# Required Reading About Bullies

**TOPIC** Relational aggression

**RATIONALE** Relational aggression is a form of emotional bullying that occurs frequently during early and mid-adolescence, involving rumors, exclusion, intimidation, the silent treatment, and more. It can be especially devastating to an adolescent who values peer acceptance above all else. This intervention will help to empower the targeted person and reduce the fear of the bully.

**MATERIALS** A copy of the Required Reading About Bullies story and Required Reading About Bullies Tips

**PROCEDURE**

1. When your client tells you about her problem with another student who is emotionally bullying her, encourage her to tell you more about this, including how she feels, behaves, and reacts when she is targeted.
2. Then share the share the Required Reading for Bullies story. After she has read it, ask her in what ways her situation is similar or dissimilar. Discuss the fact that the type of bullying described in the story is called *relational aggression,* which is a form of emotional bullying. Just as in the story, it is important to remember that the target (person being bullied) and the bystanders (observers) have a choice in how much power they allow the bully to have.
3. Next ask what she has tried in order to help her deal with this problem. After she shares her ideas, give her a copy of the Required Reading for Bullies Tips, discussing each one, asking her if she thinks any of the tips could work for her, and inviting her to commit to trying one or more of them to help her deal more effectively with this problem.

**NOTE** If time permits, search YouTube for brief videos on relational aggression to discuss with the client.

## Required Reading About Bullies

Morgan was really excited to go to school today! Nikki had written her a note that said that she was allowed back in the group and could sit with the girls at lunch today. It had been two weeks since Nikki had banned her from sitting with her friends, and it seemed like it had been a year. She knew the other girls felt bad about what Nikki had done because they had called Morgan at home to apologize for not sitting with her, but they were afraid to upset Nikki. And even though Morgan's feelings were really hurt by being excluded, she actually understood why they went along with what Nikki wanted because she was also afraid of making Nikki mad.

Morgan knew from experience that when Nikki was angry with you she could make your life miserable. First, she would give you the "burning stare" that almost burned a hole right through you! Next she would say mean things about you to your face, not just behind your back. In fact, last week she said Morgan's top looked like something the dog threw up on. She said this to Morgan but also in front of a whole group of kids, including some boys. Morgan was so embarrassed she was tongue-tied. And as if that wasn't bad enough, Nikki told the whole group not to speak to Morgan. And of course that's exactly what they did, because Nikki had so much power that if they went against her wishes she would declare war on them next.

But the very worst thing Nikki did was "lunch isolation." Before lunch, Nikki told the group not to speak to Morgan. When Morgan went to sit in her usual seat at lunch, all her friends looked pretty uncomfortable. Then Nikki told Morgan to get away from their table and sit somewhere else because nobody wanted to eat with her. Morgan looked at her friends, but none of them would look back at her, so she left the lunchroom and spent the rest of the lunch period in the bathroom crying. After that, Morgan just sat by herself every day for two whole weeks. She was miserable.

But then Morgan got a note from Nikki giving her permission to sit with the group again, starting tomorrow. What a relief! Now maybe things would get back to normal. But when she went into the lunchroom, she found out that Nikki had declared war on Christa, another friend in her group, which meant that Morgan and the others would be expected to give Christa the silent treatment and go along with lunch isolation, just as Nikki demanded. But, having been through it all herself, Morgan just couldn't do it to someone else, especially a friend. So Morgan decided to defy Nikki and sit with Christa at lunch. Morgan was really scared to do it. As soon as she sat down by Christa, she noticed Nikki giving all the other girls "the stare," but one by one, they got up from their spot at Nikki's table and came over to join Morgan and Christa until Nikki was sitting all by herself!

Apparently, bullies only have the power that others give them. And when others decide to take it back, things change rather quickly!

## Required Reading About Bullies Tips

*If bystanders and targets follow these tips, bullies will have less power, and the school will be safer and have less bullying. Remember, there are more bystanders and targets than there bullies, so take back the power.*

### What Bystanders Can Do

1. Take away the bully's power by refusing to laugh or join in with the bullying.
2. Don't give him or her power by doing what he or she says. If the bully says not to talk to someone, ignore it. If you are afraid you will receive the same treatment, talk with the people in your circle of friends and agree to support each other.
3. Support the target (the person being bullied) either during or after the bullying and let him or her know that you saw or heard what happened (the bullying) but didn't know exactly how to help at the time. Tell him or her that you don't think it is right and that if he or she wants to talk to an adult about it, you would be glad to go along as backup.

### What Targets Can Do

1. Bullies feed on the fear of others, so don't feed the bully's power by looking or acting afraid.
2. Tell the bully that you don't like it and you want her or him to stop. Use a firm, respectful tone and don't sound like you are afraid, even if you are. If she or he repeats the behavior again, say nothing, walk away, and report the incident to an adult.
3. Be observant! If the bully is picking on you, chances are he or she is doing it to others.
4. Look around to see who those people are and make them your allies. Agree to back each other, and in this way the bully won't have as much power.

# Dear Abby Letter

**TOPIC** Self-acceptance

**RATIONALE** At this stage in development, adolescents can be highly self-conscious and overly sensitive to every comment that is made about them. It is not surprising that they will often engage in a lot of self-criticism as a result of low self-esteem. This intervention works quite well to help them see that self-criticism is not helpful and that it is preferable to have a more realistic sense of self.

**MATERIALS** A copy of the Dear Abby Letter

A sheet of paper

A pen or pencil

**PROCEDURE**

1. When a client starts putting himself down, saying he isn't good at something or doesn't deserve something because he is not worthy of it, give him a copy of the Dear Abby Letter and ask him if he ever heard of the famous Dear Abby newspaper column. If not, you might want to do an Internet search so that he can see what it is, explaining that people write in to Dear Abby asking for advice. Tell him that you would like him to be a Dear Abby consultant and respond in Dear Abby fashion to a letter written by a fictitious middle school student.
2. Have the client read the letter and discuss his reaction, focusing on the following:
   - What does he think about the friend's advice to the author of the letter?
   - Does he believe that anyone is totally without good qualities, as the author of the letter seems to think he is?
   - Despite the fact that the author thinks he has no good qualities, what are some of his good qualities?
   - What does the author of the letter focus on when describing Becky? Is it possible that she had negative qualities that he was just choosing not to think about or look at?

- In contrast, what kind of qualities is he focusing on regarding himself? Why do you think he continues to put himself down? What purpose does that serve?

3. Have the client write a response to "Loser," giving him advice as Dear Abby would.
4. Invite the client to compare the author of the letter with himself. What commonalities does he see? Does he put himself down the way the author of the letter does? If so, what purpose does that serve?
5. Give the client a sheet of paper and a pen and ask him to think about his negative qualities and write them on paper. Go over the list with him, challenging him on overgeneralizations, such as "never does anything right," by emphasizing the never—"you mean you have *never, ever* done anything right?" Continue in this manner, asking for proof that he is stupid, lazy, and so forth—whatever he comes up with. The objective is to help him see himself more realistically.
6. Next have him think of three to five good things about himself and write these on his sheet of paper. Then ask him to turn the page over and write a piece of advice for himself to help him to remember to think about himself more realistically.

# Dear Abby Letter

Dear Abby:

I am writing to you because I promised my friend that I would, but I feel like I am wasting your time even having you read this letter, so I apologize. I am an eighth-grade boy, and I really like Becky, a girl in my social studies class. I have known her for a long time because we live in a small town and have grown up together. She is perfect in every way: beautiful, smart, a great athlete, and really nice. Even though she is very popular and has a lot of friends, she still talks to me. My friend thinks I should ask her to go to a movie, but I think he is crazy because no one like her would ever go out with me because I am the school loser. I don't know anyone else who makes as many mistakes as often as I do. It seems like everything I do ends up a mess because I am an accident waiting to happen. I don't get very good grades, I'm a klutz on the soccer field, and I don't do anything else well.

I have a really good friend who always tells me that I am good at a lot of things, like being a good friend, for instance. He said that Becky is nice to me because I am nice to her, so I am good at making other people feel good. He says I need to be as nice to myself as I am to other people. I don't know. I can't think of anything good about myself, and I think he is just being a good friend when he says nice things about me. I don't know if I should ask Becky out because if she says no, that will just prove that I am a loser. What do you think I should do? Thanks for your help!

Sincerely,

Loser with a Good Friend

# Science Fiction Hits Home

**TOPIC** Trust

**RATIONALE** Adolescents who have had a relationship loss in their lives often find it difficult to entrust their feelings to someone again. They frequently make the assumption that the same thing will happen next time. As a result of this fear, they sometimes adopt behaviors that push others away. However, the obvious drawback is that they are missing a wonderful part of life: a loving, trusting relationship with another human being. Reflecting upon this film and the two main characters in it will help clients see that it is well worth the courage it takes to let others in so as to experience the rewards of a loving relationship.

**MATERIALS** The movie *Martian Child* (available for purchase, rental, or authorized download)

**PROCEDURE**

1. When your client expresses uncertainty and perhaps anxiety over a new relationship because she is afraid that she will be hurt as she has been before, invite her to share more about her anxiety and what makes her think that just because she was hurt before she will be again. Then ask her if she has seen the film *Martian Child.* If not, read the following short synopsis of what happens in the film from the beginning up to the point of the first film clip.

   David is a popular science fiction author who lost his wife two years ago. Before she died they had started the process of adopting a child. David now thinks he is ready to initiate that process again as a single parent.

   He is matched up with Dennis, a five-year-old orphan. Dennis has been in and out of several foster homes and now lives in a group home. He is an interesting child with some very unusual issues. He thinks he is from Mars and is allergic to the sun, so he hides in a big box when he is outside. He wears a special belt that he made to keep himself from "floating away" because

he thinks the earth's gravity will not hold him down.
He only eats Lucky Charms, he has no social skills,
and he steals.

2. Show film clip 1, starting about 1 minute 26 seconds into the movie and ending at approximately 10 minutes, 10 seconds. Ask the client for her overall reaction to the clip, discussing the following:

    - Why do you think Dennis acted so strangely?
    - Do you think he really believed he was from Mars?
    - Why do you think Dennis stayed in that box when there were other kids playing outside whom he could have joined?
    - When David asked the social worker why she thought he would be a good match for "a boy who spends his time in a box," she answered, "Because he thinks he's from another planet." What did she mean by that?

3. Now play clip 2, starting approximately 13 minutes into the movie and ending at 16 minutes 20 seconds. After viewing the clip, discuss the following questions:

    - How did David get Dennis to come out of the box?
    - Why do you think that Dennis was so afraid to trust people? How is it that David was able to get Dennis to trust him when others couldn't?

4. Now turn the discussion to the client's relationship, asking her if she sees any parallels between the film and her own life. Is she afraid of taking the risk to trust? Help her to examine some of her recent relationship problems for indicators that she may be sabotaging them because she feels vulnerable and is afraid to trust. Suggest that she may want to rent *Martian Child* and give this idea more thought as she watches more of the film.
5. If time permits, you may want to share the following clips with her from the same film:

    - Clip 3: Beginning approximately 54 minutes 21 seconds into the movie and ending at about 56 minutes 25 seconds. Discuss: Why do you think David had Dennis break the plates?
    - Clip 4: Beginning at approximately 1 hour 32 minutes into the movie and ending at about 1 hour, 38 minutes 55 seconds (end of the movie). Discuss: How did David convince Dennis that he could trust David to always be there for him?

# Don't Judge a Book by Its Cover

**TOPIC** Expressing emotions

**RATIONALE** Adolescents can be like chameleons, appearing one way at certain times and a different way at other times, because they are good at masking their feelings. They often have difficulty being open about how they feel, they may receive mixed messages about whether or not they should be open, or they may not fully understand what they are experiencing emotionally. They also may mask who they are, appearing one way on the outside but feeling very different on the inside. This intervention will help them better understand these dichotomies.

**MATERIALS**

A copy of the Don't Judge a Book by Its Cover poem

A business-size envelope

8–10 strips of paper or index cards

A pen or pencil

**PROCEDURE**

1. When a client presents with confusion about what he is feeling or who he is, discuss these issues and then invite him to read the Don't Judge a Book by Its Cover poem. After he has finished reading it, ask if he can relate in any way to the poem, and if so, how. Point out that it is not uncommon to receive mixed messages about expressing feelings or being ourselves. For example, in the poem, he is told, "Be yourself . . . you are great the way you are." However, when he is honest about his feelings, that isn't acceptable. Ask the client if this has ever happened to him and, if so, how it affected him.
2. Next, read him the following:

> I feel like I'm leading a double life: first, the real me who is sad and depressed, and second, the fake me who acts like nothing is wrong. I can't explain

> my feelings to anyone because I don't even understand them myself. (Vernon, 1998c, p. 173)

Ask the client if he identifies with this true statement, written by another teenager and, if so, how it relates to him. Talk about the fact that sometimes people project a different image or mask their feelings because they think it might protect them from being hurt emotionally. And when people protect themselves and don't express feelings openly, they may appear one way (happy, for example), but inside they are hurting. Therefore, it is important for him not to assume that how he or others seem is how he or they really feel: He "can't judge a book by its cover" because what is on the inside may be very different from how it appears on the outside.

3. Give the client the envelope, strips of paper or index cards, and pen or pencil and ask him to think about the image he projects to others who see him at school, at extracurricular activities, at home, and so forth. Ask him to write words or phrases describing this image on the outside of the envelope. Then ask him to think about the feelings or thoughts he might be hiding, write these words or phrases on the individual slips or cards, and put them inside the envelope.
4. When he has finished, encourage discussion about whether there were any dichotomies between his inside and outside self, what purpose it serves to hide his true characteristics or feelings from others, and how it affects him to project one image but mask his feelings or other aspects of himself. Help him identify possible consequences of protecting himself or projecting another image, such as keeping others from getting close, not experiencing your true feelings, becoming "numb,"and so forth. Encourage him to continue to do the envelope activity several times to see if he develops more congruency—so people could judge his book by its cover.

## Don't Judge a Book by Its Cover

You are so great!
Just the way you are!
Just be yourself.
You will go far!
But when I cried,
At the death of Gran,
I heard, "Be tough,
My little man!"
And when I'd say,
"I'm feeling fear!
Can I have a hug?
Will you hold me near?"
They said, "Silly boy!
There's nothing to fear!
Now you get right back out there!
And I don't want to see another tear!"
So is it OK to be myself or not?
I want to know.
'Cuz a big part of who I am
Is my feelings,
And sometimes
I need to let them show!

# Achievement Autobiography

**TOPIC** Academic underachievement

**RATIONALE** It is fairly common for adolescents to fall short of what they are capable of achieving academically. Although there are a multitude of reasons for this, one of the more common is that, after years of failure in the form of low test scores, poor grades, or having one or more significant adults in their lives telling them they are not capable of doing well academically, they come to believe it. They also may have poor study habits, lack knowledge about how they learn best, or suffer from procrastination or test anxiety. This activity helps clients take the first step to improving performance by believing in their abilities and making a commitment to do their best to improve.

**MATERIALS** The movie *The Blind Side* (available for rental, purchase, or authorized download)

A copy of the Achievement Autobiography Learning Style Assessment

A pen or pencil

**PROCEDURE**

1. When a client begins talking about her lack of ability and all the "proof" she has of this, such as poor grades, low test scores, or significant adults and others who have told her that she is not smart or talented in certain areas, ask if she has seen the film *The Blind Side*. If not, share the following synopsis with her:

> *The Blind Side* is a story about All-American football star Michael Oher, who is virtually homeless while he is in high school. He is taken in by the well-to-do family of one of his classmates. The arrangement is initially for only one night, but Michael touches the Tuohy's lives as much as they

touch his, and he eventually becomes a member of the family. It is a heartwarming story, and a very unusual type of a "make a difference" tale, because in the end the people gaining the most are the ones who started out to do a good deed.

2. Next, tell the client you would like to share some clips from the film with her. Clip 1, which starts at approximately 7 minutes 50 seconds into the film and ends at approximately 9 minutes 10 seconds, shows teachers at a private school, to which the main character, Michael Oher, has applied, discussing his application.

   After watching the clip, tell the client that Michael successfully graduated with a 2.56 GPA and went on to graduate from college as well. Discuss the following points and invite her to share how each of these might apply to her situation:

   - Initially, what expectations did teachers have for Michael in their school?
   - What "proof" did they base these expectations on?
   - Were their expectations appropriate and based on good information?

3. Now show clip 2, which starts at approximately 13 minutes 25 seconds into the movie and stops at approximately 18 minutes 41 seconds. Then show clip 3, which starts at approximately 30 minutes 44 seconds and ends at 37 minutes 25 seconds. Finally, show clip 4, which starts at 38 minutes 44 seconds and ends at 39 minutes 22 seconds. Then discuss the following:

   - Initially, how did Michael think he would do in this new school? What were his expectations based on?
   - What began to turn things around academically for Michael?
   - What was the one area that Michael tested high in?
   - Why might he have tested high in this area and low in other, more academically related areas, even though, as it turned out, he had more abilities than the tests indicated?

4. Discuss with the client what talents and skills she might possess that have been overlooked or have not yet been developed. Explain that one way to discover hidden talents is by taking a learning style assessment to help her understand more about how she learns best, which can make a big difference in how successful she is academically. Give her a copy of the learning style assessment to complete. (A wealth of additional information about study skills, test taking, memory aids, and so forth is available on the Internet.)

5. After she takes the assessment, go through the results and discuss some ways she might apply the information she has learned about her learning style to improve her performance in school. Have the client pick one or two things she learned and make a specific academic action plan.

## Achievement Autobiography Learning Style Assessment

*Directions: For each item below, circle the letter for the answer that most closely describes you.*

1. When I take a test, I would rather have:
   (a) The directions in written form.
   (b) The test directions given to me verbally.
   (c) Someone who will do a sample question to show exactly what the directions mean.
2. If I need to memorize a list of items for a test, I would do best if:
   (a) I created a "study visual" with a specific place on it for each item.
   (b) I made up a song using the words on the list to help me remember them.
   (c) I actually touched each item as I was trying to memorize it.
3. If I have free time I would rather:
   (a) Read a book.
   (b) Listen to music.
   (c) Play a game or do a craft.
4. When I am trying to remember something, I:
   (a) Picture it in my mind.
   (b) Try to think about when I heard the information.
   (c) Pace around or tap a pencil to help me think.
5. In science class the way I learn best is when:
   (a) The teacher demonstrates a scientific principle (for example, does an experiment while we watch or shows us something).
   (b) The teacher tells us about scientific principles and explains how they work.
   (c) I get to do the experiments in the lab myself.
6. I would do the best on a spelling test if I prepare by:
   (a) Using flashcards of the words.
   (b) Spelling them out loud to myself.
   (c) Writing them each five times.
7. When expected to report on a topic in a group, my preference would be to:
   (a) Hand in a written report or poster to the teacher.
   (b) Present an oral report on an audiorecording to the class.
   (c) Do the report in the form of a group skit for the class.
8. When I remember an experience, I primarily:
   (a) Have pictures in my mind of what happened.
   (b) Hear sounds from when it happened in my head.
   (c) Think about how I felt during the experience.

9. Out of the following subjects, the one I like most is:
   (a) Art.
   (b) Music.
   (c) Physical education.
10. I would prefer to:
   (a) Read a story.
   (b) Have a story read to me.
   (c) Act out a story.
11. When I am learning how to do something new that is difficult, I learn best if:
   (a) I can read about how to do it (and see pictures and diagrams, if appropriate).
   (b) Someone tells me how to do it and I can talk about it and ask questions.
   (c) I can do it while I learn about it.
12. When I am not sure if a word is spelled correctly I:
   (a) Write it down to see if it looks right.
   (b) Spell it out loud to see if it sounds right.
   (c) Sound it out to see if it feels right.
13. While I am doing homework it is important that I:
   (a) Have no visual distractions, such as windows, people walking by, TV on.
   (b) Have no auditory distractions, such as noise in the next room, music, TV or radio.
   (c) Have something to fidget or play with—manipulatives for math, space to move, etc.
14. When I have to solve a difficult problem, I like to:
   (a) Draw sketches or diagrams to help me come up with ideas.
   (b) Work in groups so that I can talk and listen to the ideas of others.
   (c) Act out some of my ideas by constructing models, role playing, etc.
15. When traveling I do best if:
   (a) I have a map to follow.
   (b) Someone gives me verbal directions.
   (c) I can stop frequently so that I can get out of the car and get my bearings.

*When you have completed the assessment, count up the total number of times you circled each letter and enter that number below:*

____________ **a's** ____________ **b's** ____________ **c's**

If you circled mostly **a's** your primary learning style is VISUAL.

If you circled mostly **b's,** your primary learning style is AUDITORY.

If you circled mostly **c's,** your primary learning style is TACTILE/KINESTHETIC.

*On the next page are a few ideas for how to use this information to help you work more effectively.*

## VISUAL LEARNERS

1. Color code your notes and use highlighters to do the same to your text as you read.
2. When taking notes, include symbols to help you visualize ideas later.
3. Make flashcards with simple pictures for studying.
4. When hearing new information that you want to remember, close your eyes and visualize the information as a picture.
5. Always sit in the front of the class where you can see everything clearly.

## AUDITORY LEARNERS

1. Be sure you have a quiet place to work.
2. When possible, read your notes and assignments aloud.
3. Record yourself reading your notes aloud and listen to them when you study for tests.
4. Record class sessions and listen to them when you study your class notes. (Get permission from the teacher before doing this!)
5. Organize study groups so you talk about concepts and study with others.
6. When memorizing, use tunes to help you by putting lists and concepts you need to remember to music.
7. Use audiorecordings of books when available.
8. When you proofread, do it aloud and audiorecord it.

## TACTILE/KINESTHETIC LEARNERS

1. When you are reading, use your finger to follow along.
2. Talk to your teacher about your need for movement and explain that you need some movement to help you concentrate. For that reason, ask to be seated in the very back so you can move and not distract others.
3. When studying at home, take frequent breaks.
4. While studying your notes at home, occasionally walk around while you read.
5. Change position often while you study. Don't just sit at a desk. Try lying on your back, on your stomach, etc.
6. At school, keep a stress ball with you to squeeze.

# Book Buddies

**TOPIC** Friendship skills

**RATIONALE** Developing good social skills is a highly complex task and can be overwhelming for young children. This intervention helps them begin to develop important skills they will need to get along with their friends.

**MATERIALS** A paper bag containing bracelets representing four to six different colors, four of each color and enough bracelets for each child

A copy of the Book Buddies Story

A poster-size version of the Book Buddies Tips

**PREPARATIONS** Divide the bracelets into four to six equal color groups (or more, depending on the class size). They can be made from string, ponytail holders, rubber bands, or pipe cleaners (whatever is available in the colors you select). Create a poster of the Book Buddies Tips, including spaces under each tip to write other suggestions from students. Finally, set up four play centers, as indicated on the diagram at the end of this activity. Use masking tape to make arrows illustrating the direction in which to move from one to the other.

**PROCEDURE**

1. Introduce this activity to the class by asking them to share ideas about what it means to be a buddy, eliciting ideas that buddies do things together and are nice to each other. After some discussion, read the Book Buddies Story. At the end, ask students what they think—did the other children let Joey play or not? Then discuss how Joey tried to join his buddies versus how the other children in the story did it.
2. Invite four children to come to the front of the room. Ask one of them to play the role of Joey; the other three children will pretend to be playing a game together. Ask Joey first to try to join his buddies the way he did in the beginning of the story and then to do it by asking to join. Invite the students to comment on the difference. Explain that Joey had to use "joining skills." Ask

the group to comment on which joining skills were effective and which ones weren't. Then post the Book Buddies Tips in front of the room for everyone to see, read the first one, and ask them to think of other ways to join in. Write their suggestions on the Book Buddies Tips poster under the ideas already there. Do this for item numbers 2 and 3 as well.

3. Tell the students that they will be practicing joining skills by playing in groups. Divide them into four color groups (or more, depending on the number of children participating in the activity; groups should have no more than four children per group) by having each child reach inside the bag of bracelets and draw a bracelet to wear during the activity (the color of the bracelet will designate the group they join). Then send one child from *each* color group to *each* of the four prearranged play centers so that *each* center has four to six children, depending on how many different colors there are. When they are all there, clap or whistle to signal that they should begin the activity at the play center.
4. When five minutes have passed, clap or whistle again to signal them to stop and listen to further directions. When they are all listening, select a color (for example, yellow) and announce that the children with that color bracelet should follow the arrow to the next activity and ask, in a nice way (as discussed and modeled in the role-plays) to join in the play. (There will be one child per group rotating to the next group.)
5. After five minutes, select another color and proceed in the same manner until all color groups have had the opportunity to practice joining in.
6. When the activity is finished, discuss what they learned about joining in and how they might use these skills the next time they want to play with someone.

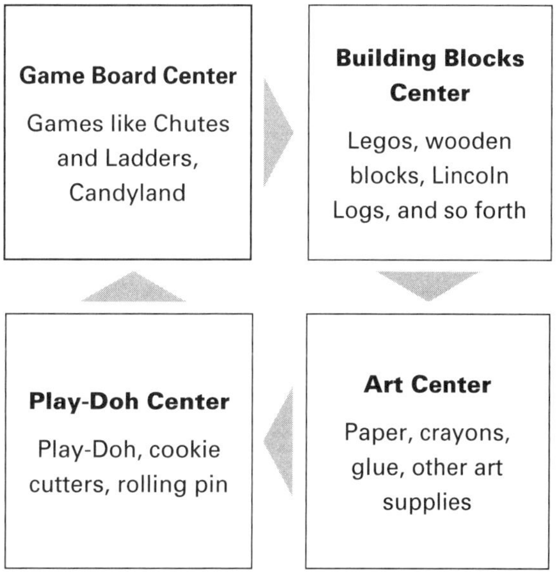

## Book Buddies Story

"Joey, you are going to miss the bus if you don't hurry up!" Joey's mom yelled from downstairs. "I hope I do miss the bus!" Joey thought to himself. Joey didn't really want to go to school today. Kids were nice enough to him in the classroom, but it was a different story when it was recess time and nobody wanted to play with him. Whenever he would try to join them in a game or other activity, they would just start shouting at him to go away. He told Mrs. Rice about his problem, and she suggested he talk to Mr. Sammons, the counselor. He liked Mr. Sammons and thought he had good ideas about friends and problems and things, so maybe he would be able to help.

"So, Joey," said Mr. Sammons, "tell me about what recess time is like." Mr. Sammons smiled and offered Joey a lump of clay to roll while they chatted.

"Well, it's pretty lonely because nobody will play with me," said Joey.

"What do you mean when you say that nobody will play with you?" Mr. Sammons looked confused.

"When I try to play with them, they all yell for me to go away and stuff like that," complained Joey.

"I'll tell you what. Why don't I just come outside and watch at the next recess, and maybe between the two of us, we can figure out what to do about this problem," Mr. Sammons offered.

Joey didn't really see how that was going to help, but he didn't want to hurt Mr. Sammons' feelings, so he agreed. The next recess, Mr. Sammons went outside to watch Joey and the other kids play. This is what he saw.

Some of the kids in Joey's class were playing soccer. Antonio went over to them and asked, "Hey, you guys, can I play, too?" Most of the kids nodded their heads, and Tommy said, "You can be on our team since we are short a player." "Great!" Antonio said, as he ran onto the field.

When Joey heard that, he thought, "If Antonio can play soccer with them, so can I," so he just ran onto the field and started playing with the other team without even asking anyone. The kids all started yelling at him, "Joey, get off the field! You aren't even in this game! We didn't say you could play with us." One of the kids was especially upset and threw the soccer ball at Joey because Joey had messed up the team's chance to make a goal. Joey felt bad that everyone was mad, but his feelings were hurt, too. He started to get mad, and he yelled, "You guys let Antonio join your team, and so why won't you let me play, too?"

That's when Mr. Sammons stepped in. "Joey, why don't you and I go for a walk and cool down a little bit."

Joey agreed and said, "See, I told you that they wouldn't let me play. It's not fair that they let Antonio play and not me."

"Joey," said Mr. Sammons, "Do you have any idea why they didn't let you play?" Joey shook his head no. "Well, what I noticed is that you just rushed in and started playing without asking your friends if you can play like Antonio did. Is that the way you usually do it?"

"Yeah, I guess I don't ask," said Joey. Mr. Sammons talked to him some more about the difference: that Joey had just run onto the field without asking or saying anything at all, whereas Antonio asked nicely if he could play and waited for them to answer. He told Joey that not asking to play was a bit like grabbing a toy away from someone without asking to play with it and asked him if he liked it when that happened to him.

"No," said Joey.

"Well," said Mr. Sammons, "apparently the other kids don't like it when you just join in without asking, so how about seeing if you can learn how to do that?"

"OK," said Joey, "but how do I learn it?" "My suggestion would be that you pretend you are a 'buddy detective' and you need to find examples of kids being buddies by asking to play. Do you want to give that a try?"

"Sure," said Joey. They started walking around and saw Jasmine waiting for a turn on the teeter-totter. When she walked up, two kids were already using it, and Jasmine said, "Can I please have the next turn?" And both kids nodded their heads yes, and in another minute, she had her turn.

Then Mr. Sammons said, "Look, Joey. There's Ben, and it looks like he is waiting to play basketball." As they got closer they heard Ben saying, "Can I play, too? I don't care which team I am on." And the kids said, "Yes, you can be on Juan's team." Mr. Sammons looked at Joey and said, "Do you think you are ready to try it yourself?" Joey looked around the playground and saw Gina and a couple other kids from his class playing four square. "OK, but only if you will come with me." Mr. Sammons gave him a thumbs-up and winked at him. Together they headed across the blacktop. Mr. Sammons stayed back a little. Joey watched the group for a minute, and then he finally decided to give it a try. "Can I play, too?" he asked Gina. And you will never, ever guess what they said!

## Book Buddies Tips

1. If you want to buddy up with another person, you can **ask** nicely:

   May I play with you?

   Can I have a turn?

   What are you doing?

   Is there room for me?

   ______________________________________________

   ______________________________________________

   ______________________________________________

   ______________________________________________

2. If you want to buddy up with another person, you can just **make a comment**:

   That looks like fun!

   That looks hard.

   You're really good at that.

   Hi!

   ______________________________________________

   ______________________________________________

   ______________________________________________

   ______________________________________________

3. If you want to buddy up with another person, You can **invite the person** to play with you:

   Do you want a turn?

   Do you want to play with this now?

   Would you like to play with me?

   I'm going to play on the swings. Do you want to come with me?

   ______________________________________________

   ______________________________________________

   ______________________________________________

   ______________________________________________

# What's in a Title?

**TOPIC** Prejudice and stereotyping

**RATIONALE** Fitting in with peers is very important to adolescents, but they often have difficulty seeing things from another's viewpoint. This intervention is intended to develop awareness of diversity and promote empathy and understanding.

**MATERIALS** The movie *Remember the Titans* (available for purchase, rental, or authorized download)

A sheet of poster paper or a chalkboard

A large sheet of clear plastic (such as overhead transparency material)

A fine-tip dry erase marker

Pictures (no larger than 8 × 10 inches) of famous people students would know and look up to who are in a minority group, such as President Obama, Michael Jordan, Serena Williams, Beyonce, Oprah Winfrey

An index card for each student

A pen or pencil for each student

**PROCEDURE**

1. Introduce the lesson by explaining that the group will be watching a clip from the film *Remember the Titans*. Read the following brief synopsis first so they understand the premise:

> Due to integration laws in the early 1970s, an African American high school and an all-Caucasian (white) high school are forced to join together. As a part of this process, a young black coach is hired to replace a very successful Caucasian as head coach for the Titans football team. There is a lot of racial tension in the town, and people are not very happy about this decision. The film clip shows the process the team goes through under Coach Boone's direction to break down the stereotypes

they have about each other and how they learn to work together as a team.

Now show clip 1, which begins approximately 14 minutes 52 seconds into the movie and stops at 19 minutes 23 seconds. After viewing the clip, ask the class if there are groups with similar divisions in their school, and, as they identify them, list them on poster paper, adding any groups that the students overlook.

2. Brainstorm with the class a list of labels and slurs they use to identify groups and individuals (for example, jocks, nerds, popular, brains) in their school. As they list examples, write them doswn on the plastic sheet with a dry erase marker. Do NOT write the words in neat rows. Instead, write them every which way, varying the angle, and as your page fills, feel free to let the words overlap, even writing some words on top of others if needed. Your goal is to cover the sheet in words. If they seem hesitant to verbalize some of the more derogatory and hurtful labels they use, encourage them to be honest so that an accurate list can be developed. Do not allow them to direct the names toward any person or to laugh and make a joke of this process. Continue to elicit labels until you think you have a thorough list, adding other labels if students don't.
3. When you feel the list is fairly complete, ask students to take a minute to write on their index cards (anonymously) a thought or reaction they have about these labels, such as remembering a time when they or one of their friends or someone they didn't even know was called one or more of these names. Or they might remember using a slur or label against someone themselves and feeling bad later. Give them some time to reflect and then collect the cards.
4. After collecting the cards, select several to read. Ask for reactions from the group, focusing on how they feel when people are labeled or called derogatory names and how they think those who are labeled like this must feel.
5. Hold up the plastic sheet with the labels. Ask them if they think it is right to judge a person or group of people before they get to know them and what the impact is if they do. Invite them to share personal stories of when they have been prejudged and how it has affected them. Introduce the word *prejudice*, which means prejudging others, and ask if they think this is fair to the person being labeled or to themselves, as it clouds their vision so that they can't see who the person really is.
6. Now show clip 2, which starts at approximately 1 hour, 26 minutes into the movie and stops at 1 hour, 29 minutes. This clip illustrates the progress that two boys made in order to break

through prejudice and stereotypes they had about each other and how they were able to develop a strong friendship as a result.

7. At this time, start holding up pictures behind the plastic sheet of famous people who have also been prejudged because of their race, religion, and so forth. Ask students to identify them. This will be very difficult because the faces will be clouded by what has been written on the sheet. As you continue to show the pictures, ask what the group might miss out on if they don't get to know a person because they have prejudged him or her, referring back to the last film clip shown about how the boys in the movie were able to look beyond the surface and stop prejudging each other.
8. Now redistribute the index cards so that everyone has one. Ask them to read what is written on the front and then on the back to write something they could do to stop that kind of labeling. As time permits, have them share what they can do to stop this type of derogatory labeling. Encourage them to put these ideas into action.

# Cyber-Safety Movie Mystery

**TOPIC** Cyberbullying

**RATIONALE** Although the Internet is a wonderful resource, it can also be a frightening jungle with practically no boundaries, limits, or guidelines to protect inexperienced adolescents. This lesson provides them with some necessary limits and guidelines to protect them from potential cyberbullies.

**MATERIALS** The film *Cyberbully* (available for rental, purchase, or authorized download)

A sheet of newsprint for each group of four to six students

A marker for each group of four to six students

A copy of the Cyber-Safety Movie Mystery Quiz for each student

A pen or pencil for each student

A copy of the Cyber-Safety Movie Mystery Contract for each student

**PROCEDURE**

1. Introduce this activity by asking students what they know about cyberbullying, encouraging discussion about their familiarity with the term and any experiences they have had and would care to share. Emphasize that anyone who goes online can be a victim and that people who have experienced cyberbullying never expected that it could happen to them.
2. Then tell them that you would like to take a quick survey, asking that they respond as honestly as possible to the following questions. Ask them to raise a hand if:
   - Someone you know has had a problem with an online bully at least once.
   - You have had a problem with an online bully.
   - You are pretty confident that your online behaviors are safe and that no one could ever harass or bully you online.

- You have ever wondered if the person you were talking to online really wasn't the person they said they were.
- You sent something to someone that you would not want anyone else to see.

Explain that if they raised their hands to any of the questions they could be a victim of cyberbullying and that the purpose of this activity is to help them learn more about what it is and what to do about it.

3. Divide them into groups of three to four students and give each student a copy of the quiz, asking them to discuss what they consider to be the best response. After they have finished, initiate discussion about their answers.
4. Next read the following short synopsis of the *Cyberbully* movie to the students:

> Taylor is a high school girl who lives with her mother and little brother. Her father left them three months ago and is in a relationship with a 26-year-old woman. Taylor has two best friends, Samantha and "Shy" (Cheyenne).
>
> At the beginning of the film, it is Taylor's birthday, and her mother gives her her own laptop. Taylor is very excited about it because, until now, she has had to use the shared family computer. Her mother does have some guidelines about the use of the new computer, however: Taylor cannot go to inappropriate sites, give out personal information, or use the Internet to be insulting or inappropriate.
>
> The first thing Taylor does with her new computer is to sign up for an account on Cliquesters, a social media site that many kids at her school belong to. The first person to "friend" her is Scott, a guy she has a crush on at school, so, needless to say, she is pretty excited about this. However, Lindsay, a girl who bullies Taylor and her friends at school, posts a nasty comment about a picture Taylor posts, but Taylor just shrugs it off.

Show clip 1, which begins at 11 minutes 20 seconds and ends at 19 minutes, and clip 2, which begins at 24 minutes and ends at 34 minutes 15 seconds. Give students a few minutes in their groups to discuss what happened in these clips and their reactions. Then give each group a sheet of newsprint and ask them to draw a line down the middle, labeling one side "Do" and the other side "Don't." Instruct them to think about what they can do to prevent cyberbullying and what they think they shouldn't do if they want to prevent it. Ask them to write their ideas under the appropriate headings.

5. Ask each group to share their lists and ask them to add the following ("PANDA") ideas, if they were not mentioned:

   **Protect your password.** Do not tell anyone what it is, not even your best friend. Also change it regularly.

   **Always be kind** to others online (even when you feel angry). Remember, anything you say on the Internet is in writing for anyone to read forever!

   **Never give out your contact information** (address, phone, school) online, not even to someone you know. It could fall into the wrong hands.

   **Don't post personal (private) information**. If it's not something you would be comfortable seeing on a billboard, then don't put it on the Internet. Remember to post only positive and kind information online.

   **Always be wary of strangers online.** Never meet with anyone you have talked with online (whom you don't already know) without your parents there.

6. Discuss the fact that taking the precautions they identified will reduce the chances of cyberbullying, but it could still occur. If this happens, ask them what they think they should do, bringing up the following:

   - Report any abuse, bullying, or harassment to the Internet service provider right away.
   - Don't reply to abusive or inappropriate messages. Instead, save and print it out as evidence and then report it to an adult right away.
   - Block the sender and/or delete him or her from your mailing list.

7. Finally, give each student a copy of the contract and invite them to sign the contract to make a commitment to follow the safety procedures while online.

8. If time permits, show and discuss the remaining film clips:

   - Clip 3, which starts at approximately 38 minutes and ends at approximately 47 minutes 45 seconds.
   - Clip 4, which starts at approximately 114 minutes and ends at 124 minutes.

# Cyber-Safety Movie Mystery Quiz

*Directions: Think about what you have learned about cyberbullying and circle a response to each of the following questions that you think represents the most effective thing to do.*

1. A classmate posted some very mean and nasty things about you on Facebook and has made untrue accusations about what you have said and done. The best way to respond to this is:
   (a) Just ignore it. The person is trying to upset you, so if you ignore it he or she will eventually stop.
   (b) Post a reply defending yourself and then "unfriend" the person.
   (c) Respond by saying that the person is "a big liar" and telling him or her just what you think.
   (d) Do not respond, but print what the person posted and report the person to your Internet Service Provider.

2. You chat online with your boyfriend/girlfriend every night. One night, he/she takes the conversation in a very "suggestive" direction, which is highly unusual. Although it makes you uncomfortable, you decide to go along with it. However, it begins to get even more personal, and he/she asks you to share some very intimate information. You decide that you should:
   (a) Share the information requested.
   (b) Express your discomfort.
   (c) Take steps to double check the person's identity.
   (d) End the conversation.

3. A classmate goes on Facebook and takes a poll of who is the "Biggest Loser in our School." He lists four names and asks everyone to vote. You decide to:
   (a) Ignore it.
   (b) Leave a comment expressing how mean and unkind it is.
   (c) Leave a comment saying that you think the author of the poll is actually the "Biggest Loser."
   (d) Print the poll for evidence and report it to your Internet Service Provider.

4. You broke up with your boyfriend/girlfriend, and now he or she is harassing you online by sending you threatening messages and posting negative comments about you. Your parents did not like him/her, so you really do not want to tell them about the situation. You decide to:
   (a) Send a reasonable and calm message asking him or her to stop, stating that if they don't, you plan to report it. (Before doing this, you save the previous messages and negative comments in case you need them later as evidence.)
   (b) Respond to the comments, telling him or her just what you think and how fed up you are.
   (c) Print the messages and comments (or save them) and then report it to your Internet Service Provider.
   (d) Block him or her from accessing your profile.

5. True or false? If someone has hacked into your Facebook or MySpace page, all you need to do is change the password and that should take care of the problem.
6. True or false? Someone sent you a "sext" message. The rumor is that the picture is of a classmate. You really want to forward it to a couple of your good friends, and since it does not have the person's face in the picture and does not mention their name you figure it is safe to forward it.
7. True or false? It is OK to share your password with very close friends whom you know you can trust.
8. True or false? People who think they are victims of cyberbullying are making too much of a big deal about it.

# Cyber-Safety Movie Mystery Contract

I, the undersigned, do hereby solemnly swear to:

**Protect my password**, not tell anyone what it is, and change it regularly.

**Always be kind** to others online (even when I feel angry), only post positive information, and remember that anything I say on the Internet is in writing for anyone to read forever.

**Never give out my contact information** (address, phone, school) online, not even to someone I know.

**Never post my personal (private) information**. If it's not something I would be comfortable seeing on a billboard, then I won't put it on the Internet.

**Always be wary of strangers** online and never meet with anyone I have talked with online (that I don't already know) without my parents being present.

**Report any abuse**, bullying, or harassment to the Internet Service Provider right away.

**Not reply** to abusive or inappropriate messages. Instead, I will save them, print them out, and then report them to an adult right away.

**Block senders** of offensive messages and/or delete them from my mailing list.

______________________________ ______________________________

(Signed) (Date)

## Chapter 6

# Counseling Through Drama

She's just a drama queen." "Spare me the drama." "I can't deal with all that drama." Chances are you have caught yourself saying these things or have heard others make similar comments. It's not surprising because life is full of drama—and not only on the stage! Like art and music, drama has been a vital aspect of every culture for more than 2,000 years, according to Degges-White and Davis (2011). Gladding (2011) draws a thoughtful parallel between drama and counseling, suggesting that the type of drama that the ancient Greeks engaged in is still practiced throughout the world and is akin to counseling in that both modalities evoke the experience and expression of emotions. In addition, he has suggested that dramatists and counselors both need to be attuned to those with whom they interact, becoming "consciously aware that what they do and how they will do it will have on effect on the audiences before whom they perform" (p. 137). He also stresses that counselors and dramatists are very conscious that what they do and how they do it will affect others. A further comparison between effective counseling and powerful drama is that drama is relationship oriented and creatively spontaneous; the "methods and techniques are secondary to personalization and imagination" (Gladding, 2011, p. 139).

According to Landy (2005), there is a natural drama to our existence; the "human ability to dramatize is inborn and unlearned" (p. 90). Landy credits Eleanor Irwin, Gertrud Schattner, and David Read Johnson as the pioneers in the development of drama therapy in the United States, although it is also used in many other countries throughout the world. Landy describes drama therapy as an eclectic approach and distinguishes between drama therapy and psychodrama, developed by Jacob Moreno in Vienna in the early part of the 20th century. Moreno's view was somewhat revolutionary because he believed that psychological change occurred through dramatic enactment rather than through Freud's theory of the "talking cure."

In psychodrama, imagination and action are integrated with verbal expression and self-reflection (Gladding, 2011). During psychodrama, protagonists act out their own problems in a creative, spontaneous manner in front of peers who participate in the drama by assuming roles or depicting significant things in the protagonist's life. Clients improve their self-understanding and develop new ways to handle problems through their own insights, as well as from feedback from others involved in the process. Gladding (2011) and Landy (2005) describe three phases that occur during psychodrama: the warm-up stage, in which participants get ready for the drama; the action stage, when the psychodrama is performed; and the integration phase, which involves processing what happened emotionally and cognitively. Reflections from the protagonist, as well as from peers involved in the psychodrama, are an integral part of the processing phase. Alternative forms of psychodrama are the monodrama, in which the protagonist switches roles and plays all parts, and the mirror approach, in which another person plays the part of the protagonist while he or she observes (Gladding, 2011). As one might assume, insight occurs with any of these approaches. In fact, Moreno believed that as people assume various roles, they "reveal aspects of themselves, but do so in a way that allows them to express and release pent-up emotion and feel more resolved having done so" (cited in Landy, 2005, p. 94).

In drama therapy, the focus is on using creative drama for symptom relief and personal growth. According to Gladding (2011), fantasy and hypothetical situations are employed to help clients gain emotional insight and incorporate this into the issues they are dealing with in their lives. Landy (2005) describes the following five-phase model: Phase 1 is dramatic play among participants and is improvisational. Phase 2 is scenework, in which the participants begin to create their fictional roles, commenting on the roles they played. During the end of this phase, those observing the drama offer reflections and feedback. In phase 3, the focus is on role-play, in which the client shifts from the fictional role to issues in his or her own life. Clients may reverse roles and play significant others, or they may play themselves. The emphasis is on developing alternative behaviors and new perspectives. Phase 4 is the culminating enactment, which is more introspective and self-revealing, with a focus on the individual within the group as his or her life is explored more in depth. The final phase is the dramatic ritual, with an emphasis on closure and the transition from the drama to real life. There may also be some ritualistic forms of closure that integrate music, movement, and imagery in order to highlight the importance of the group in this healing process.

## ADVANTAGES OF USING DRAMA IN COUNSELING

Just as with other creative arts interventions, there are numerous reasons to incorporate drama into counseling. Especially when working with children and adolescents, drama can be intriguing and engaging, and younger children in particular easily slip into roles that help them integrate concepts the counselor is attempting to convey. I recall working with an eight-year-old who thought he always had to do everything perfectly, especially with regard to his schoolwork. If his teacher returned a paper that wasn't perfect, he would tear it up and throw it on the floor. During one of our sessions, I asked him to play the part of the teacher returning papers to various students in the class, and I would pretend to be him. As Phillip (in the teacher role) gave me my paper, I complained that I hadn't gotten the answers all right. "That's OK," he said. "Missing two is still an A."

"But I have to get everything right, just like my brothers," I said.

He responded, "Are they older or younger?"

"They're older," I said, "and they always get everything right."

"Well," he said, "practice makes perfect—so when you are older, you can get them all right, too. But even if you don't get everything right, that's still OK." This last statement was music to my ears, because for quite some time Phillip had stubbornly held onto the belief that he had to get everything right. It still took some effort for him to let go of his perfectionistic standards, but referring back to the reverse role-play was a good reminder that he didn't have to be perfect.

In addition to being engaging and intriguing, other advantages to using drama in counseling include the following:

- Drama allows a safe way to express feelings, both positive and negative (Bradley, Hendricks, & Crews, 2009).
- Drama increases creativity and spontaneity (Goh, Wahl, McDonald, Brissett, & Yoon, 2007).
- In a group setting, drama facilitates social interaction (Bradley et al., 2009).
- Drama is a powerful way for clients to release emotions (Jencius, 2011).
- Drama helps clients "try on" various roles (Goh et al., 2007).
- Through role-play, clients are able to rehearse new skills and practice different responses to situations (Lane & Rollnick, 2007).
- Clients develop insight and self-awareness through drama (Gladding, 2011).
- Drama enhances concentration and communication skills (Henderson & Thompson, 2011).
- Drama provides opportunities for clients to solve problems and experiment with alternative approaches (Jencius, 2011).
- Drama therapy facilitates healing (Jencius, 2011).
- Drama helps clients change dysfunctional behavior patterns (Wiener, 2001).

- Drama helps clients become more aware of their choices—past, present, and future (Payne, Lancaster, Heil, & Pineda, 2011).

## TYPES OF PROBLEMS AND POPULATIONS THAT BENEFIT FROM DRAMA INTERVENTIONS

As previously noted, drama has been used throughout the ages as a form of healing. Furthermore, it can be used in a number of settings, including schools, mental health centers, hospitals, and prisons, as well as in work environments (Jencius, 2011), to address a wide array of problems, including the following:

- Drama has been used to help adolescents deal with grief (Slyter, 2012).
- Drama has been used effectively with adolescents to help them learn new roles and gain control over their lives (Nelson & Finneran, 2006).
- Drama has been used with middle school students to decrease bullying (Beale & Scott, 2001).
- Clients suffering from trauma benefit from drama therapy, which allows them to work through their negative history and work on a better outcome (Gladding, 2011).
- Drama therapy has been used to treat schizophrenia (Landy, 2005).
- Adolescents who have been physically or sexually abused have benefited from drama therapy (Landy, 2005).
- Drama therapy has been used with the elderly, who may have dementia or Alzheimer's disease (Malchiodi, 2005).
- Drama therapy has been effectively employed with victims of posttraumatic stress syndrome (Landy, 2005).
- Role-play has been used to help adolescents who have conflicts with parents (Bradley et al., 2009).
- Role-play has been used with children to help them deal with the cause and effect of their behaviors (Thompson et al., 2004).
- Role-play has been used to help adolescents learn more effective ways of communicating with their parents (Vernon & Clemente, 2005).
- Sculpting has been routinely employed with families to help them work through conflict and develop a more cohesive family unit (Gladding, 2011).

## DRAMA IN COUNSELING VERSUS DRAMA THERAPY

As with other creative arts interventions, there is a distinction between using drama in counseling to facilitate insight and growth and using drama therapy, which necessitates much more skill and training. As Gladding (2011) points out, drama therapists have a degree in drama therapy and are registered by the National Association for Drama Therapy. Their background in theater prepares them for helping children and adults who present with many different types of problems, such as autism, posttraumatic stress disorder (Landy, 2005), homelessness, and schizophrenia (Landy, 1997). In contrast, drama in counseling is not part of a specialized field. Counselors using this approach incorporate role-play, puppetry, videos, make-believe games, props and costumes, improvisational drama, mask making, sculpting (Gladding, 2011), and shame attack exercises (Vernon, 2011). Counselors may also involve clients in writing and performing short plays, which helps them develop perspective and problem-solving skills.

## EXAMPLES OF DRAMA INTERVENTIONS

As previously noted, numerous types of drama interventions can be employed by practitioners to facilitate growth and development. The unique aspect of this approach is that it is nonthreatening and involves "doing," which is usually appealing to young clients. As such, it is a good way to help children and adolescents increase self-understanding by thinking about past actions and choices, which in turn results in more effective ways of relating to others and to the environment. An additional benefit of this approach is that it is often conducted within a group setting, which helps develop communication and cooperation skills, as well as empathy.

Several general drama strategies are subsequently described, and more specific and detailed interventions for children in elementary, middle school, and high school and interventions for use in classrooms and with small groups follow.

### Rapport Building

Drama techniques are often employed during the get-acquainted phase of the counseling process. Especially with young children, inviting them to act something out with puppets is usually an instant rapport builder, and older elementary-age children often need no invitation if a basket of costumes or dress-up clothes is available. After playing for a few minutes, the counselor can invite them to use the puppets or costumes to act out what happened to them during the past week that they would like help dealing with.

### Show Me

Often clients have difficulty describing how they felt or how they behaved in relation to a particular issue. In these cases, an invitation to "show me" is an excellent way to get a much clearer picture of the problem. Clients can show you by using puppets, dolls, stuffed animals, or dollhouse figures to act out the problem, or they can role-play, using props or costumes to provide further clarification.

### Instant Replay

Based on suggestions in Bedford's book *Instant Replay* (1974), this technique is ideal for both children and adolescents in helping them gain understanding about their behavior and consequences, as well as learn new ways of responding. When a client describes a conflict with another person, invite him or her to act it out, as if it were an "instant replay" of the scenario, just as in sports playbacks. If you are working individually, you can first have the client act out his or her part and then the part of the other person(s). In a group setting, the client can act out his or her part and assign other parts to group members, instructing them as to how to respond. After discussing the enactment, invite the client to consider other ways of responding and act these out. This process should be followed with discussion about the consequences of the new responses in contrast to the original behavior.

### Act "As If"

This technique, based on Adlerian therapy, helps clients make behavioral changes. After discussing how they would like things to be, clients are invited to act as if that is how things are. Although this sounds too simple to be effective, experience shows us that clients are often surprised that they can actually behave or feel differently when they make a concerted effort to do so. A variation of this is to have a client draw a picture of a person he or she would like to be, then act as if he or she is that individual (Watts & Garza, 2008).

### No Words Allowed

A variation of the role-play technique is to have clients pantomime the sequence of events related to a particular issue. This can make it easier for younger children in particular to then discuss the situation and how it affected them.

## OTHER EXAMPLES OF DRAMA INTERVENTIONS

Gladding (2011) describes the family puppet interview, in which children create stories about their family by using puppets. Doing so often promotes problem resolution. Okun (2007) suggests using the empty-chair dialoging technique as an effective way to help young clients deal with conflict. This intervention involves using two chairs; the client sits in one chair and talks to the empty chair as though it is a person in his or her life. An alternative is to put a stuffed animal in the empty chair to represent the other person. Hackney and Cormier (2004) discuss a variation of a role-play in which the client plays two roles—the private self and the public self. This approach increases self-awareness, which may in turn lead to behavior change.

Video drama is another activity that is very popular with adolescents, according to Gladding (2005). In this approach, adolescents are invited to get together with several friends and enact a short play or a series of skits based on issues relevant to their age group. They videotape the production, and the client then shares it with the counselor at a future counseling session. A variation of this procedure is to videotape clients performing positive behaviors and play the tape back to them as a way of reinforcing that behavior. This is good to do in a group setting because it allows participants can look for positive behaviors in themselves and others. Gladding (2011) suggests having children perform plays that have already been written. Rather than simply reading the play, acting it out gives it much more impact. He recommends *Bullybusters,* by Beale and Scott (2001) as an excellent example of a psychoeducational drama that teaches young adolescents about the negative effects of bullying and what to do about it.

## INCORPORATING DRAMA WITH OTHER CREATIVE ARTS INTERVENTIONS

As for other creative arts interventions, drama can readily be incorporated into other approaches. For example, clients can write a story and then enact it, which makes the story more powerful. Adolescents enjoy acting out short plays and selecting music to enhance conflict, emotions, or suspense. Nonverbal clients may benefit from drawing or cartooning a sequence of events relative to a troublesome event and then pantomiming it. Most clients will benefit from drawing a picture about a dream, a disappointment, a goal, or a conflict and then enacting the scene based on the pictures.

Drama and literature can be combined in numerous ways. Gladding (2011) suggests that poetry, as well as short stories and plays, can be incorporated into an intervention that is meaningful and has strong impact. Several years ago, I worked with an adolescent who was struggling with her relationship with her boyfriend. I shared a poem written by another adolescent titled "Romantic Relationships" (Vernon, 1998c, p. 193), and my client identified with the message the poem conveyed. I suggested that it might be helpful for her to try to act out this poem and that we could videotape it to see what she might learn from watching herself. This was a helpful intervention because it revealed how desperate and codependent she appeared.

After working through some of her feelings, she identified several behavioral goals that she felt would help her develop a more positive way of relating to her boyfriend.

## CLASSROOM OR SMALL-GROUP INTERVENTIONS

As previously noted, psychodrama in particular is generally conducted in group settings, taking advantage of the group interaction to facilitate self-reflection and growth. Within a group or classroom setting, drama is an excellent tool for building group cohesion and enhancing communication and relationship skills. A get-acquainted activity that can be implemented either in a classroom or a small group with children or adolescents involves giving each group of four to six students a small paper bag filled with 8 to 10 miscellaneous objects. The task is for them to develop a skit by incorporating all of the objects in the bag. I used this intervention with a group of adolescents, giving them a bag including lipstick and makeup, several CDs, a camera, a cell phone, car keys, silverware, and a note pad and pencil. They performed a great skit about putting on their makeup while listening to music, calling friends and meeting them at a restaurant, and taking pictures of the event. A good deal of decision making and collaboration occurred as they discussed what they wanted to do and who would play the various roles.

A similar intervention that is especially good for introducing units on dealing with troublesome emotions is to give each group of four to six students an envelope containing 8 to12 index cards, each with a feelings word. Obviously, the older the group, the more sophisticated the words, but with a group of 9- to 10-year-olds, examples could include angry, scared, confused, disappointed, sad, embarrassed, and nervous. As in the previous activity, the task is for group members to make up a skit using all of the feelings words. After they perform this skit, they should then make up another skit that focuses on how to change the negative feelings to more positive emotions.

Another intervention involves developing decision-making dilemmas that group members act out. If this is done in the classroom, small groups of four to six students can take turns acting out the dilemmas while the rest of the class members guess what the dilemma is. After a brief discussion about the dilemma, all the other groups take turns acting out a possible solution. Discussion then focuses on each of the different possibilities for resolving the issue. If this intervention is done in a small-group setting, the group members can read the dilemma and then act out various solutions.

Examples of decision-making dilemmas for young adolescents include the following:

- You are standing outside after school waiting for a ride home. A kid who is in your study hall approaches you and asks if you want to go over to his house to hang out. You really like this kid and want to be friends with him, but it is your night to deliver newspapers to your neighbors. What do you do?

- You are at the mall with some friends. When you go into the music store, you see one of your best friends steal a CD. Your parents have talked to you a lot about doing the right thing, but this is one of your very best friends. What do you do?
- You and your brother are home alone while your parents are at a party. One of your brother's older friends stops by and wants your brother to leave with him and ride around town. Your brother really wants to go and says he'll give you 10 dollars if you promise not to tell your parents. You don't know what to do because you don't want your brother to be mad at you and you'd like the money. What do you do?
- You hear your parents fighting night after night, and it seems to be getting worse. You have heard them yelling about getting a divorce, but when you asked your dad about it, he says things will be all right but that you shouldn't say anything to your little sister because she is too young to understand. What do you do when your sister comes to your room in tears because she hears them fighting and asks if they are getting a divorce?

## SUMMARY

Counselors who have used dramatic activities with clients can attest to the fact that this is a powerful approach that enhances creativity, encourages social interaction, and allows clients to gain awareness, develop different perspectives, and practice new behaviors. Drama is a natural for young clients because they love to pretend and fantasize. This chapter has described a variety of drama interventions that can be used individually, as well as in classroom and small-group settings. Following are more detailed descriptions of interventions addressing friendship, anxiety, conflict resolution, anger, self-acceptance, anxiety, empathy, bullying, communication skills, and peer pressure.

# Curtains on Friendship?

**TOPIC** Friendship and jealousy

**RATIONALE** Assumptions can create many issues between friends. One assumption that frequently creates problems, particularly at this age, is the belief that you can have only one best friend. This intervention emphasizes that friends each have their own unique qualities to offer and that, therefore, one is not replaceable by another.

**MATERIALS**

A copy of the Curtains on Friendship? Puppet Play

Puppets or stuffed animals to represent T.D. (dog), C.C. (kitten), and Owl-Wise (owl)

Highlighter pen

A few additional animal puppets or stuffed animals (optional)

**PROCEDURE**

1. When your client is upset because her best friend has become friends with someone else, tell her you have a short puppet play that might help her with her friendship problems. Give her the T.D. (dog) puppet or stuffed animal.
2. In preparation, explain how to follow a script. It is very helpful to highlight the parts that the client will be reading to help her follow along and anticipate what is happening. (This can be done with nonreaders as well.) Go through the play once so that the client can anticipate what will be happening. Tell the client that any time she hears the narrator say, "T.D. was thinking" or "T.D. said," the client should move the mouth of the T.D. puppet as if it were talking.
3. Read through the play, with the client taking the part of T.D. Afterward, discuss the following:
   - Why didn't T.D. like C.C. at first when everyone else did?
   - Why didn't T.D. want C.C. in the club?
   - How did Owl-Wise help T.D.?

- Do you think there are any similarities between the situation with you and your friend and T.D. and his friends?
- What is it that your friend likes about you? Why do you think she wants to be your friend?
- Has that changed? Is there any reason to believe she no longer wants to be your friend?
- Is it possible that because your friend likes someone else you might like this person, too, if you get to know her better?
- Do you think it is possible for your friend to have other friends, too? What does that mean if she has friends besides you?

4. With clients who really respond well to the play, you might encourage them to continue to rehearse it and perform it for others. This process helps clients integrate the information more effectively, and their peers can also benefit as they learn more about friendship through the concepts presented. Another option would be for the client to invite the specific friends with whom she has concerns to come to a counseling session and participate in the puppet play with her.

## Curtains on Friendship? Puppet Play

*Directions: The counselor reads the part of the narrator, a nonpuppet role. T.D. is read by the client. C.C. has no speaking parts and just needs to look "cute and cuddly"; she can also be played by the client. Tom Cat is a one-liner read by the counselor, as is the part of Owl-Wise. Miscellaneous critters can be acted out by the counselor and/or the client.*

**Narrator:** A long time ago in a small rural town called Crittersville, there was a dog named T.D. Well, actually, his name was Andrew, but all of his friends called him T.D. T.D. was short for "Top Dog." He was the leader of the Cool Critter Club. T.D. was a really great guy, and all the critters liked to hang around with him because he was a lot of fun and he had a lot of creative ideas. He could take a boring game that everyone had played a million times and make it exciting. T.D. was really funny, too. He liked to tell jokes. As several of his friends approached him in the street, TD said . . .

**T.D.:** Hey, guys! Ya know how come the Dalmatians will never play hide and seek with us? Because they'd get spotted! Ha! Ha!

**Narrator:** T.D. told jokes like that all the time, so no matter how sad or upset you were, T.D. could get you to laugh. Before you knew it, you would be feeling better! T.D. loved his friends, and being picked as the leader of the Cool Critter Club was the best thing that ever happened to him. He knew when they voted for him to be the leader that he was very special and important to them.

But one day, something happened that T.D. was afraid would change his life forever. A new little kitten moved to town. Her name was C.C., short for "Cute and Cuddly," and T.D. didn't like her at all because suddenly everyone was paying attention to her. It was like she had magical powers that attracted everyone to her. On her first day of school, all of the other critters hovered around her and argued over who got to sit by her at lunch and play with her at recess. *(Miscellaneous puppets hover around C.C. and pretend to argue about who will get to sit by her and play with her.)* T.D. was thinking . . .

**T.D.:** Oh, well! C.C. is getting all this attention because she's new. In a day or two, things will get back to normal, and I'll be everyone's best friend again.

**Narrator:** But after nearly two weeks, it was worse than ever. All of T.D.'s friends still wanted to be with C.C. Although T.D. felt left out, he tried not to worry about it. Monday night after school, the Cool Critter Club was going to have a meeting at the clubhouse, and TD was pretty sure he would be able to get his friends' attention again. TD was thinking . . .

**T.D.:** When my friends spend some time with me, they'll realize that they've been silly to pay so much attention to C.C., and I'll be "Top Dog" again.

**Narrator:** So, on Monday at the clubhouse, TD said . . .

**T.D.:** This meeting will come to order! *(T.D. and the other puppets pantomime talking and laughing while the narrator reads what goes on at the meeting).*

**Narrator:** The room got quiet and everyone listened to T.D. They talked about the car wash and some other plans for raising money. The meeting seemed to go just fine. T.D. was very funny, and everyone was laughing *(puppets all laugh)* and having a good time. He also shared a couple of great creative ideas that the critters all seemed to like, and T.D. was thinking . . .

**T.D.:** Well, it seems as though things are finally back to normal. My friends have forgotten all about C.C.!

**Narrator:** But at the end of the meeting, T.D. asked . . .

**T.D.:** Is there anything else we need to discuss before we're done?

**Narrator:** Tom Cat, T.D.'s best friend, raised his hand and said . . .

**Tom Cat:** I would like to bring up a new critter for membership. C.C. is a new kitten in our school, and she is really cute and cuddly and nice. I think she should be in our club.

**Narrator:** All the other members started talking all at once. Several members called out things like "Good idea!" and "C.C. is the greatest!" T.D. said . . .

**T.D.:** *(To the audience or self)* Oh, no! I don't want C.C. in the Cool Critter Club! She'll ruin everything! No one will ever listen to my ideas if she's here! And they will probably want to make C.C. the leader instead of me! I have to stop this, but how?

**Narrator:** Luckily, it was getting late, so T.D. said . . .

**T.D.:** Hey, gang! It's getting late and we have to end the meeting. We'll talk about C.C. joining the club at the next meeting.

**Narrator:** And thankfully everyone agreed! T.D. was thinking . . .

**T.D.:** *(To the audience or self)* Good! This will give me time to talk with Owl-Wise.

**Narrator:** Owl-Wise was the oldest critter in Crittersville, and T.D. often talked to her when he had a problem that he needed help with. T.D. told Owl-Wise about how C.C. had moved to town and how all the other critters followed C.C. around and seemed to forget all about him. Finally, T.D. told the old owl how worried he was. He told her that if he allowed C.C. to join the Cool Critters Club, the other members would forget all about him. The wise old owl just smiled and asked . . .

**Owl-Wise:** T.D., what is it about you that your friends have always liked? T.D. said . . .

**T.D.:** Well, I am pretty creative and smart, and I really know how to make my friends laugh!

**Owl-Wise:** Have any of those qualities about you changed? Are you still creative and smart and able to make friends laugh? T.D. said . . .

**T.D.:** Well, sure. I can still do those things. We just had a meeting, and I still had lots of good ideas, and they all really liked my jokes.

**Owl-Wise:** Well then, wouldn't your friends like the same things about you now that they have always liked? Does it really make sense that your friends will stop liking you just because they like C.C.? They like you because you are smart, creative, and funny. And they like C.C. because she is cute, cuddly, and nice. And just because they like her doesn't mean they can't like you, does it? You see, T.D., everyone is special in their own way, and just because someone new comes along doesn't mean your "special-ness" goes away. In fact, if you and C.C. get to know each other, I would bet that the two of you could get to be very good friends because you each have qualities that make you very special.

**Narrator:** Wow! T.D. had never thought of it that way before! Owl-Wise was probably right. He had been so worried about losing friends if C.C. joined the club that he hadn't stopped to realize that he would be making a new one: C.C.! And he also realized that his friends could be friends with C.C. and with him, too, and they could all have fun together.

That night on the way home, he stopped by C.C.'s house and invited her to play at his house after school the next day, and do you know what? C.C., Tom Cat, and T.D. became the best of friends! One day, several months later, as T.D. was watching C.C. walk down the street to her house, T.D. was thinking . . .

**T.D.:** I can't imagine what my life would be like if C.C. wasn't my friend! I am so glad she moved to Crittersville!

# Dialogue Duo

**TOPIC** Anxiety

**RATIONALE** Developmental limitations sometimes prevent younger children from thinking sensibly about things that worry them. However, the fantasy in this intervention gives a face to the child's fear, allowing the client to stand up to the worries by disputing their credibility and creating a more rational perspective that reduces the anxiety.

**MATERIALS**

Two old socks

Yarn, buttons, crayons

Glue stick

Scissors

A sheet of paper

A pencil

**PROCEDURE**

1. When the client discloses something he is anxious about, discuss this in more detail, suggesting that he give his worry a "face." Hand him a sock and invite him to use the available materials to make a puppet. Help him along by asking him questions such as "What do you think your worry would look like if you could see it? Would it have hair? If so, what color? Would it have big eyes? Would it have ears?"
2. When the client is finished making and decorating his puppet, tell him that this puppet will be called the Worry Guy. Ask the client to have Worry Guy sit on his shoulder and loudly whisper all of the worries that he has been having into the client's ear. (While he is doing this, write down what he is saying.)
3. Now tell the client he can make another puppet and give him time to do so. Explain that this puppet will be called No Worries and that he will sit on the other shoulder. He is going to talk to Worry Guy about his worries and ask him questions to help him think a bit differently about them. At this time, give your client the list of worries that Worry Guy whispered and have the client,

as Worry Guy, tell No Worries what he is worried about, one at a time. No Worries will make a counter statement with something that he could think or do so as not to worry so much. For example, if Worry Guy says, "If I try out for the team, I'll be terrible and everyone will laugh at me," No Worries could say, "Since this is the first time you have ever tried out, how do you know you will be terrible? Lots of kids try out; some will be better than you, some will be about the same, and some will be worse." Depending on the developmental level of the client, it may be better for the counselor to initially play the role of No Worries in order to model the disputing process.

4. Continue in this manner until the client has addressed all the worries on his list. Talk with him about the differences between the Worry Guy's thoughts and No Worries' responses. Depending on the client's developmental level, discuss the concepts of blowing things out of proportion, all-or-nothing thinking, assuming the worst, and the notion of possibility versus probability of bad things happening.
5. Invite the client to take his puppets with him to serve as a reminder of how to think when he starts worrying about things.

# Drama of Conflict

**TOPIC**

Dealing with conflict

**RATIONALE**

Being in conflict with others, especially those with whom we are particularly close, can be difficult at any age, but it can be especially difficult for young children who may lack the skills to deal with or the ability to fully comprehend the situation. This intervention addresses these issues and should better equip children to deal effectively with the inevitable conflicts they will encounter throughout life.

**MATERIALS**

Drama of Conflict Scenarios

A beach ball

Fine-tipped marker

A pair of dice

**PREPARATIONS**

Number and write the Drama of Conflict Scenarios on various sections of the ball. (If you are aware of specific client conflicts, you may use those instead of the scenarios listed.)

**PROCEDURE**

1. If you are working with a client who has multiple conflicts with peers, explain that although it may seem as if conflict is always a very negative experience, it really doesn't have to be if you have the right skills to deal with it. Tell your client that you will be playing a game that will help her develop skills to handle problems with friends more effectively.
2. Begin by playing a normal game of catch or bat the ball back and forth as in volleyball. When the client drops the ball, she must roll the dice, read the conflict situation written on the ball that corresponds to the number rolled on the dice, and talk about a time when she had a similar conflict. Then have her role-play how she handled this conflict or would handle it if she hasn't experienced it. (You play the role of the person with whom she is having the conflict.)

3. After the role-play, discuss what she did. Then teach a skill that might have helped in the situation, such as an "I-message":

   I feel ______________ when you ______________________________

   because ______________ and I would like ____________________.

4. Next "rewind" and run the role-play again so the client can practice this new skill. Then brainstorm other things she might do to deal with a conflict of this nature, selecting one or two ideas and rehearsing them through role-playing.
5. Continue to play the game and role-play in this manner. If the client rolls a number and has already addressed that conflict, have her identify another example of a conflict she has had or is currently experiencing, then role-play conflict resolution strategies. At the end of the session, remind the client to keep rehearsing her new skills.

## Drama of Conflict Scenarios

1. You are first in line and someone in front of you pushes you.
2. Your best friend accuses you of telling one of her secrets to someone else, but you didn't do it.
3. Your sister asks if she can borrow your bike, and you say no because you want to ride it, but when you go inside to get your jacket, she rides away.
4. You had two new pencils in your desk this morning, and now they are gone. You think your classmate sitting in front of you took them.
5. Someone calls you a loser.
6. You are winning at a game of four square, and a kid you are playing with calls you a cheater and pushes you away.
7. You are watching your favorite TV show, and your brother changes the channel without asking if it is OK with you.
8. You are playing with your new soccer ball at recess, and another student comes up and grabs it away from you, saying it is hers.
9. You find out that Juanita told one of your friends that if she plays with you, Juanita won't be friends with her anymore.
10. Your friend borrowed a video game from you and has not returned it, even though you have reminded her twice.
11. You were not invited to a birthday party that one of your classmates is having. Your friends are talking about it in front of you.
12. During the math test, you notice that the person sitting behind you is trying to peek at your answers.

# Mask of Anger

**TOPIC** Anger as a secondary emotion

**RATIONALE** Anger is a commonly experienced emotion, but many adolescents do not realize that it often masks an underlying emotion. It is important for them to be aware of what the anger is masking so the other feelings can also be experienced and addressed.

**MATERIALS** A mask (can be a Halloween mask or a simple homemade version made with a marker and a paper plate)

**PROCEDURE**

1. When working with a client whom you suspect is using anger to mask other feelings, hold the mask up to your face and ask the client if he can tell how you are feeling right now. Discuss the fact that it actually is difficult to know exactly what others are feeling because they may not know how to express their feelings or they may cover up underlying feelings by expressing other emotions, such as anger or even happiness. Discuss this concept with him, explaining that if he covers up other feelings with anger, anger is the "secondary emotion" that masks other feelings, such as hurt, pain, guilt, embarrassment, and so forth. Explain that sometimes people choose to show anger because they think that if they acknowledged the real emotion it might make them feel more vulnerable. And if they associate anger with feeling strong and powerful, they may choose to show that emotion instead.
2. Next have the client brainstorm examples of typical things he or other adolescents might get angry about and then ask him to identify any underlying emotions. For example, he might say that he gets angry if he finds out that he didn't get invited to a party, and underneath the anger is hurt.
3. Now ask the client to think about the most recent time he got angry. Have him describe the situation to you in as much detail as possible so that you can role-play the event with him, with the client in the role of himself. Suggest that he wear the "mask of anger" during the role-play. Afterward, before he takes off the mask, ask him the following questions:

- How did it feel to reexperience the event?
- Did you feel angry this time?
- Did you notice any underlying feelings? If so, what were they?
- If you had noticed the other feeling the first time, do you think you might have acted differently? If so, how?
- How do you think the other person might have responded if you had not shown anger?

4. Role-play the situation again with the client (without the mask), this time having the client react to the primary feeling instead of trying to hide behind the anger. At the end of the session, give the mask to the client so that he can remember not to hide behind anger.

# The Many Roles I Play

**TOPIC** Self-deprecation

**RATIONALE** Adolescents often evaluate their worth based upon their performance and behaviors, and they do so in an "all or nothing" way. This intervention will help them understand the concept of accepting themselves with both their strengths and weaknesses.

**MATERIALS**

A sheet of paper

A pen or pencil

Two chairs—one for the client and one as an "empty" chair

A variety of hats

A mirror

**PROCEDURE**

1. When working with a client whose primary focus is on what she thinks are her excessive failures, ask her to list out loud all of the "hats" she wears, metaphorically speaking. For example, she is a daughter, a student, a friend, perhaps a sibling, a soccer player, a musician, and so forth. As she verbalizes, record all of the roles she mentions on paper, prompting her often to make sure the list is thorough.
2. When the list is complete, explain that just as the client may be better at one subject than another in school, this will also be the case for other roles she plays in her life: She will play certain roles better than others. Discuss the concept of unconditional self-acceptance ("USA"), which means accepting yourself for who you are and not putting a label on your whole self as good or bad. Explain that it is important to recognize that everyone has strengths as well as weaknesses and that no one can be summed up as being all good or all bad.
3. Next invite the client to try on the various hats, looking at herself in the mirror and rating how she thinks she looks in each one of them, using a 1 to 5 scale on which 5 means good. Discuss the fact that any number of people could try on the same hat and give it a totally different rating, which doesn't mean it's a bad hat, but it

just might not be a good fit for that person. The same is true for the metaphorical hats we wear (the roles we play) in life; some are a good fit for us and we do well in them, but others may not be such a good fit and are more like weaknesses instead of strengths.

4. Invite the client to look over the list of roles she plays and put a plus sign beside those she considers to be her strengths and a minus sign beside the roles she feels she does not perform as well. Then discuss the following hypothetical situation:

   > A friend of yours is a great singer and a straight-A student but not much of an athlete. Her physical education class is doing a unit on tennis right now, and she feels like a total klutz. She frequently talks about what a loser she is, saying things like "It's not rocket science! All you have to do is hit that little ball with the big huge racket, but I'm such a loser, I can't even do that!"

   The client then should address the empty chair as if her friend were there. If her friend were sitting in that empty chair, what would the client say to her about being such a loser in tennis?

5. Next have the client look at the list of roles and talk briefly about the ones with the plus sign, indicating her strengths. Then have her choose one of the roles marked with a minus sign, signifying what she considers a weakness. In the next role-play the client will address the empty chair, but this time she is to imagine that she is the person in the empty chair. What would she say to herself about being so self-critical and not being good enough relative to the weakness she identified?

6. Continue in this manner with some of the other areas that the client considers weaknesses. Before the session ends, remind the client about the concept of "USA" and encourage her to think of her varying roles as a box of hats. Many will fit, and some won't, but that's because they are just like the people who wear them: They all have their strengths and their weaknesses, but they are all still worthwhile.

# Lights! Camera! Empathy!

**TOPIC** Developing empathy

**RATIONALE** During adolescence, peer relationships are very important. However, adolescents walk the tightrope between the need to belong and the fear of rejection. This intervention uses dramatizations from a movie and role-plays to demonstrate how important empathy is with regard to peer relationships.

**MATERIALS** The movie *Bridge to Terabithia* (available for purchase, rental, or authorized download)

**PROCEDURE**

1. If your client seems to be having difficulty seeing things from others' perspectives or being sensitive to what they are experiencing, ask if he is familiar with the word *empathy.* If not, offer a brief explanation and cite some examples.
2. Tell your client you are going to show him two film clips from the movie *Bridge to Terabithia.* Provide the following synopsis, then show and discuss the two clips:

> *Bridge to Terabithia* is a story about a young boy named Jess Arrons, who is somewhat of a loner, both at school and at home. In the beginning of his fifth-grade year something happens that makes a big difference in his life. A new girl named Leslie Burke comes to town, and she will change how he sees the world forever, in more ways than one.
>
> Jess and Leslie become best friends. However, someone neither of them counts as a friend, Janice Avery, becomes a thorn in their side. She is the school bully, and just about everyone is afraid of her. At one point in the story, she steals from Jess's little sister, so Jess and Leslie design a plan to get even with Janice by embarrassing her in front of

her classmates. However, later in the story, following an unexpected turn of events, the two find themselves actually feeling bad for Janice.

Clip 1 begins at approximately 7 minutes, 30 seconds into the movie and ends at approximately 8 minutes, 18 seconds. In this clip, the focus is primarily on two characters: Leslie Burke and the school bully, Janice Avery. The scene begins on the playground at recess on Leslie's first day. She is about to have her first encounter with Janice. After showing the clip, discuss the following questions:

- How did Leslie react to Janice?
- Did she use any strategies that were successful in handling the bullying?
- If you were Leslie, how might you have reacted to Janice and why?

Clip 2 begins at approximately 51 minutes, 50 seconds into the movie and ends at at approximately 54 minutes, 30 seconds. This clip takes place later in the year. It involves Leslie and Janice again, as well as Jess. By this time, Jess and Leslie have become best friends but have also had many encounters with Janice, who has been bullying them. As the clip begins, Leslie tells Jess that she was just in the girls' bathroom and heard Janice crying. She tells Jess what she observed and suggests that maybe the reason Janice is so angry and mean is that others aren't treating her nicely. After showing the clip, discuss the following questions, making special note of how Leslie chose to respond to Janice, even though both she and Jess have been victims of Janice's bullying.

- Leslie said that what she found out from talking to Janice (which was not shown on the video) "explained a lot." What do you think she meant by this comment?
- What did Leslie say to Janice? Why was she nice to her even though Janice had bullied her and Jess?
- How did Jess react to what Leslie had to say? Why do you think he was so surprised?
- If you had been in Leslie's shoes, do you think you would have responded to the information you learned about Janice in the same way? Why or why not? If not, how would you have responded?

3. After the client has seen both the video clips and you have discussed them, ask him to talk about a time when someone has had empathy for him. Help him think of times this might have happened by bringing up typical examples, such as when he had an argument with his parents and a friend understood how he

was feeling or when he had a fight with a friend and a classmate demonstrated care and concern about what he was experiencing. Discuss why having empathy is important, how it has been portrayed in the film clips, and how it might affect his relationships with others if he develops more empathy.

4. Next engage him in an exercise called "The Mirror": The two of you will face each other, standing about 18 inches apart. Initiate the movement and tell the client to mirror (imitate) your actions, trying to match your movements exactly. Then trade roles. Discuss what this felt like and relate it to the concept of empathy in that you try to put yourself in the position of the other person.

5. Share with the client that another good way to demonstrate empathy is reflecting feelings, which is describing to the other person how you think he or she might be feeling. For example, when he sees a classmate struggling with something, he might say, "It looks like you are really frustrated!" Next encourage him to practice this skill in the following role-plays:

   - A kid in the grade above you has been harassing one of your friends on the bus in the mornings. He will take his hat or try to trip him. It is something different every day. You had decided you were going to turn around and let him have it today if he did anything, but last night you found out that the bully's dad has cancer and is dying. What could you say so that you can stick up for your friend and still show empathy for the bully? (Have the client talk to you as if you are the bully.)
   - One of your friends at school is a student in one of the special learning rooms. You and your friends frequently tease him about being in the "dumb class." It is very obvious that he doesn't like it, but he doesn't want to be called a bad sport, either, so he tries to just laugh it off. Now that you have learned about empathy, what could you say or do differently?

6. Process the role-plays by asking the client what he learned from the movie clips, the mirror exercise, and the role-plays about empathy. Ask him to give an example of how he can apply this concept in his life.

# Lead Role of Worrier

**TOPIC** Anxiety

**RATIONALE** Adolescents often do not realize the degree to which their anxieties can build up and become overwhelming and burdensome, nor are they always open about discussing anxieties because they may be self-conscious. This intervention helps them identify and analyze their anxiety and the irrational thinking that often makes it worse.

**MATERIALS**

A plastic grocery bag

20–25 potatoes

A sheet of paper

A pen or pencil

A highlighter marker

**PROCEDURE**

1. When working with a client who presents with anxiety but may not be able to verbalize what she is anxious about, give her a sheet of paper and a pencil and ask her to label it "Things teenagers might worry about." Then ask her to brainstorm a list of these anxieties. When she is finished, ask her to think about her own worries and highlight as many as apply to her. Then invite her to write any additional anxieties she has that weren't on the list of things that other teens worry about.
2. After discussing what she highlighted and additional worries she listed, ask the client to describe what it feels like when she is worried about something. Have her give a specific example of something she worries about, describing the intensity of the worry (on a 1 to 10 scale), how frequent this worry is, and how it affects her.
3. Next ask the client to stand up, and give her the plastic grocery bag. Invite her to read through the list of what other teens might worry about and also additional things that she worries about. When she reads something that she highlighted or wrote as one of her worries, she should pick up a potato and put in into the bag.

4. Now have the client walk around the room with the bag of potatoes slung over her back. Ask her how it feels to carry this burden and how it might affect her if she had to do it all the time. If she had a choice, would she rather leave it somewhere? Explain that the bag is a metaphor for her worries, noting that some worries can be motivating (worrying about what she wants to do after high school may prompt her to start exploring options, for example). Other worries are more troublesome and create more anxiety because they may be overwhelming, even if they are unlikely to occur.
5. Next take a piece of paper and divide it into two columns, labeling one "Rational" and the other "Irrational." Explain that rational worries are realistic anxieties, such as worrying about doing well on a test, whereas irrational worries are often exaggerations, such as being worried about taking a test because you know you will fail and that that would be awful and prove that you were stupid. Discuss the difference between these two types of worries, emphasizing that irrational worries are unfounded predictions ("I know I'll fail"), exaggerations ("That would be awful"), self-deprecating ("I'm no good"), and so forth. Then have the client write the worries she identified from the list in either the rational or the irrational column. For each worry that goes into the irrational column, work with her to dispute the beliefs and come up with a more rational way of looking at it. If she is able to do that, have her remove a potato from the bag. When she has finished disputing her irrational beliefs, have her pick up the bag to compare how much lighter the load is!
6. Before the session ends, review the concept of disputing irrational beliefs. Also remind her what it feels like to be burdened with unnecessary worries. Give her a copy of the list of rational and irrational worries to serve as a reminder of how to reduce the intensity of her worries.

# Curtains on Conflict

**TOPIC** Conflict resolution

**RATIONALE** Adolescents are often conflict avoidant because they don't have the skills to deal effectively with conflict in relationships. As a result, they may react defensively, making the conflict worse and upsetting themselves about how they handled it.

**MATERIALS** A copy of the Curtains on Conflict sheet

A die

**PROCEDURE**

1. When your client begins talking about a conflict that he has been avoiding, suggest that he practice problem solving with some hypothetical examples first in order to build his confidence in dealing with his own issues.
2. Give him a copy of the Curtains on Conflict sheet. Ask the client to roll the die to choose which problem to begin with (the number that corresponds to the number rolled on the die). Have him read the situation, with the goal being to think of as many ways to approach the conflict as possible, recording them in the space for responses. For example, for Situation 1 he could:
   (a) Tell Chris, "Forget it, I'm not skipping school."
   (b) Tell Chris, "Hey, man, I would really like to hang out with you, and missing school would be awesome, but I just can't risk it!"
   (c) Tell Chris, "Sorry! I just don't want to take a chance that my teachers would find out and break the trust that I have worked so hard to build with them."
3. After he has finished recording all of his responses to that situation, he should consider the probable outcome for each one and write it in the space for outcomes. Continue in this manner until outcomes have been identified for each possible response.
4. Then engage the client in role-playing his responses to the first situation. He may choose to do all responses or just pick the approach he feels he would most likely use. (The counselor plays

the part of the other person.) Afterward, process with the client how he thought the role-play went. Did the outcome match what he thought would happen? Did he say what he wanted to say? How did he feel when he delivered his response?

5. Invite the client to roll the die and play out another hypothetical conflict, following the same process: Think of all possible responses to the conflict, consider the probable outcome for each response, and pick the response he is the most comfortable with and role-play it. As time permits, have him roll the die and follow the same process for another situation.
6. Now ask the client to identify a current conflict, consider possible responses and outcomes, and role-play the situation. Discuss what might prevent him from addressing the conflict. For example, he may think it might make the situation worse if he confronts it, he might feel uncomfortable, he might fear a negative outcome, and so on. Work with him to challenge any "what if" or "awfulizing" beliefs, encouraging him to weigh the disadvantages of not speaking up and feeling uncomfortable versus confronting the conflict directly and dealing with the consequences.
7. Remind him to take the Curtains on Conflict sheet so that he can complete the rest of it and review the concepts to help him deal with real-life problems.

# Curtains on Conflict

*Directions: Read each situation, decide how you would deal with it, and write your responses and probable outcomes of the responses on this paper.*

## Situation 1

Your friend Chris wants you to skip school tomorrow so the two of you can hang out at the mall. You don't want to break the trust your teachers have in you or get in trouble with your parents. How do you handle this conflict?

***Response 1***

(a) ______________________________

(b) ______________________________

(c) ______________________________

***Outcome 1***

(a) ______________________________

(b) ______________________________

(c) ______________________________

## Situation 2

You just started to date someone new, and you really like her, but there's one thing that bothers you, and that is that she is constantly trying to kiss you in public. You're embarrassed and want to confront her about it. How do you handle this conflict?

***Response 2***

(a) ______________________________

(b) ______________________________

(c) ______________________________

***Outcome 2***

(a) ______________________________

(b) ______________________________

(c) ______________________________

## Situation 3

Lately your girlfriend has been acting strange. She avoids you at school, and what used to be hour-long phone calls are now five minutes. You think she wants to break up, but every time you tell her that the two of you need to talk, she gets huffy and either walks away or changes the subject. How do you handle this conflict?

***Response 3***

(a) ______________________________

(b) ______________________________

(c) ______________________________

*Outcome 3*

(a) ____________________________________________

(b) ____________________________________________

(c) ____________________________________________

**Situation 4**

The people you hang out with are always teasing you about your weight. They call you "Tanker" and make cracks about "weight load limits." You usually laugh, but inside it really hurts your feelings, and you are tired of it. You have decided that you've had enough. How do you handle this conflict?

*Response 4*

(a) ____________________________________________

(b) ____________________________________________

(c) ____________________________________________

*Outcome 4*

(a) ____________________________________________

(b) ____________________________________________

(c) ____________________________________________

**Situation 5**

One of your friends has been saying really bad things to you about another one of your friends. You don't like listening to it because it makes you feel disloyal. You know you need to talk to your friend about it, but you are dreading the conversation. How do you handle this conflict?

*Response 5*

(a) ____________________________________________

(b) ____________________________________________

(c) ____________________________________________

*Outcome 5*

(a) ____________________________________________

(b) ____________________________________________

(c) ____________________________________________

**Situation 6**

You are in a group in English class with Paula, who always gets As. She thinks this gives her the right to be the boss and take over the project when you work in groups. If she lets anyone else do anything, she corrects 90 percent of what they have done but then complains that no one else will do anything. Because you are always in her group, you want to confront her about this. How do you handle this conflict?

*Response 6*

(a) ______________________________

(b) ______________________________

(c) ______________________________

*Outcome 6*

(a) ______________________________

(b) ______________________________

(c) ______________________________

# Re-"Acting" to Bullies

**TOPIC** Bullying

**RATIONALE** It is important for adolescents to learn mature, rational ways of dealing with bullying because they may be faced with this problem not only during high school but also in later life in the workplace and in personal relationships.

**MATERIALS** The movies *Back to the Future* and *Cheaper by the Dozen* (available for purchase, rental, or authorized download)

**PROCEDURE**

1. If your client presents with problems related to bullying and has at times responded aggressively, discuss the fact that it was most likely the bullies' goal to get that reaction from her. If the bully can get his or her target to lose control and say or do something to get a person in trouble or show that she is frightened, then the bully has succeeded in intimidating the victim. Discuss how this applies or doesn't apply to the client's recent encounters with bullies, emphasizing that it might be more effective to try and foil the bullies' plan by not reacting as the bully might expect.
2. Tell your client you are going to show her clips from two different movies that illustrate different ways of reacting to bullying: *Back to the Future* and *Cheaper by the Dozen.* Ask her to pay close attention to the differences in the way the characters react to the bully.

   Show clip 1 from *Back to the Future*, beginning at 39 minutes 12 seconds and ending at 41 minutes 4 seconds. In this scene, Marty McFly has traveled back in time to when his dad, George McFly, was in high school. At the beginning of the scene, Marty is sitting at the counter of a soda shop next to George (to whom he has not yet spoken) when Biff, the local bully, walks in. Discuss the following questions:

   - How did George react to Biff?
   - If you had been in George's shoes, how do you think you would have handled Biff? Why?

- If you had been in Marty's shoes, what would you have done?
- What do you think about what the waiter said? ("If you let people walk all over you now, they will be walking all over you for the rest of your life.") If you agree, then what do you think George should have done?

Show clip 2, from *Cheaper by the Dozen,* starting at 55 minutes, 2 seconds into the film and ending at 55 minutes, 37 seconds. In this movie, a family with 12 children has just moved from a small rural town to a larger city. The oldest boy, Charlie (the one in this clip being bullied), is not happy about having to move. When the clip starts, he and his sister are just getting to school after dropping off their little brothers at school, which is when the bullying begins. Discuss the following questions:

- How did Charlie respond to the bully? What could he have done instead?
- When Charlie responded aggressively to the bully, what happened next?
- What did Charlie's sister do? Do you agree with what she did?
- If the sister had not stepped into the middle, what do you think would have happened?

3. Ask the client if she can think of any other movies she has seen or books she has read about bullying and how the situations were handled. Invite her to share what strategies were used and how effective she thinks they were.
4. Have a discussion of alternative ways of reacting to a bully, pointing out that there are lots of different options. Ask the client if she has ever tried reacting in a way the bully does not expect, such as these:

    - Agreeing with him or her ("Yes, I sure do have a big nose").
    - Thanking him or her for saying something ("I hadn't thought about it that way—thanks for pointing it out").
    - Distracting the bully by pointing out something totally out of context ("Oh, look—did you see that cool car go by")?
    - Totally ignoring what he or she says or does and moving away.

5. Next ask the client to talk about a couple of recent situations in which she has been bullied. Role-play these to give the client the opportunity to practice responding in more effective ways.

# The Eyes Have It

**TOPIC** Listing skills

**RATIONALE** It is not uncommon for students to believe they are good listeners when the teacher gives directions, yet when it is time to do the assignment, they don't even know what page to turn to. Being a good listener is actually a very complex skill. Therefore, it is important to start developing good listening skills at a young age. This activity is a good start to that process, showing students that being a good listener involves more of their body than just their ears!

**MATERIALS**

Tips for Listening

A CD player

A recording of the "Can-Can" tune (or any other tune from the Cole Porter musical of the same name)

Two paper plates per student and counselor

A copy of the Listening Song lyrics (optional; song appears on the CD)

**PREPARATIONS** Create a poster-size version of the Tips for Listening.

**PROCEDURE**

1. Ask students, "Who is a really, really good listener?" Most likely all will all raise their hands. Explain that you are going to teach them some important things about being a good listener, so they need to pay close attention.
2. Post the Tips for Listening poster and walk the class through each step, explaining and demonstrating. It is helpful to bring a student to the front to model each of the appropriate behaviors, and it is preferable to demonstrate the "wrong" way first and then the correct way.
3. Once you have gone through all of the Tips for Listening steps, tell them it is time for them to become the teachers. Divide students up into four groups and assign each group one of the four basic areas of listening identified on the poster:

**Group 1:** Eye contact

**Group 2:** Quiet hands and feet

**Group 3:** Quiet mouth

**Group 4:** Be an active listener

Tell each group that they are to plan and rehearse a short skit to demonstrate their skill. For example, group 1 might do a skit in which a student is late for recess because he was looking at the desk and not at the teacher, so he didn't see her motion to the class that it was time to go. But then when he starts making good eye contact, he no longer has a problem.

4. Give the groups 10 minutes to plan the skit and then have each group perform it for the others. At the end of each skit, engage students in a discussion about the skill demonstrated and how they might use it in real-life situations.
5. End the session by engaging students in "The Wacky Plate Dance," an activity that gives them an opportunity to practice eye contact:

   - Have students stand in a circle, with you (the facilitator) in the middle. Hand out two paper plates to each participant, including yourself. Instruct the students that this is an activity to practice being good listeners. There will be music playing, so they will of course be using their ears, but it will also be extremely important to use their eyes, too. They must watch you very carefully and do exactly as you do! Tell them that if they understand, they are to give you eye contact and a thumbs-up. Look around the circle to get a sign of positive confirmation from each student. Once you have it, say, "Good. Then we are ready to begin!"
   - Start the "Can-Can" music. As the students are watching, you simply make up actions to the music, incorporating the paper plates. As the music gets louder, your actions should get bigger and bolder, and the students are supposed to mirror your actions. There is no right or wrong—anything goes, and the sillier the better! You can do cymbal crashes on your head, toss the plates in the air and catch them, and so forth. When they are familiar with the activity, they can take turns being the leader.

**NOTE** If time allows, teach "The Listening Song" (on the CD). This could be taught in a follow-up session; it also makes an excellent opening for guidance classes or groups thereafter.

## Tips for Listening

1. **Make eye contact with the speaker.**

2. **Keep hands and feet quiet.**

3. **Keep your mouth silent.**

4. **Be an active listener:**

   **Let your face show that you are interested in what the speaker is saying.**

   **Raise your hand if you have a comment or a question.**

# Listening Song

*Sing to the tune of "Lightly Row."*

Eye contact, both feet flat,
Hands on desk or in your lap,
Quietly, actively.
Listen carefully.
It's as easy as can be!
Come join in and sing with me!
Quietly, actively,
Listen carefully!

# Dramatic Inflections

**TOPIC** Communication skills

**RATIONALE** Adolescents may find themselves in trouble with parents, teachers, and peers based on the way they communicate, often with an "attitude." Most are not aware that only seven percent of communication is conveyed through words and that the rest is communicated through body language and voice tone. This activity focuses on developing awareness of the subtleties of communication.

**MATERIALS** Dramatic Inflections Game Directions (one copy per group of three)

A set of Dramatic Inflections Cards

**PREPARATIONS** Copy the Dramatic Inflections Cards, glue them to tagboard, and cut apart.

**PROCEDURE**

1. Ask the students to raise their hands if any of them have ever had a parent or teacher get on them about "giving them attitude." Ask students to share examples of what they consider the attitude to be: What does it look like? How does it sound?
2. Explain that the focus of this activity is on effective versus ineffective ways of communicating. Tell the students that only seven percent of any message that we communicate is conveyed through words. Ask students how you are communicating with them at this moment other than using words, generalizing this to other examples as well. After you have gathered ideas, demonstrate or have students demonstrate other ways we communicate, such as posture, facial expressions, using hands and arms for emphasis, voice volume, tone of voice, and so on.
3. Next divide the students up into groups of three and assign each group a number. Tell them that they will be playing a game. Refer to the Dramatic Inflections Game Directions and explain them, along with the example. Place the cards in three separate piles: "Situations," "Phrases," and "Questions." Then have each group

pick three cards, one from each of the three piles. Give them 10 minutes as a group to read their cards and plan a skit. At the end of the planning time, have the groups perform their skits, starting with group 1.

4. When all groups have performed, process with the class, discussing the following questions:

    - How did students change the meaning of their words without actually changing their words?
    - Have you ever said anything that has been misunderstood because of the way you said it (i.e., you used the "wrong" voice tone or body language with the "right" words)?
    - Can you think of a time when someone has said something in a way that made you feel put down, even though the words they said were not necessarily derogatory? What was it that made you feel that way?
    - How could this information help you when working in a group? How else might this awareness of communication be helpful to you?

5. In closing, ask students what they learned, emphasizing that communication is more complicated than just words: It requires paying attention to body language, tone of voice, pitch, volume, facial expressions, and many other subtleties. Share a quote from the composer John Powell: "Communication works for those who work at it."

# Dramatic Inflections Game Directions

*Directions: Each team draws three cards: a Situation Card, a Question Card, and a Phrase Card. Each team will be improvising a role-play.*

## Explain

1. Players drawing the Situation Card may say anything they want during the role play; they "direct" where the story goes.
2. Players drawing the Question Card may ask only that question.
3. Players drawing the Phrase Card may only state that phrase. However, they can and should change the meaning of what they say by the way they say it. So each time they state it, they may:

    Say it louder or softer.

    Say it in a mean, suspicious, sarcastic, angry, or excited tone of voice.

    Use hand gestures to emphasize it.

    Jump up and down.

    Look bored.

## Example

1. The situation might be international spies on a top secret mission. So the situation players have to think about how they are going to set up that situation and keep it going. They also want to think about what their two players (question and phrase card players) have to say so they can provide opportunities for them to speak their parts.
2. The question players might have "What's that?" for their question. In their planning, they want to be thinking about how the question could be used in the situation and how many different ways they can say it—how the meaning can be changed so the message would sound different.
3. The phrase players might have "You've got to be kidding!" for their phrase. In their planning, they want to be thinking about how this phrase could be used in the situation and how many different ways they can say it. How can they change the meaning to make the message different?

## Dramatic Inflections Cards: Situations

| | |
|---|---|
| **Situation 1**<br>Being stuck in an elevator | **Situation 7**<br>Marine recruit training camp |
| **Situation 2**<br>Police detectives on an investigation | **Situation 8**<br>Being a model in a fashion show |
| **Situation 3**<br>Cheerleading tryouts | **Situation 9**<br>Astronauts stuck on the moon |
| **Situation 4**<br>Doctors and nurses on night duty in the emergency room | **Situation 10**<br>Staying overnight in a haunted house |
| **Situation 5**<br>Rock star groupies | **Situation 11**<br>Shopping in a sporting goods store |
| **Situation 6**<br>Taking a music lesson | **Situation 12**<br>News film crew on location |

## Dramatic Inflections Cards: Phrases

| | |
|---|---|
| **Phrase 1**<br>Come on, guys. | **Phrase 7**<br>I can do that myself. |
| **Phrase 2**<br>Don't blame me. | **Phrase 8**<br>I can't believe it. |
| **Phrase 3**<br>Stop that. | **Phrase 9**<br>Whatever. |
| **Phrase 4**<br>I know how you feel. | **Phrase 10**<br>I'm not doing that. |
| **Phrase 5**<br>Don't even get me started. | **Phrase 11**<br>I can't wait. |
| **Phrase 6**<br>You've got to be kidding. | **Phrase 12**<br>I don't think so. |

# Dramatic Inflections Cards: Questions

**Question 1**

What about me?

**Question 2**

Can you hear me now?

**Question 3**

Is that right?

**Question 4**

Do I look like it?

**Question 5**

Are you sure?

**Question 6**

Does that thing work?

**Question 7**

Should we be doing this?

**Question 8**

What was that?

**Question 9**

When do we eat?

**Question 10**

How ya doing?

**Question 11**

May I talk?

**Question 12**

Are we there yet?

# Cliff Hanger

**TOPIC** Responding to negative peer pressure

**RATIONALE** Adolescents are under a lot of pressure, given major hormonal and physical changes on top of social and emotional adjustments of equal magnitude. Fitting in with their peers is extremely important, which can make resisting negative peer pressure challenging. This activity will give them the opportunity to think about and prepare to respond to peer pressure.

**MATERIALS** A copy of the Cliff Hanger Peer Pressure Fact Sheet for each student

**PROCEDURE**

1. Initiate the activity by telling the students that considering the fact that it can literally be a matter of life and death, an adolescent's decision whether or not to do drugs or drink alcohol may be one of the most important choices he or she will ever make. For that reason, they need to make sure they are well-informed and have thoroughly considered all the facts. Share the following example:

> Say you were going to buy a stereo.* You wouldn't just go out and pick the one that looked nice; you probably would go to the library and look into it. You might do some research in a few magazines, ask a few friends what they thought, go to the store and listen to each stereo through multiple speakers, and finally make an educated decision.

Ask students to react to this idea. Do they think most teenagers do a thorough search to get the facts before trying drugs or alcohol, just as they would if they were buying a new stereo? If not, what prevents them from doing this? Have students brainstorm with a partner why some adolescents try drugs and alcohol before finding out the facts, and, after a few minutes, initiate discussion

*From Thinkquest, a student-created website to benefit adolescents (http://thinkquest.org/pls/htm/think.library)

about this. If peer pressure is not mentioned, introduce this as an important variable.

2. Break students into groups of three and have them brainstorm different kinds of peer pressure and tricks their peers use to try to convince them to go ahead and try drugs or alcohol. After giving them time to share their responses with the total group, hand out the Cliff Hanger Peer Pressure Fact Sheet and discuss it in the total group, comparing their ideas from the brainstorming activity with the information on the fact sheet with regard to the types of peer pressure as well as the tricks.
3. Next have two groups of three join together so that there will be six students per small group. Have each group brainstorm ways to say no to peer pressure and then ask each group to prepare a role-play incorporating these ideas and others that will demonstrate how to stand up to peer pressure.
4. After a few minutes of planning time, ask each group to present the skit, taking time after each one to process what techniques they used and how well they worked. Compare what the students conveyed through their role-plays with the suggestions on the Cliff Hanger Peer Pressure Fact Sheet on ways to say no. In closing, encourage them to apply what they learned in this lesson when they are faced with pressure from peers to use drugs and alcohol.

# Cliff Hanger Peer Pressure Fact Sheet

## Different Types of Peer Pressure

Spoken pressure: Someone actually tries to talk you into making a certain choice.

Unspoken pressure: No one says anything, but the pressure is implied, either by body language or just the fact that "everyone is doing it."

Pressure from one person: A best friend or boyfriend/girlfriend might be trying to convince you to do something.

Pressure from a lot of people: This could be the group you hang around with, or you could be at a party and everyone there could be pressuring you.

## Tricks Used By Peers

Saying or implying that they will not be your friend any more if you don't give in.

Insulting you/calling you names, such as "chicken" or "loser," because you won't try it.

Telling you why it is OK to do ("I've done it 50 times, and nothing bad has ever happened to me").

## Ways to Say No

Stand straight.

Look the other person in the eye.

Use a strong voice.

Say, "No thanks, I don't want to" (and then walk away).

Say, "I'm not into it" (and walk away).

Avoid the situation by not being around peers who pressure you.

## What Does Not Work

Using a weak voice

Mumbling

Making excuses

Avoiding eye contact

Acting like a know-it-all

Putting the other person/people down

Threatening them

## CHAPTER 7

# Counseling Through Activity-Based Experiential Interventions

If we buy into the premise that an outcome of good counseling is learning new ways of thinking, feeling, and behaving, then we also need to take into consideration how people learn so that we can maximize the benefits of our counseling interventions. Think about how you learn best: Is it by hearing something? Or do you also need to see it? Or do you learn best if you are more actively involved in the learning process? I remember taking a human sexuality course as a graduate student and having to memorize how many sperm were in a teaspoon, a fact that I remember to this day. The reason is that, prior to reading the chapter about sperm, the professor divided us into groups and gave each group a small jar filled to the brim with sequins, which he said represented sperm cells. Then he gave each group a teaspoon and told us to make an educated guess as to how many sequins it would take to fill that teaspoon. For me, this activity was much more effective than just hearing the fact in a lecture—and after all these years, I still remember the answer! In case you are wondering, I learned that there are 300 million, but an Internet search reveals that it can actually range from 180 million to 500 million.

In the 1990s, Myrick (1997) stressed the importance of taking learning style into account during the counseling process. According to Myrick, counselors must be "flexible, adaptive, and learn how to use different counseling approaches" (p. 111). The learning style approach is based on the premise that individuals have unique learning patterns and that if these aren't accommodated in the counseling process, a mismatch occurs that can negatively affect the effectiveness of the interventions.

If we think about the keys to successful learning, we need to look first at the learning environment. Just as in my graduate course, in which the professor generated interest in his topic, counselors need to do the same, creating an environment that is engaging and perhaps a bit unpredictable. This is the reason that counselors who use magic tricks are so successful—they keep their clients intrigued by "pulling a rabbit out of a hat," so to speak, at the least predictable moment. Counselors who are strong advocates of using magic maintain that magic can be a good way of connecting with clients, as well as reducing resistance if used in a group. It can be motivating and promote mastery, and it also provides numerous opportunities to illustrate concepts such as success and failure, frustration tolerance, and persistence.

Aside from magic, there are other things counselors can do to provide a stimulating (but not overstimulating) environment. First, they can have an inviting office space with furniture that is appropriate for younger clients. Next they can have objects that clients can pick up and "fiddle with," such as a Slinky, a Koosh ball, or other things that they can manipulate. A basket of toys or stuffed animals always puts younger children at ease, and adolescents seem to like having their high school yearbook on a table in plain view—and you can learn a lot about them as they chat about various friends, activities they are involved with, and so forth. The key is to develop a comfortable space and vary the format of the sessions so that clients look forward to coming back because they don't know for sure what to expect. That is why activity-based interventions, as described in this chapter, are so effective: They not only involve the client in the process, they are also interesting and a bit out of the ordinary.

One of my favorite interventions to use with adolescents who repeatedly engage in self-criticism is to give them a big dry sponge and ask them to pick it up to see how it feels. Then we talk about what happens when they soak up all sorts of criticism and believe that every bad thing that someone says about them is true, without separating fact from fiction. I then instruct them to soak the sponge in a pail of water to illustrate how they "soak up" the negative but tell them that if they want to stop the self-deprecation that results in hurt and depression, they need to "wring the sponge out" by asking themselves whether what others are saying is true and, even if it is true, does that make them awful, worthless people? They leave that session armed with the metaphor of the sponge, and in the next session they write down the put-downs that aren't true on narrow strips of paper, stuff them in balloons that they blow up and tie, and then go outside and let the balloons go. Interspersing verbal processing with the activity-based interventions is far more interesting and effective than just talking about self-criticism.

Another component of successful learning is retention, according to Jackson (1995). In his book on using active learning, Jackson notes that students will remember 5 to 15 percent of what they hear, 10 to 20 percent of what they see, and 40 to 50 percent of what they both hear and see. More important, if they have some personal involvement, the retention rate climbs to 90 percent. It is understandable that creative arts interventions are effective because, as Malchiodi (2005) notes, the expressive therapies involve the "purposeful, active participation of the individual and are often complemented by verbal interventions" (p. xiv). Furthermore, because many creative arts interventions, and activity-based interventions in particular, involve multiple modalities, there is a greater chance of retention.

Jackson (1995) emphasizes that the needs of different types of learners are addressed when counselors use active learning methods. He notes that visual learners learn best if they see information, so bibliotherapy would be a good intervention with this type of learner. Auditory learners need to hear the information, so listening to music that conveys messages of hope, problem resolution, and so forth would work well with them. Kinesthetic learners learn by doing—through touch or movement or something that actively involves them, such as role-playing or playing a game. As Jackson notes, active learning, or using activity-based interventions, combines all three of these learning processes.

Although many of the creative arts interventions described in earlier chapters of this book are activity based or experiential, the interventions in this chapter emphasize using props, concrete images, metaphors, and other active techniques that can complement the interventions presented thus far.

## ADVANTAGES OF USING ACTIVITY-BASED EXPERIENTIAL INTERVENTIONS IN COUNSELING

Roaten and Schmidt (2009) contend that experiential interventions can be very powerful, benefiting clients in many ways. Counselors who use activity-based interventions can attest to the fact that they are much more meaningful to clients, both young and old. An intervention I have often used with younger children who present with anger issues is a spin-off of the commercial game Twister. I made my own "anger board" using a solid light-colored flannel-backed plastic tablecloth divided into 20 squares. Using five different colors, I put four Xs of each color randomly in the squares on the board. Then I developed two sets of cards: "anger buster" cards and directions cards. These cards were also marked with Xs, four for each color. For example, a directions card might read: left foot blue, right elbow red; right hand green, left hand yellow; right knee black, left foot green; left elbow purple, right hand blue. The anger buster cards were also color coded, four of each color. Examples included "Calling names is a good way to handle anger," "If someone hits me, I should hit them back," "I can control my anger if I . . . ," "I have to get angry if someone teases me," "It's fun to get angry," and "Talking things out helps me feel less angry." In implementing this intervention, the child first draws a directions card and moves on the board according to the directions. Then he or she draws an anger card—placed in one of five piles according to the color of the X on that card and matching the color of the X on the directions card. After reading the anger card, he or she is asked to give a response. Clients like this game because it is engaging and gets them moving, as well as helping them to think about their anger and to identify more helpful ways to deal with it.

There are certainly many advantages to activity-based experiential learning, and it is important to stress that these types of interventions are not just fun and games: They are implemented for a specific therapeutic purpose. Although clients are learning by doing, the debriefing that occurs afterward is an essential part of the intervention. Roaten and Schmidt (2009) note that debriefing should not only include processing feelings but also engage clients in cognitive discussion to stimulate critical thinking and transfer of learning to real-life situations. They also emphasize that experiential interventions must have a clear purpose and be contextually related to the needs of the client. Christopher Old, one of the therapists interviewed by Shallcross (2011b) for an article on active interventions, states:

> The main idea is that as the therapist, you tailor the activities and the debriefing based on what the client is bringing into the session and what the therapeutic goal is for the session. . . . It is a very intentional use of activities versus just game playing. (p. 29)

A unique aspect of these interventions is that they can occur in or out of an office or school setting, although Jeff Ashby, another expert interviewed by Shallcross (2011b), expresses concern that confidentiality is broken by going outside in a school setting and even in other settings if they are not private. Fortunately, for many years I had a private practice in my home, which was in a remote wooded neighborhood, so inviting clients who had difficulty opening up in an office setting to take a walk did not jeopardize their privacy and, on many occasions, proved to be an effective way to get them to talk.

Jackson (1995) has identified the following advantages of active learning:

- It is a good way to learn while having fun.
- It is process as opposed to outcome oriented.
- It puts the responsibility for learning on the client.
- The concepts are reinforced through debriefing what has been experienced.
- If implemented in a small-group or classroom setting, everyone can be involved.

Shallcross (2011b) describes other advantages:

- Active interventions promote awareness that might not occur in traditional talk therapy.

- In a group setting, group members can process what they observe and provide feedback to other group members.
- Counselors can observe clients' behavior in the moment without having to rely on feedback from teachers or parents.
- Active interventions that include processing help clients generalize the experience to other aspects of their lives.
- These types of activities can result in clarifying thinking and increase the amount of dialogue that occurs within the session.
- A variety of skills can be developed using various activity-based approaches.
- An active learning approach enhances the client-counselor relationship.

## TYPES OF PROBLEMS AND POPULATIONS THAT BENEFIT FROM ACTIVITY-BASED EXPERIENTIAL INTERVENTIONS

As has been previously mentioned, traditional verbal approaches to counseling are often ineffective, particularly with children and adolescents whose language skills may not be well developed, whose attention spans may be limited, and whose primary learning styles may not be auditory. Increasingly, counselors are "getting off the couch," as Shallcross (2011b, p. 28) notes. Active interventions are becoming more popular, not only with clients but also with counselors.

Many different types of problems can be addressed through this approach, as counselors from around the country interviewed by Shallcross (2011b) describe. These experts shared how they used these types of interventions with the following client populations:

- Unmotivated adolescents who struggle to concentrate at school
- Clients with mood disorders, including anxiety and depression
- Clients with eating disorders and weight issues
- Clients with PTSD
- Clients dealing with abuse
- Clients with substance abuse problems
- Clients with low self-esteem
- Clients dealing with grief and loss
- Adolescent males who have difficulty opening up during counseling sessions
- At-risk youth
- Families working on communication and cohesion
- Clients with multiple self-defeating behaviors

According to Shallcross (2011b), clients of all ages are appropriate candidates for active interventions. Groups and families also benefit from these types of interventions, which range from experiential activities in the counseling office to outdoor counseling interventions such as ropes courses, yoga and walking sessions, wilderness adventure-based counseling, and adventure hiking and skiing. D.B. Palmer, another therapist Shallcross interviewed, expressed the belief that it is good to "shake things up" (p. 35) because, as a society, we sit too much, and getting clients active has many health benefits in addition to therapeutic effects. Furthermore, he noted that, as a therapist, he is more perceptive and connected with his clients when he and his client are "off the chair" (p. 35).

## TRAINING AND PREPARATION

It is essential that counselors be adept at making children and adolescents feel comfortable with this alternative style and be skilled at processing on both an affective and a cognitive level. Counselors themselves must also develop a comfort level with this approach. For some, activity-based interventions may seem challenging, especially if they are used to more traditional approaches and are not comfortable "counseling outside the lines." Counselors working with children and adolescents most likely have employed various forms of experiential learning with their clients because it is what works best for this population, so adding more active interventions to their toolboxes shouldn't be a big stretch. Some forms of activity-based interventions are more specialized and require additional training, however. For example, counselors who use wilderness therapy and ropes courses need more advanced training. In addition to confidentiality issues that differ to some degree from traditional counseling approaches, there are also safety issues, depending on the type of activity. For these reasons, it is ethically imperative that counselors have adequate training or certification, if necessary, when using these approaches with clients.

## EXAMPLES OF ACTIVITY-BASED EXPERIENTIAL INTERVENTIONS

The sky is the limit when it comes to developing activity-based interventions with young clients. We invite you to consider the following, adapting them to your clients as appropriate:

### Rapport Building

Unless something is really out of a client's comfort zone, which is possible, most activity-based experiential activities facilitate the development of rapport. An example of a quick and easy intervention is to toss a ball back and forth; each time you or the client has the ball in hand, you share something about yourself related to a category (a list posted on the wall). Examples include favorite color, favorite animal, favorite thing to do, or favorite school subject. Depending on their sophistication, the activity can work with adolescents if the questions are adapted so that they are more complex—for example, "Who is your favorite sports figure, and what do you admire most about him or her?" "What is something you believe in very strongly?" "What type of music do you most enjoy listening to?" and "What matters most to you in life?"

### Take a Toss

I developed this intervention for a 10-year-old who was having difficulty staying on task at home and at school. Because he liked sports, I made several beanbags, and then put aluminum pie plates at various points around the room. The object was for him to stand behind a line and try to get a beanbag in the pie plates. Each plate had a different colored X in the center, and I made cards that also included a colored X. When the client successfully got a beanbag in a plate, he drew a card from the pile that matched the color on the plate and responded to questions such as "When it's hard to concentrate, one thing I can try is . . ." "If my friend is talking to me when we are supposed to be listening, I can . . ." "To help me remember to take my homework home, I can . . ." and "Something I can do to help me remember to take my lunch money to school is . . ." Writing the answers on the back of the card was a visual reminder of things he could do to help himself be more successful in school.

### Jump for Joy

Working with children who seem chronically sad is difficult, but research is clear that getting sad and depressed clients moving is therapeutic. This intervention engages clients in a physical activity while at the same time helping them discuss and identify things they can think or do to help them feel better. The strategy is simple: Give the client a jump rope and tell him or her that you will be the secretary as the two of you talk about sad feelings and how to deal with them. Ask the client to think about the past week and what he or she was sad about as you write it down. Then explain the idea of "jumping for joy," which means that as he or she jumps, the challenge is to think of something to think or do that would be a way to make the sad feelings go away or not be so strong. Encourage the client to use the phrase "When I'm sad, I can jump for joy by giving this a try" and then to identify something. I have found it helpful to write down the ideas, and then work with the client to include them in the following jump-rope chant:

> *When I'm sad, I can jump for joy*
> *And give ________ a try (one of the ideas).*

*And one thing more that I can do*
*Is ________, which might work, too!*

This can be repeated until all ideas are incorporated into the chant.

### Shake, Rattle, and Roll

This intervention can be adapted for various problems, but I used it with an 8-year-old who needed to develop better social skills. I gave her a milk carton that was sealed at the top and contained a cup of dried beans, a rattle (or you could use a maraca), and a beach ball. I told her that I would be reading some examples of friendship behaviors to her. For each behavior read, she was supposed to shake the carton if she thought it was a good idea, rattle the maraca if she thought it was a bad one, and roll the beach ball if it was something she had tried that had worked for her. Examples included telling a classmate you don't like what she is wearing, inviting a classmate to sit by you at lunch, talking about a classmate behind his or her back; stealing a classmate's pencil, cutting in front of a classmate in the lunchline, and telling a classmate you like her new haircut.

### Tug of War

Many of my adolescent clients have struggled with decision making, especially those involving moral dilemmas. With one client, rather than just talk about it, I developed several dilemmas based on issues the client might be dealing with and invited her to take hold of one end of a sturdy rope. I then read the dilemma and instructed my client to pull one way, giving an argument for or against a decision, while I pulled on the other end and played the opposite role. For example: "You are invited to a party and you know there will be alcohol there. Your parents have explicitly stated that you should never attend parties of this nature. You want to fit in with your friends, so what do you do?" I pulled on one end and said, "How would my parents find out unless the party gets raided?" The client pulled on the other end and said, "But what if it did get raided? What would happen?" I pulled on the other end and said, "If I don't go, how will my friends treat me?" This tug of war was a concrete way to help her think about the dilemma she was facing, which we discussed after the intervention.

## OTHER EXAMPLES OF ACTIVITY-BASED EXPERIENTIAL INTERVENTIONS

Jackson (1995) has developed an intervention to help clients with anger management. He used it in a classroom setting, but I adapted it as follows for use in individual counseling: First, give the client a big balloon and ask him or her to blow it up part way and hold it there, explaining that the balloon represents how angry he or she gets. Then ask the client to talk about what he or she gets angry about as you write the responses on paper. Then read each item separately, instructing the client to blow into the balloon each time you read one of the items, varying the amount of air blown into the balloon depending on how much anger he or she attaches to a particular item. Be aware that it may explode, but if it doesn't, hide a small pin in your hand and reach over to pop it after everything on the list has been read. Discuss why the balloon popped and why some of the items on the list provoked more anger than others. Next give the client a second balloon and instruct him or her to blow it up very large but not to let it pop. As the client talks about some things he or she could do to reduce the anger, ask him or her to let some air out of the balloon for each anger management idea. Debrief by focusing on anger management techniques and how the client can apply these to his or her own problems with anger.

Shallcross (2011b, p. 29) describes an intervention used by Christopher Old, called "Minefield," with a client who struggled in school. Old developed various obstacles—such things as showing off for friends, not managing time effectively, or talking too much in class—and wrote these on sheets of paper and placed them on the floor. He then invited the client to imagine that he was in a minefield and that his goal was to avoid the obstacles. First, he was allowed to do this with his eyes open, which was easy, but then he had to try it with his eyes closed, which became much more challenging. Then the counselor said he would try it with his eyes closed, but he asked for help to guide him through it and was successful in avoiding the obstacles. He invited his client to try it this way, which proved to the client that asking for help was a viable way to manage his problem.

Another activity-based intervention that helps adolescents clarify values is called "Walk the Line" (Vernon, 2009, p. 32): Place a strip of masking tape on the floor, designating one end as "like me" and the other end as "not like me." Tell your client that you will be reading a list of characteristics and that he or she should move to whichever end of the line best describes him or her. Examples include "good at sports," "favorite subject is math," "loves school," "tries to be perfect at everything," "good at saving money," and "likes lots of alone time."

## INCORPORATING ACTIVITY-BASED INTERVENTIONS WITH OTHER CREATIVE ARTS INTERVENTIONS

As Slyter (2012) notes, a significant trend in employing creative arts interventions is to combine them with other expressive approaches because they work so effectively in concert. For example, when working with clients who have issues with perfectionism, hand them three pencils: one with a sharp point but no eraser, one with an eraser but a very dull point, and one that has a decent eraser and a fair point but that is all chewed up. Ask the client to pick the perfect pencil. The client will realize an ideal doesn't exist with this sample of pencils. Then ask the client to make up a limerick, a song, or a short skit to represent what he or she learned about perfectionism from the pencil activity. Debriefing can focus on what being perfect means to the client and how to be realistic about personal demands for perfection (adapted from Vernon, 2002, p. 97).

Another strategy combines bibliotherapy or cinematherapy with an activity-based intervention designed to help clients address issues related to depression. When depressed, clients often feel "blue," so this intervention involves giving the client a jug of water, a bottle of blue food coloring, and a clear bowl: Invite the client to pour an amount of water into the bowl and then to add food coloring, matching the intensity of the color with how depressed he or she felt during the past week. Next invite the client to discuss in more detail what was depressing and how he or she dealt with it; then focus on what else could be done to diminish the depression. If the client identifies anything that he or she has tried or something that might help, ask him or her to add more clear water to the blue bowl to symbolize lessening of the depression. As a follow-up, invite the client to read a book or watch a movie that identifies ways to overcome depression (adapted from Vernon, 2002, p. 126).

Jackson (1995) has used an inflated beach ball to help clients who struggle with self-esteem issues. He explains that the beach ball represents an individual's self-esteem, hands the ball to the client, and asks him or her to push it and drop it, noting what happens. They discuss the fact that the ball is resilient because, as the client just demonstrated, even when the client pushes or drops it, it bounces back. Jackson then asks the client to identify things that would "deflate" his or her self-esteem and instructs the client to let a small amount of air out of the ball each time he or she identifies something. He asks the client what happens when the deflated ball is pushed or dropped (it doesn't bounce). He suggests to the client that it is possible to raise self-esteem, and they discuss various things the client could think or do to feel better. With each suggestion, the client blows some air back into the ball. This activity could be combined with art by having the client make a collage of his or her strengths or a "Me Bag" with pictures on the outside of positive attributes and words or phrases inside the bag of things the client likes best about himself or herself.

## CLASSROOM OR SMALL-GROUP INTERVENTIONS

Activity-based experiential activities are ideal for small-group counseling and classroom guidance, focusing on communication and cooperation, decision making, self-esteem, problem solving, managing troublesome emotions and stress, substance abuse, bullying, cultural diversity, and many other topics. One activity that works well with adolescents and addresses problem solving and communication is to provide students with a roll of masking tape, a big pile of newspapers, a medium-sized cardboard box, and three bricks. The task is to build a bridge that is high enough so that the box will fit underneath and strong enough to support the bricks. The bridge must be free standing. During the 10-minute planning stage, students can talk and touch the materials, but during the building stage (20 minutes), they must communicate nonverbally. Discussion afterward focuses on how they decided what to do, how they communicated once they could not talk, who assumed leadership roles, and so forth (Hawley & Hawley, 1975).

Jackson (1995, pp. 102–105) has developed the "Balloon Bash" to help students learn stress management techniques. In the activity, the group is divided into teams of four or five players and instructed to line up facing each other, as in the game Red Rover, three feet behind a piece of masking tape on the floor. The person in the middle of each line is given a blown-up balloon and, using a marker pen, each team member writes something that stresses him or her on the balloon. These stressors are read out loud before play begins. To begin the game, the person in the middle of each line hits the balloon and tries to keep it in the air, using his or her teammates to help. Each round is played for 20 seconds. When a balloon hits the ground on the opposing team's side, that team gets a point, and any player can put the balloon back in play next to where the balloon hit the floor. Only hands can be used to hit the balloons. Before beginning the second round, each team is given another balloon. Once again, each player writes a stressor on the balloon and reads it out loud. Play resumes with four balloons instead of two. For the third round, two more balloons are added, and the same procedure is followed. Rather than continuing to write stressors, however, I would adapt the third round by asking participants to write how they handle stress. This could be repeated with a fourth round. Discussion could focus on what it was like trying to keep the balloons in the air, with major emphasis on how much more difficult it is to handle stress when there are multiple stressors, just as it is to keep multiple balloons in the air. Further discussion could emphasize stress management techniques.

Jackson (1995, pp. 80–82) has developed another activity that addresses problem solving. Students form partnerships, and each "team" receives 10 drinking straws and 25 inches of masking tape. Each team has seven minutes to build a raft using the straws and masking tape. At the end of the building time, teams take turns putting their rafts in a baking pan filled with water; on top of the raft, they put pennies, one at a time, adding them until the raft sinks. Discussion focuses on how they decided what to do, how well they worked together, and how they could apply what they learned to real-life problem-solving situations.

An experiential activity designed to build rapport and help students learn about other cultures is "Cultural Bingo" (REACH Center, 1993). A bingo sheet with specific cultural activities or customs written on each square (e.g., "celebrates Hanukkah," "observes the Day of the Dead," "celebrates Chinese New Year") is given to each student, and students walk around the room, handing their bingo sheet to others who can initial squares that apply to their culture or religion.

## SUMMARY

If you work with children and adolescents who seem to learn best by doing, activity-based interventions should be added to your counseling toolbox. Most young clients respond well to this approach, but it is imperative that adequate time be allowed for debriefing so that concepts can be thoroughly discussed and reinforced. As noted previously in this chapter, even though these interventions are engaging, they are not just fun and games; they are developed with a specific goal in mind. As you will note, the following activity-based interventions involve a lot of play, games, and experiential activities, while at the same time incorporating a variety of other expressive-arts interventions.

Additional activity-based experiential interventions are described on the following pages, addressing self-acceptance, friendship, expressing feelings, problem solving and decision making, managing negative emotions, dealing with peer pressure, postsecondary planning, procrastination, communication and assertion, self-awareness and values clarification, and group collaboration. These can be modified to address the client's specific issues or developmental level. As stressed previously, to ensure effectiveness, care should be taken to select activities within the client's comfort zone.

# Catch It If You Can!

**TOPIC** Self-acceptance

**RATIONALE** During this period of development, young children are learning new skills at a rapid rate. Mastering them can be difficult, especially when children put pressure on themselves to be perfect. This intervention is intended to help them accept themselves as individuals with strengths and weaknesses.

**MATERIALS**

A beach ball

A whistle

A baseball cap

A set of Catch It If You Can Cards

**PREPARATIONS** Copy the Catch It If You Can Cards, glue them to red, white, and blue tagboard, and cut apart.

**PROCEDURE**

1. When working with a client on self-acceptance issues, engage her in an activity-based intervention that will help her remember that there are things she can do well, things she cannot do, and things that she can do but not very well.
2. First, invite her to play a game that goes like this: When you blow the whistle, she draws a card out of the baseball hat and reads it out loud (or you read it for her if she isn't able). If it is a red card, she throws the ball to you, and you throw it back to her. Once she has the ball, she answers the question. If it is a white card, she throws the ball up in the air and then catches it before she answers the question. If it is a blue card, she throws the ball to you, you throw it back, and then she throws it up in the air and catches it before she answers the question.
3. After she answers each question, encourage her to elaborate with other examples, engaging her in discussion that emphasizes that learning is a process, that there will be things she masters better than others, and that her worth as a person isn't contingent on her performance because everyone has strengths and weaknesses.

# Catch It If You Can Cards

## Red Cards

| | |
|---|---|
| What is something that you do really well? | What is something that you can do now that you couldn't do last year? |
| What is something that you aren't very good at? | What is something that you see others doing that you wish you could learn to do? |

## White Cards

| | |
|---|---|
| What is something that you don't do well at all? | What is something that is really hard for you to do? |
| What is something that you want to learn to do better? | What is something that you don't think you will ever be good at doing? |

## Blue Cards

| | |
|---|---|
| What is something that you are proud that you can do? | Do you think it is a good idea to get mad at yourself when you don't do something well? |
| Do you think there is anyone who can do everything really well? | What does it say about you if you can't do everything well? |

# You've Got a Friend

**TOPIC**

Friendship

**RATIONALE**

Socialization in the context of a peer group is a key issue during middle childhood. Because relationships with friends can involve positive as well as a negative experiences, it is important to help children develop social skills, empathy, and rational thinking. These competencies can increase their ability to maintain good peer relationships.

**MATERIALS**

A CD player

A CD with tunes that appeal to children

A sheet of paper

Crayons or colored pencils

A copy of the You've Got a Friend Dilemmas page

Paper plates

**PREPARATIONS**

Copy the dilemmas, cut apart, then glue to 10 paper plates, one per plate.

**PROCEDURE**

1. When a child presents in counseling with issues related to friendship, ask him to draw a picture that illustrates one of the problems he is having. After he has finished drawing, invite him to discuss the problem and other related friendship issues.
2. Next invite him to play a game that is somewhat like musical chairs. Point out the paper plates that are placed in a circle on the floor, face down. Explain that there will be music playing as he walks slowly around the circle of plates and, when the music stops, he should pick up the plate nearest to him, turn it over, and read what it says out loud. After he answers the question, invite further discussion. In particular, reinforce rational thinking or challenge him if he says he's a loser if he doesn't get invited to a party or isn't allowed to play in a game, for example. Also reinforce the concept of empathy—putting himself in someone else's shoes to get a clearer idea of how another person might

feel. Before starting the music again, have him toss the plate out of the circle. Proceed in the same fashion until all the plates have been picked up, discussed, and discarded.

3. Upon completion of the game, discuss what he learned and how he can apply this to his relationships with friends.

## You've Got a Friend Dilemmas

1. You and your best friend usually sit together during lunch, but today he is sitting with someone else, and there is no more space at that table.

   **What do you think, how do you feel, and what do you do?**

2. You whisper to one of your friends that your mother is going to have a baby but that your friend shouldn't tell anybody because it is a secret. A few minutes later, another friend tells you that he knows your secret.

   **What do you think, how do you feel, and what do you do?**

3. At recess, you want to join in a kickball game, but one of your classmates says that you can't play because there are too many players.

   **What do you think, how do you feel, and what do you do?**

4. Your best friend comes to school with a very short haircut. Kids start making fun of him, saying that he looks like a sheared sheep. In front of him, one of them says to you, "Hey, have you ever seen anything uglier?"

   **What do you think, how do you feel, and what do you do?**

5. One of your friends is having a birthday party, and you aren't invited. You don't know for sure who else is going, but you've heard several other friends talking about it.

   **What do you think, how do you feel, and what do you do?**

6. Someone in the other class has been teasing you, calling you names, and saying things about you that aren't true.

   **What do you think, how do you feel, and what do you do?**

7. You want to play with your friend after school, but he says he was invited to go to someone else's house.

   **What do you think, how do you feel, and what do you do?**

8. You ask a classmate to play soccer with you during recess, and he says he doesn't want to.

   **What do you think, how do you feel, and what do you do?**

9. You invite a friend over to play in your tree house, but he doesn't want to do that. Instead, he says he wants to stay inside and play board games.

   **What do you think, how do you feel, and what do you do?**

10. Your best friend raises his hand to answer a question, but he doesn't get it right. Another classmate whispers to you that your friend is really dumb.

    **What do you think, how do you feel, and what do you do?**

# Feelings Fling

**TOPIC** Identifying and expressing feelings

**RATIONALE** Developing a feelings vocabulary and learning positive versus negative ways of expressing feelings is a cornerstone of emotional development. This intervention encourages vocabulary development and also helps children understand the relationship between feelings and behaviors.

**MATERIALS**

Masking tape

Two beanbags

Two shoeboxes, one with a plus (+) on the front and the other with a minus (-) on the front

Two empty vegetable cans, one labeled "Feelings Cards" and the other labeled "Actions Cards"

A set of Feelings Fling Feelings Cards

A set of Feelings Fling Action Cards

**PREPARATIONS** Copy the two sets of cards, glue to tagboard and cut apart, then place in the appropriately labeled cans. Place a masking tape line two or three feet away from the cans.

**PROCEDURE**

1. When working with a young client who has difficulty identifying and expressing feelings, engage her in this experiential intervention designed to facilitate her emotional development.
2. First, tell her that she gets to play a game called "Feelings Fling." Explain that she will first draw a card from the Feelings Card can, read it, and explain what it means. Next she will draw a card from the Action Card can. If she thinks the action is a good way to express the feeling she drew, she will stand on the masking tape line, take a beanbag, and toss it into the shoebox that has a plus on the front. If she thinks it is not a good way to express the feeling, she will stand on the line and toss a beanbag into the shoebox with a minus on the front. If she tosses it into the box with the minus sign, she should identify a better way of expressing that feeling.

After each round, have her retrieve the beanbags so that she can use them again.

3. Let her play the game and engage her in discussion about the meaning of the feelings words, when she has experienced them, and how she expresses them. Focus on positive, appropriate ways to express feelings and discuss consequences of expressing feelings in negative ways, such as throwing tantrums, hitting others, and so forth.

## Feelings Fling Feelings Cards

| | |
|---|---|
| Angry | Worried |
| Sad | Excited |
| Happy | Upset |
| Scared | Confused |
| Jealous | Grouchy |
| Guilty | Disappointed |

## Feelings Fling Action Cards

| | |
|---|---|
| Cry | Write about it |
| Scream | Pout |
| Shout for joy | Throw a tantrum |
| Hit someone or something | Call someone bad names |
| Talk to someone about how you feel | Draw a picture that describes how you feel |
| Jump up and down | Talk to someone about how you feel |

# It's "Up" to You

**TOPIC** Problem solving and decision making

**RATIONALE** Young adolescents are faced with a myriad of decision-making challenges. Because they tend to think in the here and now and may not take into account salient aspects of the situation when they make a decision, their ability to make the right decision and use effective problem-solving strategies may be compromised. This intervention focuses on effective problem-solving and decision-making strategies.

**MATERIALS** 12–15 balloons (extras in case some break)

A ball of string

A marker

**PROCEDURE**

1. When an adolescent presents in counseling because he has made some bad decisions that had negative consequences, encourage him to talk about the decision he made, how he feels about the consequences, and what problem-solving process he went through as he made his decision.
2. Next give him the balloons and ask him to blow them up and tie them with string. Ask him to think about another problematic decision that he needs to address and write it on one of the balloons, also drawing a circle around what he wrote.
3. Ask him to take five balloons and on each one write one factor he needs to consider before making this decision, numbering the balloons NC1 to NC5 (needs to consider). Then have him take five more balloons, and, for each of the factors he needs to consider before making the decision, identify a possible consequence (positive and/or negative), numbering these C1 to C5 to correspond with the specific factors he needs to take into account.
4. Now have him toss his balloon with the problematic decision in the air and try to keep it in the air as you take the first "needs to consider" (NC) balloon, read it out loud, and proceed to toss it in the air. Instruct the client to keep this balloon in the air as well.

Continue to read out loud the other balloons with factors to consider and toss them into the mix, telling the client to keep them all in the air as long as possible.

5. Depending on how successful he is in keeping all the balloons in the air, stop this process after a couple of minutes and ask what it felt like to try to consider all these factors related to the problematic decision.
6. Next ask the client to take the first consideration balloon, read it, and toss it in the air as you take the "consequence" balloon associated with this consideration balloon, read it out loud, and throw it into the air. Ask the client to toss these two balloons back and forth between his hands, verbalizing as he does this what the consideration is and what he identified as a consequence. After a minute or less, tell him to stop. Repeat the process with the rest of the consequences.
7. To process, ask your client what it was like to balance the considerations and the consequences, discussing other possible factors to take into account and generating additional alternatives that he might not have thought of. End the session by asking him to write his decision on another balloon and throw it up in the air, telling him that the decision is "up to you."

# Mood Management

**TOPIC** Managing negative emotions

**RATIONALE** Young adolescents can become easily overwhelmed by the frequency and intensity of negative emotions that tend to be common during this stage of development. Learning how to manage their moods is an essential skill, given that they are also impulsive and often overreact to situations, which can sometimes result in self-destructive behavior.

**MATERIALS**

Three clear plastic cups filled with water

Three Alka-Seltzer tablets

Three bottles of food coloring: red, blue, and green

Six clear (empty) plastic cups

Six to eight index cards

A pen or pencil

**PROCEDURE**

1. When a client presents with problems related to managing negative moods, discuss which emotions are most troublesome, how often she experiences them, how they affect her, and so forth. Explain that during this period of development it is quite common to have intensely negative emotions and that you will help her work on ways to deal with this.
2. First, hand her three cups of water and the Alka-Seltzer tablets, inviting her to put a tablet into each cup of water, noting what happens. Liken this bubbling that gradually subsides to emotions that may seem to be bubbling intensely for a while and then become less intense. Discuss whether or not she has experienced anything like this.
3. Next ask her to identify three of her most troublesome emotions and designate a color of food coloring to each emotion. Typically anger (red), depression (blue), and anxiety (green) are identified, but the colors can stand for any emotion. Ask her if her emotions vary in intensity, which is common, and invite her to put drops of food coloring into each cup to indicate the approximate intensity

of the three emotions she is focusing on (one color per cup). As she does this, encourage her to talk more about how she experiences these emotions.

4. Then talk about what she has done thus far to manage her moods, focusing on what has or has not worked for her. Ask her to imagine that she is giving advice to a friend who has similar emotions: What does she think might work for her friend? Brainstorm other possible options with her and have her write each of these suggestions on an index card.
5. Next ask her to close her eyes and try to visualize herself feeling one of the emotions she identified as being very intense. Then ask her to try to visualize herself trying some of the mood management suggestions she came up with to try to reduce the intensity of the emotion. If she is successful, she can open her eyes and pour some of the water representing that emotion into an empty cup, symbolizing a less intense emotion. Do the same for all three feelings she identified.
6. Debrief by focusing on whether she gained any additional insight about her moods and how to manage them and how she can apply this to help her deal with intense negative emotions.

# Fearless Friends

**TOPIC** Peer pressure

**RATIONALE** Striving for social acceptance is paramount at this age, so peer pressure becomes a salient issue as young adolescents strive to fit in with their peers. "Just saying no" is not easy, yet the ramifications of engaging in activities with negative consequences can be significant. This intervention helps clients think about these issues.

**MATERIALS**

A cloth bag, such as a supermarket recycling bag

A five-pound bag of potatoes

A copy of the Fearless Friends Activity Sheet

**PROCEDURE**

1. When you are working with a client who is struggling with issues related to his peers and dealing with pressure to conform, encourage him to share more about these situations, talking about his need to be accepted versus doing what he thinks is the right thing. Also discuss the consequences of giving in to peers, particularly when risky behaviors are involved.
2. Give him a copy of the Fearless Friends Activity Sheet and invite him to read the first scenario, discussing whether this is something that he has experienced or possibly could experience. Next ask him to identify several consequences if he did give in to the peer pressure and write those in the space provided.
3. Then give him the cloth bag and the bag of potatoes. Tell him to imagine that the potatoes represent the severity of the consequences of succumbing to peer pressure and that he should carefully select as many potatoes as there are consequences (relative to the first scenario) and put them in the bag. Ask him to talk about what the consequences could be and then pick up the bag so that he can feel the weight of the consequences. Before moving to the next scenario, have him count the number of potatoes in the bag and write that number beside the scenario. Then he should

dump out the potatoes, read the second scenario, and follow the same procedure.

4. After he has completed several scenarios, as time permits invite him to discuss how these scenarios are like or unlike ones he is presently dealing with. Discuss how he identified the consequences and, in particular, discuss the scenarios that had the most severe consequences, focusing on what he would gain and lose from giving in to peer pressure.

# Fearless Friends Activity Sheet

*Directions: Read each scenario and identify possible consequences if you give in to peer pressure.*

1. You are invited over to one of your good friend's homes, but you don't know until you get there that his parents are gone. You know your parents would be upset if they knew that, but you figure that they won't find out. Besides, his older sister is there with her friends, and you think they are really cool. At first you and your friend just stay in his room and listen to music, but then the two of you get hungry and decide to go to the family room and raid some of their food. As soon as you start down the stairs, you think you smell smoke, but you just keep on going. When you get to the family room, you find them smoking not just cigarettes but also pot. They ask you and your friend if you want to get high, and you both say no, but they keep persisting, so finally your friend agrees to try it. They ask you again if you want to try it.

   **Identify possible consequences if you give in to peer pressure:**

   ______________________________________________

   ______________________________________________

   ______________________________________________

2. You are at the shopping center with your friend and see a video game that you really want. It's very expensive, and you don't have enough money to buy it. Your friend is also looking at one and says he can't pay for it, but since nobody is looking, he says he's going to stuff it under his shirt, and he thinks you should take one, too.

   **Identify possible consequences if you give in to peer pressure:**

   ______________________________________________

   ______________________________________________

   ______________________________________________

3. Your dad and his girlfriend are at a movie, and your brother is staying overnight with your cousin. You are grounded and are not supposed to leave the house, use the computer, or talk on the phone. You are sitting on the porch when an older kid that you are just getting to know drives by and stops. He comes up on the porch and asks if you want to ride around and hang out. You think it's pretty cool that an older kid would want to hang out with you, and you really want to go. You tell him that you're not supposed to leave the house because you are grounded, but when he asks if your dad is home and you say no, he says he can get you back in an hour, well before the movie would be over.

   **Identify possible consequences if you give in to peer pressure:**

   ______________________________________________

   ______________________________________________

   ______________________________________________

4. You are spending the weekend at your grandparents' house while your parents are out of town. You are really bored and want to get out of the house, so you ask your grandma if you can walk to the library because you have some studying you have to do. It's not very far, so she says all right but that you can't go anywhere else. When you get there, some of your friends are hanging around outside, and they suggest that you all go to the café for a coke. You don't see any problem with that, so you go along. On the way there, one of the guys pulls out a cigarette and offers one to you and the two other guys. You don't really want to smoke, but you don't want to be the only one who isn't smoking.

   **Identify possible consequences if you give in to peer pressure:**

   ______________________________________________

   ______________________________________________

   ______________________________________________

5. You are in eighth grade and you have a crush on your older sister's friend, who is 16. One night when your sister and your parents are gone, this girl comes by with a couple of her friends and asks for your sister. You tell her that your sister is gone but she'll be back soon, so if they want to come in and hang out, that'd be cool. They ask if your parents are home, and you say no, that they won't be home until pretty late. They come in. One of them is carrying a paper bag with beer in it. They pop open the beer and start drinking and ask you if you want one. You really want this older girl to think you are cool.

   **Identify possible consequences if you give in to peer pressure:**

   ______________________________________________

   ______________________________________________

   ______________________________________________

6. Your friend calls to invite you to a movie, but you tell him you spent all your allowance for the month, so you can't go. He says he's out of money, too, but he is just going to take some from his mother's purse because he's done it before and she's never caught on. He thinks you should do it, too. You really want to go to the movies, so you start thinking about taking some money.

   **Identify possible consequences if you give in to peer pressure:**

   ______________________________________________

   ______________________________________________

   ______________________________________________

# Better Think Twice

**TOPIC** Decision making and consequences

**RATIONALE** During their teenage years, adolescents must make numerous decisions that affect them in the present, as well as the future. Although they are for the most part better able to generate alternatives and think more logically at this stage in their lives, it can still be difficult for them to think clearly about consequences or understand the "domino effect" that can occur when a decision made at one point in time affects future courses of action.

**MATERIALS**

A set of dominos

A sheet of paper

A pen or pencil

**PROCEDURE**

1. When working with a client who has difficulty making decisions and thinking about alternatives and consequences, invite her to talk about a decision she is struggling with and what alternatives she is considering.
2. To illustrate, give her the set of dominos and ask her to select one, laying it flat on a smooth surface. Tell her that this domino represents a decision she is struggling with. Then ask her to select another domino and look at the number of dots on it. For each dot, she needs to identify an alternative, laying additional dominoes, one for each alternative, underneath this "decision" domino as illustrated (this will vary depending on the number of alternatives she needs to identify). These dominoes should be placed vertically under the horizontal "decision" domino. As your client identifies the alternatives, draw a graphic of it on a sheet of paper and record each alternative. Do the same with the consequences, which she will identify in steps 3 through 5.

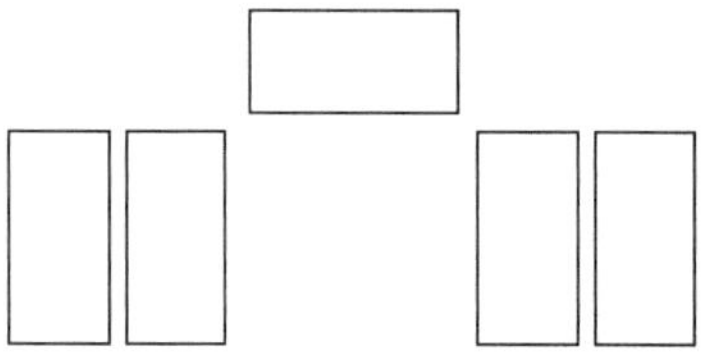

3. Next she needs to identify at least one consequence for each alternative by first selecting a domino and laying it underneath the alternative, as illustrated.

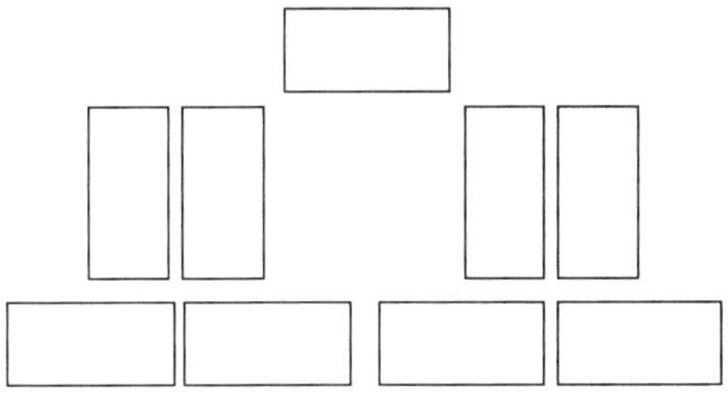

4. Then ask her to identify any other consequences for each of the alternatives by selecting other dominoes and playing them vertically under the first consequence, as illustrated.

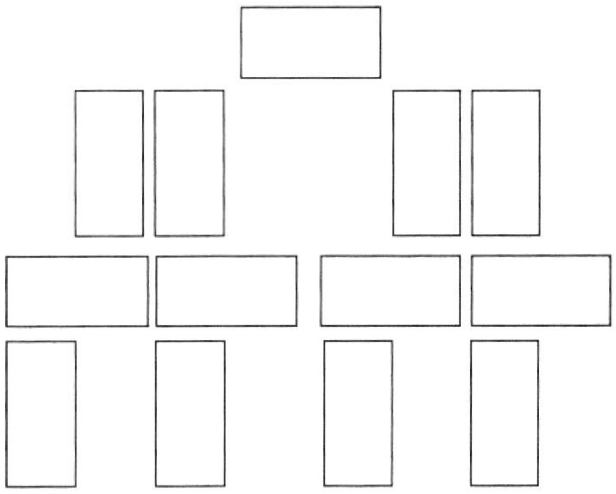

5. Continue in this manner, with the client identifying additional consequences or generating other alternatives and consequences that may be identified through discussion about factors involved in making this decision.
6. When she thinks she has identified all alternatives and consequences, hand her the sheet of paper with the annotated illustrations. Ask her to think again about her decision and withdraw any alternatives from the domino board that she no longer sees as viable after thinking carefully about the consequences. Discuss her decision-making process and help her work through each of the remaining alternatives and consequences until she has clarified the decision she needs to make.

# Finding My Way

**TOPIC** Postsecondary planning

**RATIONALE** High school graduation is a "marker" transition, signifying increased independence and various changes as adolescents make important decisions about this next step in their lives. This intervention is designed to provide further clarification as options and their advantages and disadvantages are addressed.

**MATERIALS**

Six to eight blank sheets of computer paper (you may need more depending on how many options the client identifies in step 1)

Six to eight sheets of paper (or more, depending on the number of identified options)

A pen or pencil

A marker

**PREPARATIONS** Fold six to eight sheets of paper in half lengthwise; on one side of each sheet write "Advantages" and on the other side, "Disadvantages."

**PROCEDURE**

1. When working with a client who is indecisive about his future, help him work through the decision-making process by first asking him to talk about what he sees as his options after graduation and write them (in large letters) on separate sheets of computer paper. After he has recorded all the options he has thought of at this point, take them from him and spread them around the floor, suggesting that these possibilities represent a type of maze that he must work his way through in order to get a clearer picture of his future.
2. Take one of the folded sheets of paper labeled "Advantages" and "Disadvantages," making sure to write one of the options at the top of the page. Ask him to walk to the first stop on the maze and invite him to talk about this option in more depth: why he is considering it, what about it appeals to him, and what might be the advantages and disadvantages. As he talks, record the

advantages and disadvantages he identifies on the folded sheet of paper. Place this sheet beside the first option on the maze and then have him walk to the second option, following the same procedure. Continue in this manner—recording advantages and disadvantages—until all possible choices have been discussed.

3. Next ask him to walk back through the maze to the first option he identified and look at the lists of advantages and disadvantages. Have him take a marker and put a large X beside those that seem most important to consider. Follow this procedure until he has walked through all parts of the maze.
4. Now ask him if there are any alternatives that he thinks he can eliminate based on what he has been thinking about as he has made his way through the maze. If he can eliminate any, ask him to remove those sheets from the maze and talk about how he arrived at that decision. Have him continue to walk around, weighing the advantages and disadvantages of the remaining choices and putting additional Xs on any that he sees are significant. Continue to engage him in discussion to help stimulate his thinking about other advantages, disadvantages, or consequences of the various options.
5. When he has walked the maze and eliminated as many alternatives as possible, engage him in a discussion about whether or not this intervention clarified anything for him and discuss how he feels about the remaining choices. Give him the remaining option sheets with the accompanying advantages and disadvantages lists and continue to work with him as he weighs his options.

# Get Out from Under It

**TOPIC** Procrastination

**RATIONALE** Many high school students have a lot going on, juggling time with friends, work, school, and extracurricular activities, among other things. If they become overwhelmed, they may procrastinate about doing things they would rather not do, which leads to further complications. This experiential intervention addresses this problem.*

**MATERIALS**

A large pile of newspapers

10 index cards

A pen or pencil

A copy of the Get Out From Under It Activity Sheet

A beach or large bath towel

**PROCEDURE**

1. When a client is referred or self-refers with issues related to procrastination, ask her to share more about the problems it creates and how she feels about it. To help her clarify some of the reasons she puts things off, ask her to complete the Get Out from Under It Activity Sheet.
2. Engage her in a discussion regarding her responses to the questionnaire, exploring in more depth why she puts things off, how she feels when things begin to pile up, and whether or not it seems as if she can't get out from under the pile.
3. Next ask her to think about things she procrastinates about and have her write them on separate index cards. Collect these cards, and then place the towel on the floor and invite her to lie down on her back. Explain that you are going to read what she procrastinates about, one item at a time, and then place a stack of newspapers on her stomach so that she experiences the feeling of things piling up.

*This intervention has been adapted from Vernon, 2002, pp. 183 and 188–189.

4. After each card has been read and the newspapers have piled up, discuss how she feels and talk about what happens when she lets things get to this point. Then explain that you will help her get out from under the pile if she can identify something she can think or do relative to the things she procrastinates about.
5. Take the first card, read it, and as she comes up with a strategy, write it on the back of the card to serve as a visual reminder of what she can try. Then remove a small stack of the newspapers. Proceed in this manner with the remainder of the cards. After she has gotten "out from under it," ask how she feels and whether she thinks the ideas she generated will help her deal with procrastination in the future.

# Get Out from Under It Activity Sheet

*Directions: Read the following questions and check your response for each item.*

| | Yes | No | Sometimes |
|---|---|---|---|
| 1. I procrastinate about things I don't like to do. | ☐ | ☐ | ☐ |
| 2. I procrastinate because I figure I can get it done later. | ☐ | ☐ | ☐ |
| 3. I procrastinate because I don't like to do things that are too difficult or frustrating. | ☐ | ☐ | ☐ |
| 4. I procrastinate because I don't know how to start tasks. | ☐ | ☐ | ☐ |
| 5. I procrastinate because I can't help it. | ☐ | ☐ | ☐ |
| 6. I procrastinate because I think I might be more in the mood to do it later. | ☐ | ☐ | ☐ |
| 7. I procrastinate because it's something I've always done. | ☐ | ☐ | ☐ |
| 8. I procrastinate because I get too anxious and can't start. | ☐ | ☐ | ☐ |

# Tell It Like It Is

**TOPIC** Communication and assertion

**RATIONALE** It goes without saying that good communication skills are survival skills. Similarly, assertive communication is far more effective than aggressive or nonassertive communication. In this experiential intervention geared for elementary grades, students can practice communicating effectively.

**MATERIALS**

A sheet of newsprint

A marker

A chair for each student

**PROCEDURE**

1. Introduce this lesson by asking students to identify some characteristics of effective communication: eye contact, speaking clearly, showing interest in what others are saying, and so forth. Write their suggestions on the newsprint.
2. Next ask if they understand the difference between assertive, aggressive, and nonassertive behavior. Explain it by using the following analogy: If you are nonassertive, you are like a mouse—weak and timid. You are afraid to stand up for what you think or feel because you don't want others to be upset with you. If you are aggressive, you are like a monster—mean and controlling. You don't care if you hurt people; you just want your way. If you are assertive, you aren't timid and you aren't mean. You aren't afraid to say what you think and feel, but you do it in a nice way that doesn't hurt others' feelings.
3. Divide the students in half and ask one group to take one chair each and to place the chairs in a straight line with a little space between each chair. Then instruct the other group to place their chairs across from the group whose chairs are already in place, leaving about two feet between them. Each student should be sitting directly across from another student.

4. Assign one group to be the "monsters" and the other group to be the "mice." Each person in the monster group is supposed to look glaringly at his or her partner, who is sitting across from him or her, and say mean things in a menacing tone of voice. The mouse responds timidly, agreeing with the monster or denying it, but doing it in a very soft voice without making eye contact.
5. Stop the process and ask how the mice felt. Solicit feedback about the difference between the two messages. Next explain more about an assertive message: that it can begin with an "I feel" statement about what the other person said or did, or it can begin with "When you ________ (behavior), I feel ________ (feeling)." Explain that this is effective because others can't argue with how someone else feels. Assertive messages are delivered using good eye contact and in a calm and firm voice. Give examples, such as "I feel hurt when you say mean things about me" or "I don't like it when you call me names." An assertive message can contain a request: "I don't like it when you call me names, and I would like you to stop." Explain that just being assertive doesn't mean that you will get what you request, but you will have much better communication if you don't respond like a monster when someone acts like a monster with you.
6. Now begin round 2. For this round, the monsters say something mean to their partners, but the partners are no longer mice—now they respond assertively. When finished, discuss the difference and how the mice felt when they no longer responded in a timid, deferential manner.
7. For round 3, switch roles so that the members of the monster group become mice and the mice are now the monsters. Repeat the same process as before, first with the aggressive-timid response and then with the aggressive-assertive response.
8. For the final round, instruct the monsters to deliver an aggressive message, the mice to respond assertively, and the monsters to respond as they feel they might to the assertive message. Discuss whether or not the monsters tended to be less aggressive when responding to an assertive message.
9. Process the intervention by asking students to describe the difference between these three communication styles, which they think is most effective and why, and how they can apply these concepts to their own lives.

**NOTE** Monster and mouse analogies are taken from the book *The Mouse, the Monster, and Me* (Palmer, 1977). If you wish, you may read this book to the group.

# Identify Yourself

**TOPIC**

Self-awareness and values clarification

**RATIONALE**

A major developmental task for young adolescents is identity development. In many ways they are like chameleons, trying on many different ways of thinking and behaving as they clarify their values, develop greater awareness of their strengths and weaknesses, and learn more about their interests. This experiential intervention is designed to help facilitate identity development.

**MATERIALS**

A set of Identify Yourself Role Cards

Masking tape

16 sheets of newsprint

**PREPARATIONS**

Copy the role cards, glue to tagboard, then cut apart. Print the following in large letters, one phrase per sheet of newsprint:

1. Being good looking
2. Being very religious
3. Hanging out with friends
4. Smoking cigarettes or pot
5. Being preppy
6. Being liked by teachers
7. Getting along well with parents
8. Having musical talent
9. Being in a rock band
10. Drinking beer or other alcohol
11. Being your own unique person
12. Helping others
13. Being popular
14. Being a loyal and supportive friend
15. Getting good grades
16. Having lots of money

Hang these sheets around the room in the order listed, with space between them (students will be walking to these spots throughout the activity).

**PROCEDURE**

1. To begin this activity, ask for eight volunteers: four girls and four boys. Take them aside, give each of them a separate Identify Yourself Role Card, and ask them to familiarize themselves with that role so that they can describe themselves to other classmates as the person depicted on the card.
2. Next explain to the rest of the students that these eight students are their peers and will be explaining who they are and what is important to them. Point out that around the room are 16 sheets of newsprint, each with a different phrase describing key factors relative to the eight students' values and priorities.
3. Ask one of the volunteers to stand in front of the group and read his or her role card in the first person—for example, "I am Juan Carlos. I was recently selected as the best soccer player out of all the leagues in the city. I am very good looking and popular, and religion is very important to me." Then have the student read the two phrases written in bold on the card and instruct the student to select one of those phrases that is the most important to him or her and to walk to that sheet of newsprint. (The other students in the room should also do this.)
4. Before moving on to the second role card, ask students to look around to see how many are at each spot, engaging them in a discussion about how difficult it was to choose between the two, how they decided where to go, and so forth. Follow this same process as the other role cards are read.
5. In conclusion, ask students what they learned about themselves and their values and priorities as they participated in this lesson.

# Identify Yourself Role Cards

**Juan Carlos**

Juan Carlos was recently selected as the best soccer player out of all the leagues in the city. He is **very good looking** and popular and **religion is very important** to him.

**Mary Catharine**

Mary Catharine thinks school is boring, and she doesn't see why getting good grades is important. She would rather **hang out with her friends** and **smoke cigarettes and pot** when she can get it.

**Ben**

Ben's parents have a lot of money, and some kids call him **preppy** because of the way he acts and dresses. He gets really good grades and the **teachers all like him** because he always volunteers in class.

**Paula**

Paula **gets along with her parents**, even though she thinks they are too strict and old fashioned and she is sometimes embarrassed to be around them. She is **very good in music** and has won several competitions for her piano performance.

**Peter**

Peter is the lead **singer in a rock group** that he and his friends started last year. He and his friends hang out with a lot of older kids, so it is easy for them to **get beer, which they usually drink** after their band practices. He doesn't get very good grades because he spends most of his time practicing with his band and has no time for homework.

**Maria Luisa**

Maria Luisa hates preppy kids, so even though her parents have plenty of money, she buys her clothes at the Salvation Army so that **she can be unique in the way she dresses.** She **likes helping others**, so she volunteers after school at a day care center where she reads and plays games with young children.

**Marcus**

Marcus is **very popular** and was just voted class president. He is also the captain of the basketball team. He is a very **supportive and loyal friend.**

**Anna**

Anna gets really **good grades** and wants to go to medical school so she can be a doctor and **make lots of money.**

# We Can Work It Out

**TOPIC** Group collaboration

**RATIONALE** It is a given that successful employees are those who are effective collaborators and can get along with others in the work setting. As adolescents prepare to leave high school and begin the next stage of their lives, which at some point will involve being employed, learning group collaboration skills is an important part of future planning.*

**MATERIALS**

A large stack of newspapers

A roll of masking tape per group (4–6 members)

A copy of the We Can Work It Out Group Process Sheet for each student

A pen or pencil for each student

**PROCEDURE**

1. Introduce this activity by sharing the purpose of the intervention and asking the students to identify what they consider effective collaboration skills. Next divide them into groups of four to six and explain that each group is going to collaborate in order to build a freestanding shelter that they can all fit inside. Inform them that they have 15 minutes to plan what they will do and 15 minutes to build the shelter. They may talk during the planning stage but not during the building stage. They also should not look at what other groups are doing (if possible, have the groups in different rooms or far apart from each other).
2. At the end of the 30 minutes, have each group look at the other shelters and then get inside theirs.
3. Debrief the activity by asking them to reflect generally on what the process was like for them. Give each student a We Can Work It Out Group Process Sheet to be completed and then discussed in each small group.

*This intervention is based generally on an activity described in Hawley and Hawley, 1975, p. 59.

4. Initiate another discussion with the whole group about how well they worked together, what types of factors inhibited or enhanced their work as a group, how leaders and followers were identified, and so forth. Focus on what they think could have improved their group performance and how skills such as these will be applicable in their future.

## We Can Work It Out Group Process Sheet

*Directions: Complete the group process sheet based on your experience working in your group to build the shelter.*

1. Who assumed the leadership role in your group—the person(s) who got the group organized and perhaps offered the most ideas?

2. Who were the followers?

3. Were there any group members who blocked your progress by not participating, not collaborating, or negating ideas?

4. Who were the encouragers?

5. How did you determine how you would build your shelter?

6. What was the most difficult part of this process?

7. What do you think it would have been like if you had had to do this by yourself?

8. How would you rate your level of productive participation in this group on a 1 (low) to 5 (high) scale?

9. How do you think the group could have improved their performance in completing this task?

10. What did you learn about yourself as a group member by doing this?

Chapter 8

# Case Studies

It's one thing to read about creative arts interventions, but they really come alive when applied to actual cases. In this chapter, several school and mental health counselors have contributed cases based on real clients, with names and other identifying information changed to preserve confidentiality. Their contributions provide a foundation that should give the reader a clearer picture of how the seven types of creative arts approaches described in this book can be applied to many different types of problems during childhood and adolescence. We appreciate the generosity of Jane Balvanz, Shelly Klaas, Dave Berns, Michelle Bruty, Rebecca Lins, and Lynne Staker for taking time to contribute to this book.

This chapter includes three case studies for each level: elementary, middle school, and high school. The majority of these cases portray more serious situational problems as opposed to typical developmental problems, which were the primary focus in the previous chapters. When I read these cases for the first time, I thought about how difficult it must be for many of these clients, who are dealing with varying degrees of family disruption or dysfunction over which they have no control: incarcerated parents, parents who have abandoned the family and have no contact with the children, death of a close relative, parental divorce, and homelessness. Anger, aggression, anxiety, depression, and underachievement are prevalent reactions these young clients manifest as they struggle to deal with their life circumstances. At the same time, they still have typical developmental issues to contend with, as several of these cases illustrate: codependent romantic relationships, indecision about the future after high school, relationships with peers, and school performance.

For each case study, contributors provided background information relative to the client's age, family configuration, academic performance, and social-emotional adjustment. I reviewed each case, identified the targeted problems, and developed an intervention using each of the seven creative arts approaches for each case study. If the contributing counselor identified interventions he or she used, these were noted. The interventions are described in the order in which they were presented in the previous chapters of the book: play and games, music, visual arts, expressive writing, literature, drama, and activity-based experiential interventions. In real life, there may be reasons that a school or mental health counselor may not choose to use an intervention from each category: It might not match the client's learning style, the counselor might not be comfortable with that approach, or a particular intervention might not be the most appropriate choice for that problem. However, by presenting each modality, I wanted to illustrate the wide applicability of the creative arts interventions to a variety of problems.

As emphasized in the beginning of this book, creative, expressive counseling approaches may be used as the primary therapeutic method or as a complement to a predominantly verbal interaction with the client. As you read the case studies, consider which of the approaches you think would be most effective and how you might modify them or come up with additional ideas that you think would effectively address the targeted problems.

As has been stressed often throughout this book, these interventions are not just fun and games but rather have been developed for a specific purpose. However, as also has been emphasized, the approaches described in this book can benefit clients from all backgrounds and cultures in that they are concrete, engaging, and empowering—and they address multiple learning styles. They are a powerful means to stimulate awareness and growth, and they have an impact on clients in ways that traditional approaches do not. For children and adolescents in particular, whose ability to conceptualize their problems and express them verbally may be limited, using interventions that make it necessary for practitioners to "counsel outside the lines" can significantly enhance the process.

After you read the following case studies, try taking an example from your own caseload and identifying creative arts interventions for each of the seven modalities. Then put them into action with your client! If you are not already using these types of interventions, you will likely soon be convinced that counseling in this way can have much greater impact, which is what it's all about—making a difference in kids' lives.

## ELEMENTARY CASE 1: ANNIE

*Contributed by Jane Balvanz*

### Background Information

Annie is a bright, energetic 7-year-old who lives in a midsized Midwestern community where Annie's father is a construction worker and her mother is a nurse's aide. Annie attends a small neighborhood elementary school, and her brother, age 14, is in middle school. Annie takes ballet and piano lessons and is also in soccer. She and her brother spend quite a bit of time with their grandparents, who live on the other side of town.

Annie is very social and has generally been well-liked by her peers, although there have been some problems recently because she is having trouble staying focused. Although Annie's school performance was good last year, for the past two months she has been having a great deal of difficulty concentrating. The teacher has used various methods to try to address this behavior problem, including letting her earn points for special privileges, moving her desk to the back of the room, and putting her in time-out, but nothing has really helped. She is just like a jumping bean in class, as well as on the playground, where she flits from one activity to another, always in perpetual motion. Her behavior is beginning to distract the other students, and several have started to complain that they can't get their work done if they have to be with Annie at a learning center or in a small-group activity.

Annie was referred to the school counselor by her second-grade teacher and at the request of her mother. Whereas the teacher referred Annie for counseling because of her distractible behavior, her mother said that she and her husband were getting a divorce and that she thought Annie's inability to focus was related to this—although Annie hadn't verbalized this at home when both her mother and father tried to talk to her. Annie's mother told the counselor that Annie was having difficulty getting to sleep at night, which was unusual for her, and she had noticed that lately Annie hadn't been eating as well as she typically did. She did note that Annie was spending more time in her room, which was not typical behavior for her because she usually liked to be right in the middle of things at home or out in the neighborhood playing with her friends.

The mother shared with the counselor that her husband was the one who had initiated the divorce and indicated that this had probably come as a major surprise to the children because she and her husband never fought or acted disagreeably with each other; they had simply grown apart, and her husband no longer felt that he could live with her. She suspected that her husband might be experimenting with drugs because he was associating with a totally different group of people who had a reputation as users, but she didn't really have any firm indication of this. She thought that they were both pretty committed to making the children's adjustment as good as possible and that if the drug issue didn't become a problem, she had no qualms about their ability to coparent, communicate, and act in the best interests of the children. They planned to have joint custody; the children would live with her during the week and be with their father on weekends.

## Targeted Problems

Because Annie had gotten along socially, behaviorally, and academically the previous year in first grade and in kindergarten as well, according to the school counselor who reviewed her cumulative file, it seemed apparent that the pending divorce was resulting in her problems with distractibility. It is not at all uncommon for younger children to express themselves behaviorally if they aren't able to verbalize their thoughts and feelings. Therefore, the main problem to target was the family situation, and it was anticipated that once Annie was able to work through this, she would be able to focus again. If not, the behavior problems would need to be specifically addressed.

## Interventions

### Play and Games

As noted in a previous chapter, play is the language of the child and is an especially effective approach for a youngster who expresses her feelings behaviorally instead of verbally. Unstructured play might be a preferred approach initially and involve making available dolls, family figures, costumes, a dollhouse, a play telephone, and other toys related to families. The counselor could invite Annie to play with the toys and note what she selects and what she expresses, both verbally and nonverbally. This approach would most likely be used over the next several sessions so that even if Annie didn't verbalize much as she played, the counselor could observe what struggles Annie might be having with the pending family changes by noticing the toys she selected and what she chose to do with them. The counselor could reflect back to the client what she is noting at intervals during the unstructured play periods and identify additional interventions based on what emerged during the unstructured play.

### Music

The counselor could use music to address the concept of family changes. At the time of this writing, a very engaging short music video called *We Are Family,* is available from www.wearefamilyfoundation.org. Sesame Street characters sing the catchy song that reinforces the idea that families come in different forms, but they are still a family. This could be an important message for Annie to hear because her family configuration will soon be changing.

### Visual Arts

For children who have difficulty with verbal expression, the visual arts can be an effective way for them to convey what they are feeling. An invitation to use art supplies to create something that illustrates how Annie feels is an open-ended approach that the counselor might find appeals to Annie. The counselor could simply put out various art supplies, such as construction and wrapping paper, yarn, colored pencils, glitter, buttons, and so forth, and invite her client to use them. The contributing counselor actually did use this intervention with her client. The client cut out four paper hearts (two that were larger than the other two), and each heart was torn in some way.

When the counselor asked her client if she could say more about the broken hearts, she didn't say anything but turned them all over. The counselor noted lots of teardrops on the two smaller hearts and not quite as many on the larger ones.

### Expressive Writing

Numerous expressive writing interventions can be effective for young clients dealing with losses associated with divorce. In this case, it might be good to combine this approach with the visual arts and literature and read *I Don't Want to Talk About It* (Franz-Ransom, 2000), a story about a little girl who learns that although some things will be different about her family because of the divorce, her parents still love her and they can work things out. After reading and discussing the book, the counselor could invite Annie to write her own book, suggesting that Annie might also want to illustrate each page. Given Annie's age, the counselor might need to serve as the client's secretary, Annie could dictate what she wanted to say, and the counselor would write it down and then let Annie draw the pictures.

### Literature

Literature can be an excellent way to help clients deal with issues related to divorce and family change because clients can identify with what the characters in the story are feeling and gain insight about how to handle the changes. The counselor could read *Dinosaurs Divorce* (Brown & Brown, 1998) to her client, stopping throughout the book to engage Annie in discussion about how her situation is like or unlike that of the dinosaurs. Although Annie might not expound much, she could learn some key concepts relative to divorce that might be helpful to her. Another book, *Divorce Happens to the Nicest Kids* (Prokop, 1996), dispels some of the myths about divorce. This book is a bit more informational and is intended to be read to the client. Using these books in conjunction with each other should help Annie understand more about the upcoming family changes and provide her with coping strategies.

### Drama

Puppets can often be used to help young clients express their feelings and experiences. With Annie, the counselor could put out a basket containing several different puppets and invite her to play with them. After a while, she could ask Annie to pretend that one of the puppets is the mom who is talking to the other puppet, Annie, about the divorce. Young children usually readily contribute back-and-forth dialogue, and Annie might be able to ask "Mom" questions about what is happening and why. This process could be repeated with a "Dad" puppet.

### Activity-Based Experiential

For this intervention, the counselor could develop a game by making up a set of cards having to do with divorce-related topics and then put paper plates in a zigzag pattern around the room. She could invite Annie to draw a card and read it (or read it to her) and respond to the question before jumping to the next paper plate. Examples of cards include the following:

When my parents told me they were getting a divorce, I felt . . .

What will change when my dad no longer lives with us is . . .

What I wish could happen is . . .

What I worry about most is . . .

Something I would like to tell my parents is . . .

Something I can do when I feel sad is . . .

The counselor could then develop other interventions to address specific issues resulting from Annie's responses during the game.

## ELEMENTARY CASE 2: KEVIN

*Contributed by Shelly Klaas*

### Background Information

Kevin is a nine-year-old fourth grader who lives with his mother and preschool-age sister. He has no other siblings; his parents were never married, and he has had extremely limited contact with his father, who lives overseas. He doesn't have grandparents or other relatives who live close by. Kevin lives in a suburban community of approximately 33,000, where his mother works as a white-collar professional. He attends a school that houses preschool through fifth grades, approximately 320 students. There are 22 students in his class.

Kevin is an extremely bright student who has very high expectations for himself in both academics and sports. He is a gifted athlete who is very involved in extracurricular activities such as soccer, baseball, and Boy Scouts but struggles when he loses and when things do not go the way he wants them to. He also has considerable difficulty with some social cues, and although overall he is generally well liked by his peers, he loses control at times and becomes physically aggressive. As a result, other students sometimes steer clear of him, expressing fear in relation to these incidents. He does have one classmate he considers his best buddy. They spend a lot of time together both in and outside of school. Kevin's mother is extremely involved and supportive, often taking Kevin and his friend to their extracurricular activities or Scouting events.

Kevin's mother requested that he work with the school counselor because he has problems with anger management and impulse control. He also can be extraordinarily oppositional, both at home and in school. These problems are not new: In kindergarten and first grade, he experienced similar problems. During that period of time, he would frequently have temper tantrums and, because he is large for his age, he would occasionally hurt another student, although usually without intending to do so. In second grade he was referred to the school-based mental health therapist because, although there had been definite improvement in his self-regulatory skills, Kevin still had difficulties with impulse control. He was subsequently diagnosed with ADHD and was put on medication, which has helped to some extent.

Third grade seemed to be a bit better year for Kevin, but now that he is a fourth grader, things have gotten worse again. He periodically has major meltdowns in class, which usually correspond to his being asked to do something he doesn't want to do. Although these episodes are not frequent, when they do happen, they are quite intense and can be very intimidating to the other students, as well as to the teacher. Kevin really struggles with the concept of fairness in relation to what he and others are allowed to do. If he perceives that another student is getting special treatment or is acknowledged more than he is, he goes into a rage. This seems to be particularly true when another very gifted classmate seems to be getting special attention. During these times, Kevin's anger escalates much more quickly and explosively than it does with other students.

As can be surmised, Kevin also struggles with any sort of competitive situation because he has difficulty being a good sport if he loses. This is unfortunate because he is a very good athlete. However, it is unlikely that he will find success in this arena if he cannot learn to be a good team player. This problem carries over from sports to games in the classroom and during recess. When Kevin gets angry, he goes into a rage, screaming and throwing things, although at times his whole body goes rigid; he clenches his teeth and quietly stares at the object of his anger.

To help him avoid major altercations involving his peers, Kevin begins his day in the school office, reading quietly and then going to his classroom when the bell rings. Although this helps some, Kevin really doesn't think he has problems and isn't especially motivated to do anything about them, even though his mother is very concerned. The following interventions could be used by the school-based mental health counselor, who sees Kevin on a fairly regular basis, albeit against Kevin's wishes.

## Targeted Problems

Because Kevin is a very bright student who struggles emotionally and behaviorally but not academically, targeted problems are anger management and impulse control. Because medication apparently worked initially and helped Kevin control his impulsivity, it would be important to have a doctor review the dosage to see if any changes need to be made.

## Interventions

### Play and Games

Because Kevin has issues with fairness and competition but is a gifted athlete, it is important to address these issues so that he will be able to participate in sports activities, as he seems inclined to do. It would be most effective to put Kevin in a small group of three to four of his peers and invite them to play a variety of board games or card games. Prior to playing, the counselor could ask the group members how they deal with losing, what it says about them if they lose, what characteristics they most like to have in peers they are playing games with, and so forth. During the game, if Kevin or others struggle with issues of fairness or are not handling competition or losing well, the counselor could stop the game and process the issues, focusing on how to play games without getting so upset if they are losing, and so forth.

Many commercial games deal directly with anger management. The Anger Solutions Board Game (Childswork/Childsplay), which would also be played in a small group, is about controlling behavioral responses to anger and is suitable for children Kevin's age, as is Furious Fred (Franklin Learning Systems), in which players earn points when they identify positive ways to deal with anger.

### Music

Making "mad music" could appeal to Kevin and serve two purposes: to release some negative energy and to initiate discussion about effective ways to express and manage anger. If feasible, this intervention would be most effective when Kevin was having one of his episodes. Pots, pans, small metal garbage cans, and various drumming utensils could serve as the musical instruments. After the music making, the counselor could work with him to create a song about anger and how to deal with it. Taking a familiar tune such as "Jingle Bells" and working with him to write new words could help Kevin think more about his anger and how it affects him. Here is one example:

*I'm so mad, I'm so mad,*
*It's really getting bad.*
*It's no fun to play with kids if I can't always win.*
*I must win, I must win, I cannot stand to lose,*
*But if my temper takes control,*
*I'll lose the game and my friends, too.*

## Visual Arts

Any number of visual arts interventions could be helpful for the targeted problems. First, Kevin might benefit from drawing cartoons that illustrate anger management tips. He could also draw or paint pictures of things that make him mad. The illustrations could be combined with expressive writing; he could make a book by compiling the illustrated pages and writing something on each one, describing what he is angry about and how he might deal with it. He could then refer to his "anger book" when he needs advice on how to manage his anger. If he continues to make books over time, he could see a decrease in the number of pages, signifying that he is not experiencing as much anger.

## Expressive Writing

It would be effective to use a worksheet as a form of expressive writing with Kevin, asking him to take time immediately following an incident in which his anger has gotten control over him to write what happened, using a structured format: what triggered his anger, how he behaved, how he felt about the way he reacted, what the consequences were, and things he might have thought or done to avoid the out-of-control response. The activity would be most effective if Kevin shared the worksheet with the counselor, but even if he is unwilling, the writing experience itself could be helpful.

## Literature

There are some excellent books for children on anger management and impulse control that the counselor could use with Kevin. *What to Do When Your Temper Flares: A Kid's Guide to Overcoming Problems with Anger* (Huebner, 2007) includes some what-to-do guides that are very helpful for this age group. *Chillax! How Ernie Learns to Chill Out, Relax, and Take Charge of His Anger* (Craver, 2011) is also a good selection for children this age. The counselor could suggest that Kevin make a list of ideas he thinks might help him manage his anger, and they could discuss them together and develop an action plan.

## Drama

Given that Kevin needs to learn how to manage his impulses and his anger, role-playing could be a very effective intervention. Kevin could set up the scenario based on a recent incident in which he had trouble controlling his impulsive behavior or his anger, and then he and the counselor could take turns role-playing or reverse role-playing until he could respond more effectively to the reality-based scenarios. Puppets could be used in a similar manner, although someone as bright as Kevin might consider this approach beneath him.

### Activity-Based Experiential

It might be effective to use "Adios, Anger" with this client (Vernon, 2009, p. 206). First, the counselor could have Kevin make a list of things he gets angry about or loses control over. After discussing this, the counselor would set down a hopscotch board (drawn with a marker on a bedsheet or flannel-backed tablecloth). The counselor would inform Kevin that she will read each of the things he wrote, one by one, and if he can identify something he could think or do to calm himself down and avoid letting his anger get out of control, he may jump ahead to the next set of squares. His goal would be to jump to the end and say "adios" to his anger. A commercially available or counselor-made anger control ball, with different anger management strategies written on it, could be fun for Kevin and the counselor to toss around and discuss.

## ELEMENTARY CASE 3: AMY

*Contributed by Dave Berns*

### Background Information

Amy is 12 years old and a sixth grader at Western Hills Elementary. There are approximately 400 students in her school. Amy lives with her mother, her stepfather, a six-year-old stepsister whom she claims to hate, and a one-year-old half-sister whom she adores. Amy and her family live in a community of 30,000, where her stepfather works at a local manufacturing plant and her mother is a clerk at a local convenience store. Her mom also does tax returns. Amy's biological father is in the area, but she has had very limited contact with him since her parents divorced five years ago, and in the last two years she has not seen him at all. The mother and stepfather have been married for approximately two years. Amy attended Western Hills Elementary from kindergarten to fourth grade, then moved out of state for two years, and has now returned for sixth grade.

Tension and conflict characterize the family dynamics. Amy has considerable anger toward her mother and has never liked nor gotten along well with her stepfather. There is sibling rivalry between Amy and her stepsister for Mom's attention and affection. There are also communication and trust issues between Amy, her mother, and her stepfather. Her mother does not get along with her parents (Amy's grandparents), whom Amy is very close to. Amy's mother's relationship with her parents has always been contentious, and although they live in the area, Amy's mother limits the contact they can have with her daughter. The grandparents dote on Amy, and Amy feels that her grandparents truly understand her and that they are on "her side."

At one time, Amy and her mother had been extremely close. After the divorce, they lived together for more than two years, and then Mom started dating her current husband, which is when Amy's anger and resentment surfaced because her mother had made some promises about not dating or remarrying, which she obviously didn't uphold. When her mother started dating, Amy was left out and thought her future stepfather was a bad influence on her mother because he drank too much. Apparently Amy's grandparents felt the same way because they said something to their daughter, which only further alienated them from her.

As her mother continued to date her future stepfather, Amy became increasingly hurt and angry. She resented both of them because she felt like she was losing her mom. She wanted things to be the way they used to be before the divorce, but that wasn't in the cards. After they had dated for six months, during which time the conflict between Amy's mother and grandparents continued, Amy's mother and her boyfriend moved out of state, taking 10-year-old Amy with them. Amy was very upset about the move and pleaded with them to let her stay with her grandparents. Amy didn't win that battle. Her future stepfather got a job offer and had to report immediately, so they left without giving Amy time to say goodbye to her friends. Shortly after they moved, her mother and stepfather got married and later had a baby.

Now that Amy is back at her old school, she prefers to have a few close friends rather than belonging to a large group and actually associates more with boys than with girls in her class. Her best friend is her neighbor, who moved across town shortly after Amy moved back to the community and now attends another school. They still maintain close contact. The girls she does hang out with in school have some issues with her because she has gradually become more "goth" in her appearance. Amy is not afraid to stand up for what she believes, has strong standards for how she thinks others should treat her, and can be stubborn and somewhat rigid in her thinking. She holds onto grudges, and if someone turns against her, it is hard for her to forgive. She tends to blame others for her problems rather than take any personal responsibility, and she spends a great deal of energy dwelling on the past and getting bogged down by her negative emotions.

At school, teachers have also noted Amy's up-and-down moods. They contend that she has average to slightly above average academic ability and is stronger in reading and language than in math and science. They think she could do better, but motivation can be a problem for her. Until recently she has usually completed her homework, but that has changed in the past month. Now she complains that school is boring and that she doesn't feel like doing her homework. Consequently, her grades are starting to slip.

Amy has not been able to move past her hurt, anger, and resentment. She wants to punish her mom for breaking her promises. Despite her mother's attempts to connect with her, Amy pushes her away; at the same time, she says she wants a better relationship with her mom, but she doesn't seem able to put any effort into making this happen.

Amy requested to see the school counselor to talk about issues relating to her family. Her mother also requested assistance, indicating to the counselor that she was concerned about Amy's emotional state and possible depression. Amy's mother noticed that Amy has become quite withdrawn lately and spends a lot of time alone in her room. She also remarked that Amy's moods shift very quickly and that Amy tends to be very negative and argumentative with her as well as her husband.

## Targeted Problems

Based on the information provided by the school counselor, it appears that Amy needs to learn how to deal more effectively with her anger and how to manage her moods in general. She is most likely depressed, which at this age is not uncommon. If left untreated, however, depression can become very problematic.

## Interventions

### Play and Games

Amy is just on the cusp of being too old for games, so the counselor needs to be cautious to avoid selecting anything that would be inappropriate for this client. Something that may work is "Pick Up Straws." The counselor could take thin strips of paper, write unfinished sentences on them relating to Amy's issues with her mother and stepfather, and insert them into the straws. Examples might include "I wish my mother would . . ." "One of the reasons I resent my stepfather is . . ." "Something I wish would be different about my family is . . ." and "Something I can do to help myself when I feel sad is . . ." The straws should be dropped randomly on the table and Amy could pick them up, taking care not to move another straw in the process. If she moves a straw, she wouldn't pick it up but instead would say something about herself that the counselor couldn't tell by looking at her. Then she could try again to pick up a straw and, if successful, finish the unfinished sentence.

### Music

To target the depression, the counselor could invite Amy to keep a music journal, selecting songs that represent how she feels at given intervals during the day throughout the week. The counselor could encourage Amy to play these songs so that they could discuss the meaning they hold for Amy and how they reflect her moods. Amy could also find uplifting songs—ones that make her feel good—and make a plan to listen to those each day to help elevate her mood.

## Visual Arts

Because Amy has so much anger and resentment toward her mother, the counselor could ask Amy to draw a timeline from the time of her earliest recollections of her mother to the present. The counselor could explain that Amy should divide the timeline into years and for each year list positive and negative things about the relationship, citing specific examples as much as possible. Amy could draw arrows above the line and write in positive remembrances, with arrows below the line representing negatives. As is common for many people, it is easier to remember negatives when there is considerable anger, but the visual representation of memories is often very enlightening because positive memories are also included. After the timeline has been discussed, a good follow-up intervention would be to have Amy find pictures of times she and her mother spent together over the years. This is often a good reframing technique, opening the client's eyes to the fact that the relationship hasn't been all negative.

## Expressive Writing

Several expressive writing interventions could be helpful to this client, including keeping a journal or writing poetry, both of which can be very cathartic. Another possibility would be to have her write a letter to her mother in session so that the counselor could discuss it with her. Based on the intensity of Amy's anger, it is likely that the first draft will be very accusatory and negative, so the counselor would be advised to keep it until they have done more work to decrease the anger, at which point it might be appropriate for Amy to revise the letter and share it with her mom. Provided the client is willing to share, journaling, poetry, and letter writing should give the counselor more insight into this client's anger and depression so that other interventions could target these two areas more specifically.

## Literature

There are some exceptionally good anger management books for children and teens, including *Hot Stuff to Help Kids Chill Out* (Wilde, 1997), which includes several short surveys about anger, information about the negative effects of this emotion, explanation about anger-causing beliefs and how to challenge them to reduce anger, and other anger management suggestions. Amy could be encouraged to put some of these ideas into practice and then write her own chill-out book, writing additional suggestions of things that have worked for her. Literature could also be used to address her depression. *What to Do When You're Sad and Lonely: A Guide for Kids* (Crist, 2006), might also be very beneficial to Amy because it addresses depression and how to deal with it, including 10 specific "blues busters" and other relevant information.

### Drama

Given that Amy has anger issues with her mother, role-playing might be a very helpful intervention after teaching this client about assertive versus aggressive messages. Amy could make a list of some of her resentments and rank-order them from most to least resentful. The counselor could then invite Amy to play herself while the counselor plays her mother. The counselor could coach Amy to first state her resentments in an aggressive manner and then see if she can switch and be more assertive, noting the difference in the way the message is delivered and received. This intervention would need to be repeated over several sessions until Amy learned to differentiate between the two types of responses and had a chance to air her resentments.

### Activity-Based Experiential

To address Amy's depressed feelings, the counselor could use an activity-based intervention called "Crying Takes the Sad Out of You" (Vernon, 2009, pp. 120–121). First, Amy and the counselor could talk about what she is sad about, and then Amy could take a pan of water and squeeze drops of blue food coloring into the water, each "tear" representing her sadness. The counselor could point out that once the "tears" hit the water, they eventually disappear, so the goal for Amy is to figure out ways to feel less sad. The two of them could talk more about her sadness and what she could try to reduce the level of intensity. As she identified things she thinks might work for her, she could pour some of the blue water down the drain. This same intervention could be used to address anger, using red food coloring to represent that emotion.

## MIDDLE SCHOOL CASE 1: GARY

*Contributed by Kathryn L. Barry*

### Background Information

Gary is 13 years old and lives with his father in a small rural community, where his father is a factory worker. Along with his father, Gary and his mother and 10-year-old sister moved to this small community last year just before Gary started middle school. Initially, things were going well. He seemed to like his new school and made friends right from the start because he had good social skills and was very outgoing. He was doing fairly well academically and went out for football. However, about two months after school started, Gary's life changed dramatically, when one day when his mother picked up his younger sister from school to take her to a dental appointment and never returned. Gary and his dad soon learned that Gary's mother and sister had moved across the country and had no plans to come back. Gary's mother filed for divorce almost immediately, and neither she nor Gary's sister have had any contact whatsoever with him and his father.

As the year progressed, Gary was involved in multiple incidents at school requiring office referrals, most of which involved some kind of violence on his part. Although he always appeared remorseful after such incidents, it didn't prevent him from getting out of control again. In fact, he was suspended from school after one such incident, and some parents forbade their children to associate with him. He was also excluded from some school events out of concern for the safety of other students. As these incidents increased in frequency and intensity, Gary was referred to the school counselor by the problem-solving team.

According to cumulative file records, Gary had a history of similar behavior problems in his previous school. School records noted that he had the ability to do well academically but that his performance was erratic because his emotional and behavioral issues interfered with his ability to concentrate. Apparently, there was no counselor at his previous school, but it had been noted that several teachers had suggested to his parents that they seek outside counseling for their son. There was no indication that they had followed through with this. This was in fact confirmed by Gary's father when the counselor at the new school called him for further information. According to Gary's father, the teachers at the previous school were exaggerating the severity of Gary's problems. In his opinion, Gary had a temper and sometimes got into trouble for being too physical with some of his peers, but Gary's father thought his son was just a typical boy whose anger got out of control at times. Because the counselor had heard about Gary's mother's disappearance and the impending divorce, she asked the father about how Gary was handling this and whether he thought this had a bearing on Gary's behavior problems at school. The father said that he had forbidden Gary to mention his mother's or sister's names in his presence: "They left us, so to me, they are as good as dead." His father didn't appear to be too concerned about Gary's grades—he said he hadn't been a high achiever in school, and as long as his son passed to the next grade, he wasn't going to worry about it.

The father was also not happy about the fact that, due to the severity of the problems, the problem-solving team was recommending counseling, either at school or from an outside agency. He reluctantly agreed to counseling at the school but reiterated that he didn't think Gary really needed it.

## Targeted Problems

Because Gary had had problems with anger and aggression prior to his mother's and sister's abandoning him, it was apparent that these issues needed to be addressed, but the loss issues could not be ignored. Whether these issues were contributing to the anger and aggression could be debated, but their significance needed to be explored.

## Interventions

### Play and Games

Because Gary was quite resistant about counseling, a game format might be effective. The counselor could invite him to play Chinese checkers, which actually is quite challenging but also engaging. They could play the first round as a regular game, but during the second round the counselor could introduce some "trips my trigger" anger cards that Gary would need to respond to each time he made a move. Examples of cards include the following:

Something that really makes me angry is . . .

I can't stand it if things aren't fair because . . .

It makes me mad when people say things like . . .

I hate people who . . .

When I get mad I just want to . . .

My temper flares up when . . .

Additional interventions could be developed to address anger management and other issues brought up during the game.

### Music

The counselor could use music with this client in the following ways. First, she could invite him to identify "mad music"—music that Gary tends to listen to when he is mad. The counselor could invite him to write out the lyrics of these songs, and they could talk about how they reflect themes in his own life. Once he has had a chance to talk through some of his anger, she could encourage him to find other songs that might be more uplifting.

### Visual Arts

Photography can be an excellent way to help clients deal with loss, and after several sessions, the counselor could invite Gary to bring some pictures of his mother and sister to share if he felt comfortable with this. Over the course of several sessions, he and the counselor could talk about various pictures, memories, and good times together. The counselor could also invite Gary to make a memory mobile, taking some of the loose pictures, punching a small hole in the top of each one, and tying them with string to a hanger.

### Expressive Writing

To address loss, the counselor could ask Gary if he would write a letter to his mother and one to his sister, explaining how he feels about them leaving him and his dad. The counselor should tell him that it is often helpful to write letters of this nature even if he doesn't send them because it is a good way for him to express how he feels about something that must be confusing and painful. The counselor could give him two envelopes and tell him that when he is finished he can share the letters or not, but putting them in the envelopes is a good way to keep them private.

Another expressive arts intervention to help Gary deal with the loss is to invite him to write his own book of memories about his mother and sister or about his family when they were all together. Because Gary is not very expressive, it may be necessary for the counselor to give him suggestions for some of the pages. Ideas could include the following:

Fun things my sister and I used to do

Things my mom and I used to do together

Things we did together as a family

Something special about my mom

One of my happiest memories about our family

I wish . . .

### Literature

Literature could be used to address both the anger and the loss. First, the counselor might use Ron Potter-Efron's (1993) *How to Control Your Anger Before It Controls You.* This short book contains a good checklist about anger and suggestions about how to control it, primarily by changing the way you think about anger triggers. After Gary completed the checklist, the counselor could discuss Gary's responses and work with him on how he could change his thinking to better control the angry thoughts that frequently resulted in aggressive behavior.

The counselor could also give him a copy of *Help for the Hard Times,* by Earl Hipp (1995). This book, specifically written for teens, covers all types of loss and gives suggestions about how to move on and grow from negative experiences. Gary could be invited to read it and, if he chooses, he and the counselor could discuss it. If he would prefer, he could write his reactions or keep his thoughts to himself.

### Drama

To address Gary's aggressive behavior, the counselor could engage the client in role-playing. The counselor could ask Gary to write out several different scenarios that trigger his anger and aggressive behavior, prompting him with recent examples. When he generated several, the counselor could invite Gary to play the role of the other kid while the counselor played Gary, encouraging him in his role of a classmate to taunt "Gary" or behave in ways that might really trigger

Gary's anger. The counselor would then act as Gary typically does, flying off the handle and responding physically. This intervention would be even more powerful if these role-plays could be recorded and played back for Gary to observe. It would also be good to switch roles so that the counselor played the role of the classmate and Gary played himself, trying to respond in a less angry or aggressive manner. This could continue over several sessions to help Gary learn alternative ways of feeling and behaving.

### Activity-Based Experiential

The counselor could adapt an intervention used by Christopher Old (cited in Shallcross, 2011b, p. 29) called "Minefield," developing various obstacles that represent things that trigger Gary's anger, such as other boys paying too much attention to his girlfriend, the referee not making a fair call, his teacher being on his case for not turning in his homework, and so forth. The counselor could write these on sheets of paper and place them on the floor around the room and then invite Gary to imagine that he is in a minefield and his goal is to avoid the obstacles. First, he could do this with his eyes open, which is easy, but then he could try it with his eyes closed, which is much more challenging. Then the counselor could try it with eyes closed, asking for Gary's guidance through the maze and being more successful in avoiding the obstacles. The counselor then could invite Gary to try it this way, which would prove to him that asking for help is a viable way to help him learn to manage his anger and aggressive behavior.

## MIDDLE SCHOOL CASE 2: KYLA

*Contributed by Michelle Bruty*

## Background Information

Kyla is 14 years old and attends Bradford Middle School. There are approximately 385 students in her eighth-grade class, with a total school population of almost 1,100 students in grades 6 through 8. She lives with her mother, her 9-year-old half-brother and her 5-year-old half-sister. Kyla's father is not presently living with the family, although at times he will move back in and stay for a few months at a time. According to Kyla, her dad has had 13 children with several different women. He moves between these women, living with one for a few months and then moving in with another for a period of time. He is unemployed. Kyla's mother works the night shift at a local convenience store.

Over the past three years, Kyla's family has been homeless for periods of time and has had to move in temporarily with her mother's parents. Kyla is very close to her maternal grandparents and often goes to their home after school with her younger brother and sister. She especially idolizes her grandmother, who has a good job as a secretary for an insurance agency. Kyla is particularly close to her because she spent the first six years of her life living with her grandparents because her mother was still a teenager when Kyla was born. Things appear to be pretty stable at Grandpa and Grandma's house, in contrast to her own home, with Dad in and out and her mother working at night, leaving Kyla in charge of her siblings.

As a result of spending considerable time on the responsibilities associated with caring for her brother and sister, Kyla is not involved in any extracurricular school activities, which contributes to some isolation from peers. She is also quite shy and is extremely obese, weighing 320 pounds at age 14. Her mother is also very overweight. Kyla often brings large bags of Cheetos or other junk food to school and eats it for both breakfast and lunch, so the weight gain can be attributed to a poor diet, as well as lack of physical activity.

Kyla was placed in a homeroom for at-risk students because of her lack of a connection to school and consistently failing grades, attributed in part to failure to do her homework. She has average ability but doesn't apply herself. This has been a pattern for many years, although it has become much worse in the last two years. She has been scheduled for Saturday school several times to help her get caught up with her assignments, but her mother always calls in to say that her daughter is sick. Kyla's mother has agreed to attend numerous meetings with the teaching team to develop a plan to help Kyla be more successful, but she has never shown up for any of the scheduled meetings.

The school nurse noted several health concerns due to Kyla's weight, including very high blood pressure and borderline diabetes. She contacted the mother with these concerns when Kyla was in seventh grade, but they were apparently never addressed because Kyla has in fact gained 25 pounds since the end of seventh grade. The school counselor also contacted Kyla's mom to suggest that Kyla participate in an after-school wellness group for students. This contact did not go well. Kyla's mother became very defensive and stated that Kyla could not do this because she was needed at home to help care for her brother and sister.

Kyla has very few friends, partly because she is not involved in any extracurricular activities and also because of her weight. Classmates have teased and taunted her, and because Kyla is very shy, she simply withdraws. In part because her mother can't afford to buy her nice clothes and also because she is so heavy, she always wears unattractive, baggy sweat suits. She has poor hygiene, and her self-esteem is very low. Although Kyla denies being depressed, both the counselor and the nurse think she probably is because her life circumstances are very challenging. Given that she is a teenager, she is probably more susceptible to depression than she had been in previous years.

## Targeted Problems

Obviously, there is great concern about Kyla's health, and because her mother has made it known that she cannot afford to take her daughter to an outside agency for supportive services, school personnel are going to do what they can to help Kyla. Thus, wellness and weight control are key problems to target, as well as academic achievement, self-esteem, and probable depression.

## Interventions

### Play and Games

Because of Kyla's shyness and the sensitive nature of the problems this client needs to address, the counselor might be wise to use games as a rapport builder, while at the same time trying to get a better understanding of what is going on with Kyla. The counselor could use Totika, a commercial game similar to Jenga. In this game, the client attempts to build a structure without knocking it over and responds to questions on cards. With this client, the counselor could use cards from both the icebreaker and self-esteem decks. Self-esteem could be addressed more directly by having Kyla make a puzzle of herself. The counselor could give her an envelope containing shapes cut out of card stock. The counselor could ask Kyla to put the puzzle together, explaining that there are many different pieces that make the whole, which is also true for her. After Kyla puts the puzzle together, the counselor could then ask her to write personal strengths on each of the pieces.

### Music

The counselor might also learn more about this client though music, and music might also provide some insight for the client. The counselor could suggest to Kyla that she keep a music journal, finding a song each day that reflects how she feels. Although this won't address any of the targeted issues specifically, the counselor could gain a clearer picture of what Kyla might be feeling about herself and her life through this approach, and listening to the music could be therapeutic for her.

### Visual Arts

The counselor could buy a disposable camera for Kyla and invite her to take some pictures of what she likes about her life now and pictures that represent things she wishes were different. She could be encouraged to make a collage of these, separating what she likes from what she wishes were different so as to have a good picture of things she might want to work on to change. Kyla could repeat this process after several weeks, giving her a visual reminder of what changes she has made and what she still could work on.

## Expressive Writing

With a shy client like Kyla, writing could be very effective, but because Kyla doesn't take academics seriously, short writing exercises might be more successful than having her journal, for example. The counselor could develop a list of unfinished sentences to target self-esteem in particular. Examples such as the following could be used:

I would describe myself as . . .

What I like about myself is . . .

If I could, something I would like to change about myself is . . .

One of the most difficult things about being me is . . .

When I look in the mirror, I see . . .

When I look in the mirror, I would like to see . . .

Additional interventions could be developed to address issues that are brought up as a result of this intervention.

## Literature

Because Kyla struggles academically, traditional bibliotherapy might not work well with her. Instead, the school nurse could talk to her about her health issues and weight problems, and the counselor could find several short articles about weight management and healthy eating to share with Kyla, engaging her in discussion about what she has read and whether any of the ideas would be helpful to her. The counselor could follow this up with a visual arts intervention, asking Kyla to cut pictures out of magazines and paste them on three different sheets of paper: one for healthy foods, one for foods that wouldn't be good for her, and one for "caution" foods—which she could have only in moderation.

## Drama

An empty-chair dialogue could be a helpful intervention to address the issue of academic underachievement. Sitting in one chair, Kyla could "talk" with the other chair about why it is important to put more energy into her schoolwork, then switch chairs and counter with why it doesn't matter. After she switches back and forth several times, the counselor could engage her in discussion about anything she learned as she carried out the dialogue. This intervention could be followed up with a visual arts strategy to help Kyla look objectively at the advantages and disadvantages of working on her underachievement. The counselor could give Kyla a strip of paper with the statement "Decided not to do my homework" written on it. She then could instruct Kyla to think of consequences of not doing homework and write each on separate strips of paper. Then she could have Kyla staple each strip together to form a ring, slip them inside each other, and staple them again, forming a paper chain. Kyla could then make a chain for the statement "Decided to do my homework" and follow the same procedure, discussing which "chain of command" she would like to follow and how to do it.

### Activity-Based Experiential

One way to address the underachievement issue could be to have Kyla interview her grandmother, whom she admires, about what it takes to be a successful professional and how to succeed in school. The counselor may need to help her client generate some specific questions to help guide the interview. Another strategy to address probable depression could be to have Kyla make a depression toolbox, by making a list of things that make her feel happy, finding an artifact to symbolize each one, and then making a plan to do one or more of these things each day to try to help improve her mood. She could also look in the box when she is depressed to help remind her of happier things, which will hopefully elevate her mood.

## MIDDLE SCHOOL CASE 3: BRITTNEY

*Contributed by Rebecca Lins*

## Background Information

Brittney is 14 years old and lives with her biological dad and stepmom. Her grandparents raised her for the first 13 years of her life because her father was in prison, but she recently moved from their small community to a larger town to live with her dad and stepmother. She now visits with her grandparents one weekend a month. During the time she lived with her grandparents, she did have regular visitation with her stepmom, and with her dad after he got out of prison, but the grandparents were still her legal guardians. Brittney had an older brother with special needs whom she adored, but he died about a year and a half ago. She also has two younger half-siblings, an 8-year-old sister and a 6-year-old brother. Neither her father nor her stepmother is employed at present. Brittney has no idea where her biological mother is and hasn't seen her in many years. Despite the fact that she hasn't lived for extended periods of time with her stepmother and her father, she has a good relationship with them, and the family is quite close, especially since the death of Brittney's brother.

The death of her brother started Brittney's spiral into depression and anxiety. She seems to have a difficult time grieving and also transitioning to the oldest sibling role. She gets along well with her parents, especially for a teenager, but she is now experiencing some separation anxiety. Her fear, especially since losing her brother, is that her parents will suddenly disappear and leave her like her brother did. This irrational fear contributes importantly to Brittney's anxiety and also has resulted in frequent absences from school because she does not want to leave her parents. In fact, she has missed 22 of the first 39 days of school this year.

In addition to dealing with her brother's death, Brittney also has had another challenging circumstance in that she had to change schools when she moved to live with her dad and stepmother. Not only did she have to leave behind several close friends, but as a new student in a much bigger school, she feels lost and alone while at the same time struggles with depression and anxiety. This has been a huge uphill battle for this client. At Brittney's new school, Jackson Junior High, there are approximately 200 students in her class, with a total school population of approximately 600. The fact that there are so many students contributes to Brittney's anxiety about fitting in and meeting new friends.

Brittney is very self-aware. She knows she has a problem with depression and anxiety and needs help. She is very honest and recently shared with the school counselor that she had suicidal thoughts and thought she should be hospitalized. When the counselor called her dad to report this, he followed up immediately, and Brittney stayed in the psychiatric ward for three days, after which time she was referred to a mental health counselor in the community. Brittney's parents admit that they are desperate to know how to help her and no longer know what to do. They are aware that they have enabled her school avoidance problem but have chosen not to use a tough-love approach because they know Brittany is vulnerable because of the loss of her brother and her difficulty making friends and adjusting to a new school. They will participate in some family counseling at the same agency Brittney goes to for individual help.

## Targeted Problems

Brittney has multiple problems, and it seems that loss and transition are at the core, contributing to the anxiety and depression. All of these issues need to be addressed at some point. The assumption is that once these are dealt with, school attendance will improve.

## Interventions

### Play and Games

As a 14-year-old, Brittney may not be amenable to games, but the counselor could try using the Bright Spots Memory Garden sentence completion game, available from the Self-Esteem Shop, with her. This game deals with grief and facilitates healing as clients talk about their losses. This game is actually suitable for children from age 12 into adulthood.

### Music

As a teenager, Brittney probably listens to music on a regular basis, so the counselor could use Gladding's (1995) "Line Spacers" activity, which involves finding examples of songs that inspire hope or provide suggestions about how to deal with difficult circumstances. If Brittney wrote the lyrics to each song and then made a list of words or phrases that are encouraging or helpful, she would have ready access to some suggestions to help her when she is feeling depressed or anxious.

### Visual Arts

The counselor could have Brittney make a memory tree, taking a large sheet of poster paper and drawing a tree trunk with multiple branches. On the branches, she could paste favorite pictures of her brother and times they shared together, or write words and phrases on index cards that express how she feels about him and paste those on the branches. She could hang this in her room as a remembrance. Expressive writing could also be combined with the visual arts; she could write a story about life with her brother and either illustrate it or find pictures to paste on the pages, compiling it into a book and giving it a title. This would be another good way for her to commemorate her sibling. The counselor could also use "When You Need a Helping Hand" (Vernon, 2002, pp. 131–132) to help this client deal with her depression and/or anxiety. The counselor could ask Brittney to draw around her hand. On each finger, she should write something that she is depressed or anxious about, and after talking more about it, she could write a suggestion for coping with the anxiety or depression in between the fingers.

### Expressive Writing

It could be very helpful for Brittney to complete a loss experience timeline (adapted from Humphrey, 2009), in which she would be encouraged to write the following stimulus questions down the left side of a sheet of paper and, on the right side, respond to them:

What loss did you experience, and how old were you?

What thoughts and feelings did you experience?

How did you cope at the time?

Who was involved in this experience, and how were they involved?

What messages did you get about grief and loss?

What impact did the loss have on you?

How is the loss still affecting you today?

How do you cope with this loss?

The counselor could invite Brittney to talk in more detail about each of the categories and continue to explore how the loss of her brother affected her and how she is dealing with it. They could also discuss the losses brought about by the move to a new school and leaving her grandparents' home.

## Literature

Earl Grollman's (1993) book on death, *Straight Talk About Death for Teenagers: How to Cope with Losing Someone You Love,* would be good for Brittney to read because the author not only discusses common reactions and emotions but also provides suggestions about how to work through grief and begin living without the loved one. The counselor could encourage her to take notes or write reactions to what she reads so they could discuss it. Cinematherapy also would be good to use with this client; the counselor could search the Internet for short film clips on YouTube or rent a movie dealing with the death of a sibling.

## Drama

Empty-chair dialoguing might be good to help Brittney not only deal with the loss of her brother but also assist her with leaving her grandparents and her old school and friends. She could take each of these losses separately and identify others if necessary, "talking" to the empty chair as if it were her brother, her grandparents, her friends at her old school, and so forth. This could be an effective catharsis for her regarding her losses and the impact they have had on her.

## Activity-Based Experiential

To help Brittney deal with anxiety and depression, the counselor could use props such as a large sponge and two buckets, one filled with water and the other empty. The counselor could first ask Brittney to make a list of things she gets anxious about, wording them as "What if . . ." (something bad happens to my dad while I'm at school). After Brittany has listed several things, the counselor could ask her to dip the sponge in the bucket of water and describe how it feels (heavy), then hold it over the other bucket and wring it out while verbalizing something she could say to herself or do to lessen the anxiety. The counselor might need to help her with this, of course. The same technique could be used to address the depression, although in this case Brittany would identify what depresses her. When she wrings out the sponge, she and the counselor could identify things she could think or do that might help alleviate the depression.

## HIGH SCHOOL CASE 1: DAKOTA

*Contributed by Lynne Staker*

### Background Information

Dakota is 15 years old and a freshman in high school. Her parents divorced five years ago, and she and her sister, age 9, and her 6-year-old brother live with their Native American mother and her significant other, who has been part of the family for the last four years. Dakota gets along well with her mother and the partner, but there is family conflict between the two younger siblings, who act out. Dakota's sister has learning disabilities and receives special services, including being seen in individual therapy at a local agency. When the divorce occurred and Dakota and her siblings were living alone with their mother, her mom expected her to coparent, so shifting out of that role was somewhat difficult when her mother's boyfriend moved in. Dakota's parents get along relatively well when it comes to parenting, and she and her siblings have regular visitation with their father (who is not Native American) and the woman he has lived with for the past five years. This woman's children, ages 9 and 14, live in Dakota's dad's house full time. Although Dakota sees her dad on a regular basis, she thinks he doesn't have enough time to give her the individual attention she wants. She is aware that he is working long hours in order to meet his family obligations, both with Dakota and her siblings and his new family. Dakota feels guilty about this, but she is a quiet and compliant teen who internalizes her feelings rather than acting them out, so she has never told her dad how she feels.

For the most part, Dakota gets along with her mother but feels that she is too overprotective. Most of her friends have boyfriends, but Dakota wasn't allowed to have one until just recently. However, she decided she wasn't all that interested in him because he was not very attentive, so she gave up on that and started doing more with her friends.

Dakota, along with her mother and siblings, are very close to their Native American relatives and participate in rituals. They still attend powwows, and, until a few years ago, Dakota was a tribal dancer. During the past year, however, Dakota has not been as connected to her roots. She is not really clear about the reason for this except that she just doesn't feel like doing much. She would like to get back into the dancing and start going to the community center on a more regular basis.

There is history of alcohol abuse on both sides of the extended family, and Dakota's mother was in a treatment center as a 12-year-old for self-mutilation (cutting). There has also been some trauma history: the death of a young relative four years ago, her great grandmother's death a year ago, and witnessing the physical assault of her maternal aunt in the recent past.

Dakota is a B and C student but is not consistent in completing assignments. She is somewhat shy but has some good friends now;

while in seventh grade, however, she was a victim of some harassment, primarily in the form of verbal aggression by her classmates. When this was occurring, her tendency was to get quiet and withdraw, and she didn't talk about it very much. One of her teachers was aware of what was happening and mentioned it to Dakota's mother, but the problem seemed to go away on its own.

Dakota is in counseling at a local agency to help her deal with her emotions. She reports being angry and moody and is often tearful. She says she feels helpless and hopeless and worries excessively about almost everything. She has difficulty sleeping. In the past she has used pencils and scissors to make cuts on her wrist, and she yells loudly at her siblings, slams doors, and isolates herself.

## Targeted Problems

Treatment goals should include stabilizing the anxiety in order to increase Dakota's ability to function more effectively on a daily basis. In addition, the depression must be addressed, and her deficient coping skills need to be replaced with healthier strategies.

## Interventions

### Play and Games

A game could be used as a way of building rapport with Dakota, as she is quite reserved and not very verbal. The counselor could use a familiar commercial game, the Ungame, selecting teen cards and family cards that might be appropriate in addition to the cards that are more general in nature. This game emphasizes communication and sharing and should be a good way to learn more about Dakota. Although the cards are geared for teens, the game would be used only if the counselor felt it was age appropriate for the client.

### Music

Because this client is a former tribal dancer, it is likely that music, or at least drumming, would appeal to her. And as a typical teenager, Dakota probably listens to music with considerable frequency. Based on these assumptions, the counselor could invite Dakota to make a musical collage that depicts how she feels on any given day. The counselor could suggest that Dakota bring this collage with her to the next session so they could talk about anything relevant that resulted from the activity. If Dakota is willing to do this over time, she will likely see that her musical collage conveys more positive than negative lyrics. The counselor could also ask Dakota if she would be comfortable sharing a video of her dancing, which might provide more insight into this client and help develop rapport and trust.

## Visual Arts

The counselor could use one or both of the following visual arts interventions to help this client address her anxiety. The first one, adapted from Gladding (2005), is a word cluster that would be a concrete way of helping this client get more in touch with her *anxiety.* The counselor could invite Dakota her to write the word anxiety in a large circle in the center of a blank sheet of paper and then think about all the things she associates with anxiety—events, people, thoughts, other feelings, and so forth. She could write or draw a symbol of as many of these as she can in smaller circles attached by lines to the large central circle, as the diagram shows. She and the counselor could talk more specifically about these anxieties when she has completed the activity, then identify coping strategies.

The second intervention could involve making a mask. As is true for many teens, it is likely that Dakota sometimes "hides behind a mask" so that others won't know how she feels. This may be particularly true with her father, from whom she wants more attention; she keeps her feelings bottled up inside because she doesn't know how to tell him that she needs more from him. The counselor and client could talk about this, and then the counselor could put a large sheet of card stock and other art supplies on a table and invite Dakota to make a mask to symbolize how she masks her feelings. Dakota could write words on the inside of the mask to describe what she is hiding.

## Expressive Writing

For a shy, relatively quiet client like Dakota, journaling or writing poetry could be a very effective intervention. The counselor could encourage her to try one or both of these media, noting that they are often a good form of catharsis and can promote better self-understanding and coping skills. If Dakota is open to this suggestion, the counselor could give her the option of either unstructured journaling, whereby Dakota could write whatever came into her mind each day, or more structured journaling, in which the counselor could give her a list of suggestions to guide the writing, such as the following:

My life would be happier if . . .

Things I worry about are . . .

I get angry about . . .

What depresses me is . . .

How I'd like to feel is . . .

What I can do to help myself is . . .

The counselor could also suggest that if it is difficult for Dakota to write, she might try turning on the tape recorder and do her journaling that way.

## Literature

A particularly helpful book about depression written specifically for teens is *Beyond the Blues: A Workbook to Help Teens Overcome Depression* (Schab, 2008). The counselor could give a copy to the client and invite her to read it, explaining that this book not only discusses what depression is but also has lots of different activities to help teens better understand their depression, identify their own signs and symptoms from a list provided in the book, and, most important, learn to better manage this powerful state. This book should be very useful to Dakota because she can learn a lot about her depression and how to deal with it without having to try to put her feelings into words, which appears to be somewhat difficult for her.

## Drama

Because Dakota is shy and not very assertive, she probably keeps a lot inside, especially as relates to her relationship with her parents. In particular, she wants more from her relationship with her father but doesn't have the courage to say anything. Sharing some information with her about assertive communication might be helpful because when she is nonassertive, negative emotions build up and become overwhelming. After some dialogue about the difference between assertion, aggression, and nonassertion, the counselor could engage Dakota in role-playing to help her hear the differences in the three styles and also to practice assertive communication strategies that she can apply with her parents.

## Activity-Based Experiential

To address Dakota's anxiety, the counselor could invite her to identify some of the things she is anxious about and write these on individual strips of paper. After discussing them at length, the counselor could ask her client if she could rank order them, from most to least anxiety provoking. After discussing what differentiates the high rankings from the low rankings, the counselor could help Dakota identify some of the beliefs associated with them, such as "I'll for sure flunk the test" or "My friends will definitely think I am so weird if I start doing the tribal dancing again." The counselor could help her dispute these and ask her to change any of her rankings if appropriate. Then the counselor could invite Dakota to select three or four worries that she thinks she could let go of and stuff each one into a balloon, blow it up and tie it, and then let it go to symbolize letting go of some of her anxiety. Dakota could use this strategy again when she is ready to let go of other things she gets anxious about.

## HIGH SCHOOL CASE 2: STACIE

*Contributed by Ann Vernon*

### Background Information

Stacie is a 16-year-old high school sophomore in a midsized community. She has lived her all her life with her mother, father, and younger sister. Her grandparents, an aunt and uncle, and several cousins close in age live about 30 minutes away. Stacie sees them quite often and enjoys her time with them. Stacie's father is in sales, and her mother is an accountant. There have been some marital problems that Stacie is aware of, and she suspects that her mother has had, or is having, an affair. She is quite angry about that because she thinks her dad is a pretty nice guy and doesn't deserve this. Her beliefs about her mother's betrayal, which she has never actually verified, have contributed to some negative interactions with her mother, and they fight with some degree of frequency. She gets along better with her dad, but he isn't around much, and she does not perceive him to be as controlling and hard to get along with as her mother is.

Stacie could be a very good student because she is bright and perfectionistic, but she puts so much pressure on herself to perform well that she ends up procrastinating and often doesn't turn work in when it is due. This then becomes problematic for Stacie, because she gets very down on herself. Despite these problems, she does maintain a B average, which, in her opinion, is not good enough.

At her mother's insistence, Stacie attends the youth group at church. She also is a member of the high school choir and plays the flute in the band. She just got a part-time job working a few hours a week at a local supermarket because she wants to start saving money for next year's choir trip.

Stacie is generally outgoing and has quite a few friends, although in many ways she is immature and therefore manifests some of the same insecurities about relationships that younger teens typically exhibit. For example, she gets very upset if friends don't always return her calls immediately, suspecting that they might be with other friends and not want anything to do with her, which usually turns out not to be the case. Stacie has a boyfriend, Tim, and they have been going out for over six months. Her parents don't exactly approve of the relationship, but they don't prevent her from seeing him as long as she continues to socialize with her friends as well. This has become somewhat of a problem because Stacie wants to be with Tim most of the time and doesn't have as much interest in spending time with her friends as she does with him.

For the most part, Stacie is not defiant, except occasionally with her mother. She is conscientious about obeying school rules, even though she sometimes breaks house rules by coming in past her curfew. For the most part, however, she could be described as pretty compliant and responsible.

Stacie initiated contact with the school-based mental health counselor, whom she had seen during middle school to help her deal with anxiety and depression, this time to discuss her relationship with her boyfriend. According to Stacie, the relationship had been very good for the first few months, but lately they have been arguing so much that she fears he will break up with her. Whenever they go out, she constantly wants reassurance that he cares about her, which irritates him, and they end up fighting. When he doesn't call when he says he will, she gets anxious, assuming he is out with other girls, that she's not good enough for him, and that others are more important to him than she is. If he doesn't return her calls, she is even more anxious, assuming the worst. Her response to this situation is to sit at home and wait for his phone calls, to call his friends to see where he is, to stay awake at night thinking about the situation, and to cling to him when they are together. She feels quite anxious.

## Targeted Problems

Anxiety and codependency are the problems that seem most critical to address at this point.

## Interventions

### Play and Games

To address the anxiety, the counselor could engage the client in playing "What If . . ." Based on this client's anxieties related to friends, her boyfriend, and her need to be perfect, the counselor could write statements such as the following on index cards (one per card):

What if my friends don't call me?

What if my boyfriend wants to go out with his guy friends instead of me?

What if I don't get a perfect score on my test?

What if my friend invites someone else over instead of me?

What if my boyfriend doesn't return my phone calls?

What if he breaks up with me?

The counselor could have Stacie draw one card at a time, read it out loud, and then answer it. Her responses should shed more light on her specific anxieties. The counselor could then come back with "And so?" questions to help Stacie delve further into the thoughts contributing to her anxiety so the counselor could help her address them.

### Music

Music can be a very powerful way for adolescents to gain insight into their own issues. In this case, the counselor could use LeAnn Rimes's "How Do I Live Without You." This song is an excellent way to help the client understand codependency. After listening to it, the client and counselor could discuss the concepts and how these apply to Stacie's relationships.

## Visual Arts

A visual arts intervention that could be used to help Stacie learn to identify characteristics of healthy relationships is to have her make a poster, cutting words and pictures portraying healthy relationships from magazines and gluing them to a sheet of poster paper. Another possibility is to have her pick out several greeting cards that convey messages of unhealthy, unrealistic, and codependent relationships and then to have her make her own "healthier" version of a relationship card.

## Expressive Writing

Letter writing can be a cathartic and therapeutic intervention to help clients deal with a variety of issues. In this case, the counselor could invite Stacie to write a letter to her anxiety, describing what the anxiety is about, how it affects her, and what she wants to do about it. The counselor could also suggest that her client write an advice column, using her own problems with codependent relationships, writing them up as if she was asking for advice and then answering her own questions.

## Literature

To help address the codependency issues, the counselor could use a checklist of codependency characteristics (Vernon, 1998c, p. 181) to help educate her client about this and also have her identify her codependent behaviors. This could be followed up by inviting the client to read a short story about codependent relationships titled "I Need You" (Vernon, 1998c, pp. 182–184) and then discussing the concepts with her when she finishes reading the selection.

## Drama

Some of Stacie's codependency issues could be related to her need to control relationships. To make this point more dramatically, the counselor could tie some strings to her arms and legs and ask Stacie to pull on them. The harder she pulls, the more the counselor could resist. This could segue into a discussion about control. To help Stacie deal with this issue, the counselor could help Stacie make a list of things she could say to herself when she feels like she wants to control her boyfriend, such as "Will it do more harm than good to control?" "What's the worst thing that could happen if I don't control him?" and "Can I really control another person?"

### Activity-Based Experiential

To address anxiety, the counselor could use an intervention titled "Walk Away, Anxiety" (Vernon, 2009, pp. 107–108) to help Stacie learn to distinguish between the probability of something happening versus the possibility. The counselor could explain this concept to her client and then place a strip of masking tape on the floor, labeling one end "Probability" and the other end "Possibility." The counselor could then ask Stacie to make a list of all the terrible things she thought would happen relative to her friends and her boyfriend, cut the list into individual strips, and place the strips on the line that represent the probability of that happening to help her gain perspective and thus reduce her anxiety. Many of the things Stacie worries about most likely have a low probability of occurring.

## HIGH SCHOOL CASE 3: TODD

*Contributed by Ann Vernon*

### Background Information

Todd, an 18-year-old, is a senior in high school in a small rural community. He has lived there all his life, and his parents were also born and raised in the area.* Todd has a younger brother, age 12, and a sister who is 8. His father is a manager at a bank, and his mother is a secretary at the elementary school. Their family has always been very close, and as a family unit, they spend considerable time with Todd's maternal grandparents, who live on a farm just outside of town. His paternal grandparents live just up the street from Todd's family, so he also sees them on a regular basis, as well as several cousins who go to the same high school as Todd.

Todd works some evenings and most weekends busing tables at a local pizza parlor, where some of his friends also work or hang out. Up until this year, Todd was on the basketball team, but he didn't go out this year because he wanted to work more hours to earn money for college. Throughout high school, he has been in chorus and a few other extracurricular activities, including being class president last year. He has also been active in the peer counseling program and has been a "book buddy" to a sixth grader the past two years. Despite his involvement in various school-related activities, he has consistently maintained a B average. He gets along well with his teachers, and he has a lot of friends. Most of these friends have been in school with him since kindergarten, and he has some very tight relationships with many of them. Todd is popular and dated off and on during his sophomore and junior years, but this year most of his buddies aren't really dating anyone seriously, just as he is not, so they spend a lot of time hanging out together when they aren't working. He doesn't drink or smoke and has never been in any trouble.

---

* Adapted from Vernon and Clemente, 2005, pp. 219–221.

Todd initially made an appointment to meet with the school counselor because he needed financial aid forms. When he returned them, he and the counselor talked about what he was planning to do after high school. He said that he had applied at a state university two hours away, but as the end of his senior year approached, he didn't know whether he wanted to go to college. He told the counselor that all of his friends seemed excited about graduation and moving on, but he had very mixed feelings because, as he stated, "Nothing will ever be the same again." In addition, he said that because he had always lived in this community, he didn't know what it would be like to move away. His parents had never left, and they seemed perfectly happy, so he thought he might be happier if he stayed around instead of moving away. He admitted that he hadn't talked to his parents about his change of heart, sensing that they might be upset; neither of them had gone to a four-year college, and they were very proud of Todd, who would be one of the first in the extended family to attend college. Even though it would be expensive, they were willing to help him financially as much as they could. Todd said that he felt as though he would really be letting them down if he changed his plans because this was so important to them.

Sensing Todd's loss and transition issues, in addition to his uncertainty about what he would do in the future, the counselor asked Todd if he would be willing to come back so that she might help him work through his dilemma. The counselor said she was glad he was talking about this because high school graduation represents a significant turning point for most adolescents, one that is met with mixed emotions. As he is seeing with his friends, there is a sense of excitement and anticipation about the future, but this transition can also result in ambivalence and loss. Saying goodbye to friends and family and leaving the familiar behind can be complicated and often stressful. The counselor told him that there were ways to help him sort through his feelings about the future and to deal with this significant transition, reinforcing the fact that these issues are typical for someone his age.

## Targeted Problems

The most significant problems to target are transition and loss issues and indecision about the future.

## Interventions

### Play and Games

To help Todd deal with some of his ambivalence about going away to college, the counselor could suggest that the two of them toss a ball back and forth as a concrete way of identifying pros and cons about going away to college. The counselor could ask Todd to think of a reason for going to college, verbalize it, and toss the ball back to the counselor. The counselor could then think of a reason not to go and toss the ball back to Todd. Then Todd would have a choice to make: to respond or refute what the counselor said or come up with a new reason for going ahead with his plan. The counselor could then respond with a "Yes, but . . . " statement or another reason not to go. After playing this game for several minutes, they could stop and talk about whether this strategy was helping him clarify his ambivalence and discuss other "for" or "against" reasons to proceed with the college plan.

### Music

Like most adolescents, Todd probably likes music, so the counselor could suggest that it might be helpful to make a CD collage of songs that have had special meaning to him and his friends over recent years. This would help him remember special times with them and would be something that he could take with him if he chooses to go away to college.

### Visual Arts

The counselor could address the loss issue through art, asking Todd to make a list of the friends, teachers, relatives, and family members he would miss the most if he left for college and then invite him to draw pictures or use photographs to make a collage of some of his happiest memories with these people. The collage, a concrete way to remember these people, is something Todd could take with him and look at if he chooses to leave the community. They could also talk about ways to have meaningful closure with these people. Todd could also use art and make and send cards to some of the teachers, female peers, and other adults who are significant to him, and if he is hesitant to do this with his male friends because they might think it was too sentimental, the counselor could suggest that Todd make the cards but not send them. In this way, he could express how he feels and perhaps, when the time was right, he could follow through and share them. He could also identify some meaningful activities to initiate with these buddies, such as camping out or having one last backyard basketball game.

### Expressive Writing

Given that Todd seems unclear about his feelings and thoughts, other than the awareness that everything is going to change, the counselor could engage him in a transition writing exercise. The counselor could give him a sheet of paper divided into four squares, each square with one of the following labels: roles, relationships, routines, and resources (time, money, skills). The counselor could ask the client to think about how his life might change after high school in relation to each of these areas and to write his thoughts in the corresponding spaces. As they discuss his responses in more detail, the counselor could note in particular such things as loss of relationships, anxiety about money, whether he would be smart enough to make it in college and what he would major in, and how he would make new friends if he moved. The counselor could also encourage him to keep a career awareness journal to help him become more attuned to the various dimensions of jobs that he comes in contact with, sees on television, reads about, or observes, explaining that this might help him look more clearly at possible career choices so that he would know what to major in if he decides to go to college.

### Literature

To assist Todd with his career indecision, the counselor could lend him *The 10 Best College Majors for Your Personality* (Shatkin, 2011), assuming that the college path is the route he is choosing to pursue. This book might be helpful to Todd as he thinks more about what he wants to major in. The counselor could invite him to read it and come back with any questions or ideas he would like to explore further.

### Drama

Adapting the Gestalt empty-chair technique could help Todd continue to work on his ambivalence about whether or not to attend college. The counselor could direct him to sit in one chair and talk to the empty chair about why he doesn't think he wants to leave home and attend college. Then the counselor could have him switch chairs and respond to this position, repeating the switch several times until he reaches some point of clarification. It would be helpful to audiorecord the empty chair dialogue so that he could listen to it and reflect on his responses to facilitate his decision-making process.

If he makes the decision not to pursue college, it might be good for him to role-play telling his parents because he is quite anxious about it. The counselor could play the role of the parent, and Todd could pretend that he is telling them about his concerns about going to college.

### Activity-Based Experiential

Given that Todd has a lot of ambivalence about his future—not just in terms of a possible career but also about whether or not he will continue with his plan to attend college—the counselor could suggest that he take some action to find out more about his options. If he hasn't visited the campus where he has applied and been accepted, or if he has not spent a night there, which is often very helpful, the counselor could suggest that he follow through with these things. The counselor could also suggest that, if he knows anyone from his home town who attends that college, he could contact that person and interview him or her about what he or she does or doesn't like about college, how he or she has adjusted, and so forth. If at some point Todd still is not leaning in the direction of college, the counselor could suggest that he do some job shadowing to get a clearer idea of what he might like to do.

APPENDIX

# Game Board

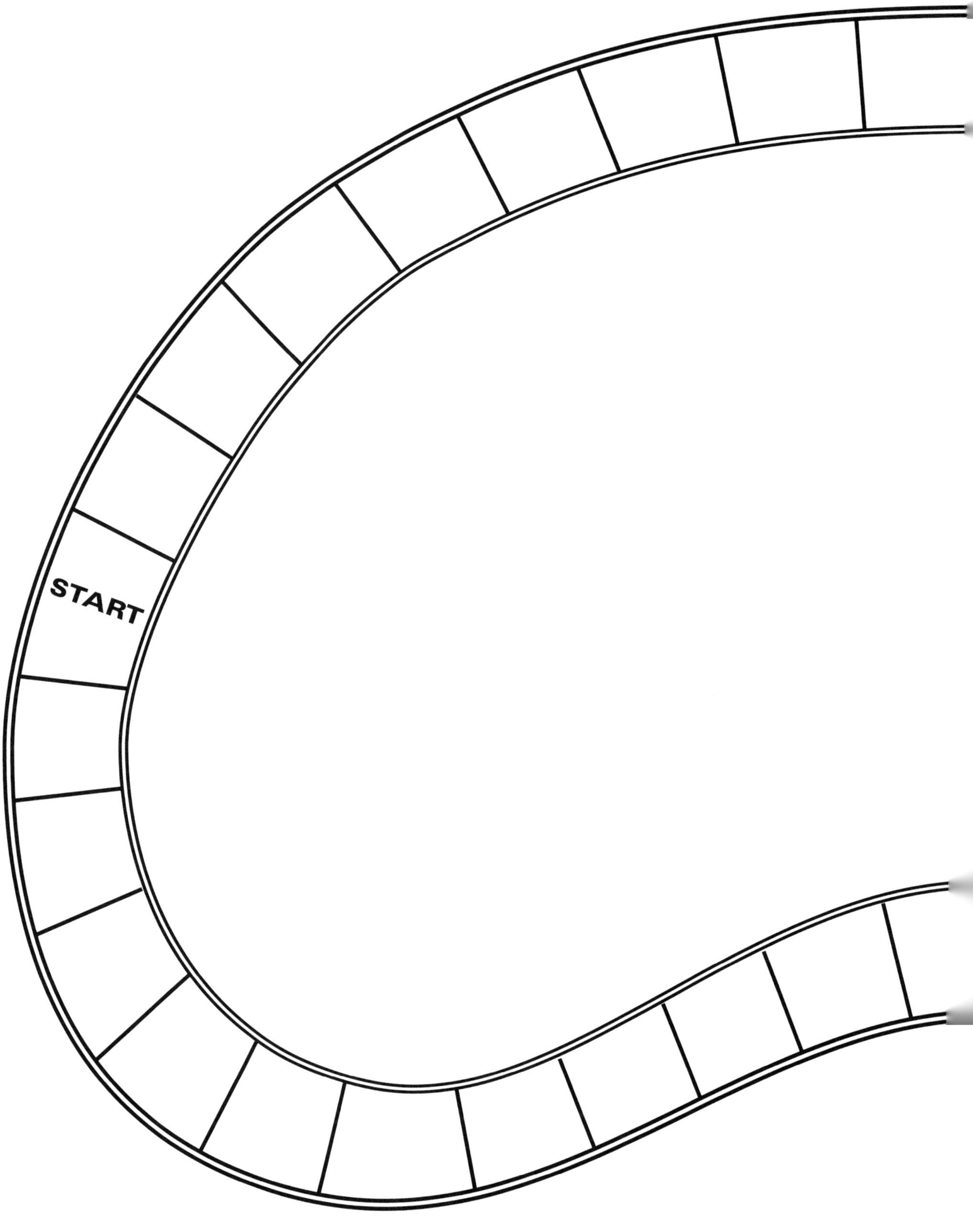
START

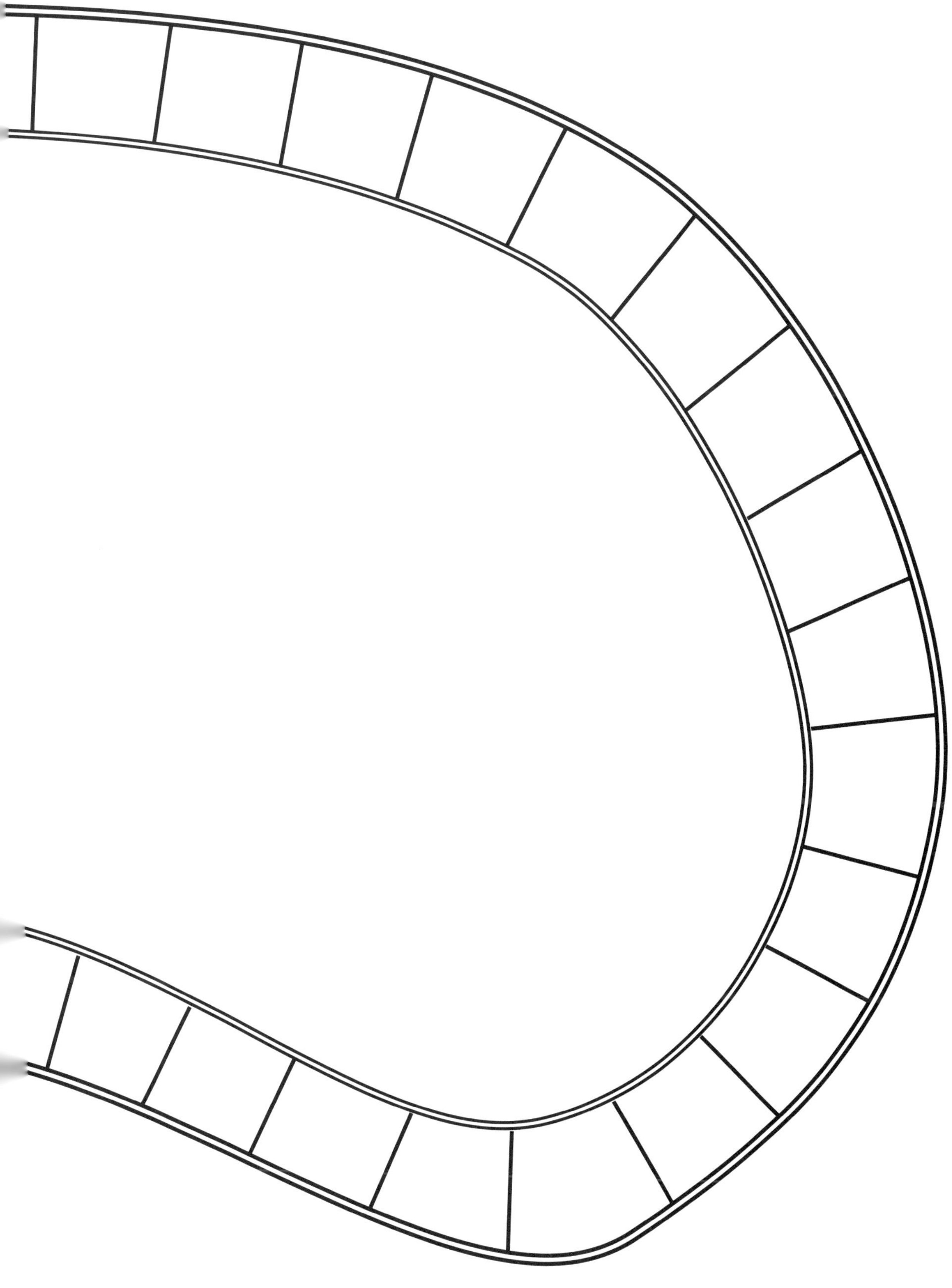

# References


Abercrombie, B., & Graham, M. (1990). *Charlie Anderson.* New York: Simon & Schuster.

Alberti, R. E., & Emmons, M. L. (1974). *Your perfect right.* San Luis Obispo, CA: Impact.

Baggerly, J. (2007). International interventions and challenges following the crisis of natural disasters. In N. B. Webb (Ed.), *Play therapy with children in crisis: Individual, group, and family treatment* (pp. 345–367). New York: Guilford.

Baikie, K. A., & Wilhelm, K. (2005). Emotional and physical health benefits of expressive writing. *Advances in Psychiatric Treatment, 11*, 338–346.

Ballard, M. B. (2012). The family life cycle and critical transitions: Utilizing cinematherapy to facilitate understanding and increase communication. *Journal of Creativity in Mental Health, 7*(2), 141–152.

Bartlett, J. R. (2003, July–August). Storytelling through the ages. *ASCA School Counselor,* pp. 19–23.

Bauer, M. S., & Balius, F. A. (1995). Storytelling: Integrating therapy and curriculum for students with serious emotional disturbances. *Teaching Exceptional Children, 27,* 24–29.

Beale, A. V., & Scott, P. C. (2001). Bullybusters: Using drama to empower students to take a stand against bullying behavior. *Professional School Couseling, 4,* 300–305.

Bedford, S. (1974). *Instant replay.* New York: Institute for Rational Living.

Black, D. W. (2007). A review of compulsive buying disorder. *World Psychiatry, 6,* 14–18.

Blanco, P. J., & Ray, D. C. (2011). Play therapy in elementary schools: A best practice for improving academic achievement. *Journal of Counseling and Development, 89*(2), 235–243.

Bowman, R. P. (2004). *Test buster pep rally* (2nd ed.). Minneapolis: Educational Media.

Bradley, L. J., Hendricks, C. B., & Crews, C. R. (2009). Expressive techniques: Counseling interventions for children and adolescents. In A. Vernon (Ed.), *Counseling children and adolescents* (4th ed., pp. 83–122). Denver: Love.

Brems, C. (2002). *A comprehensive guide to child psychotherapy* (2nd ed.). Boston: Allyn & Bacon.

Brickell, N. (2010). Family timeline. In L. Lowenstein (Ed.), *Creative family therapy techniques: Play, art, and expressive activities to engage children in family sessions* (pp. 33–34). Toronto: Champion Press.

Brown, M., & Brown, L. K. (1988). *Dinosaurs divorce: A guide for changing families.* Boston: Little, Brown.

Bullock, R. B. (2007). The crisis of deaths in schools: Interventions with students, parents, and teachers. In N. B. Webb (Ed.), *Play therapy with children in crisis: Individual, group, and family treatment* (pp. 270–293). New York: Guilford.

Burnett, K. G. (2000). *Simon's hook: A story about teasing and put-downs.* Roseville, CA: GR.

Cain, J. (2000). *The way I feel.* Seattle: Parenting Press.

Carlson, N. (1992). *What if it never stops raining?* New York: Puffin.

Caron, J. C. (2005). DSM at the movies: Use of media in clinical or educational settings. In G. R. Walz & R. K. Yep (Eds.), *VISTAS: Compelling perspectives on counseling 2005* (pp. 179–182). Alexandria, VA: American Counseling Association.

Cerio, J. (2000). *A do-it-yourself guide for practitioners.* Alfred, NY: Alfred University.

Coker, J. K. (2001). Creative arts in counseling elementary school children: A user-friendly approach. In D. S. Sandu (Ed.), *Elementary school counseling in the new millennium* (pp. 47–62). Alexandria, VA: American Counseling Association.

Conley, D. (1994). *If you believe in you* (CD). Brooklyn: Treehouse Music.

Cook, K. (2011a). Altered books and changed lives. In S. Degges-White & N. L. Davis (Eds.), *Integrating the expressive arts into counseling practice: Theory-based interventions* (pp. 28–32). New York: Springer.

Cook, K. (2011b). New chapter pamphlet stitch book. In S. Degges-White & L. Davis (Eds.), *Integrating the expressive arts into counseling practice: Theory-based interventions* (pp. 37–38). New York: Springer.

Craver, M. M. (2011). *Chillax! How Ernie learns to chill out, relax, and take charge of his anger.* Washington, DC: Magination Press.

Crist, J. (2006). *What to do when you're sad and lonely: A guide for kids*. Minneapolis: Free Spirit.

Davis, W. B., Gfeller, K. E., & Thaut, M. H. (1999). *An introduction to music therapy: Theory and practice* (2nd ed.). Boston: McGraw-Hill.

Degges-White, S., & Davis, N. L. (2011). *Integrating the expressive arts into counseling practice: Theory-based interventions.* New York: Springer.

DeLucia-Waack, J. L., & Gellman, R. A. (2007). The efficacy of using music in children of divorce groups: Impact on anxiety, depression, and irrational beliefs about divorce. *Group Dynamics: Theory, Research, and Practice, 11,* 272–282.

Dinkmeyer, D., & Dinkmeyer, D. (1982). *DUSO: Developing understanding of self and others.* Circle Pines, MN: American Guidance Services.

Doll, B., & Doll, C. (1997). *Bibliotherapy with young people.* Englewood, CA: Libraries Unlimited.

Dollarhide, C. T. (2003, July–August). Cinematherapy: Making media work. *ASCA School Counselor,* 16–17.

Duffey, T. (2007). *Creative interventions in grief and loss therapy: When the music stops, a dream dies.* Florence, KY: Taylor & Francis.

Eckhardt, K. J., & Dinsmore, J. A. (2012). Mindful music listening as a potential treatment for depression. *Journal of Creativity in Mental Health, 7*(2), 176-186.

Evans, L. (2007). *Sometimes I feel like a storm cloud.* New York: Mondo.

Forinash, M. (2005). Music therapy. In C. A. Malchiodi (Ed.), *Expressive therapies* (pp. 46- 67). New York: Guilford.

Franz-Ransom, J. (2000). *I don't want to talk about it.* Washington, DC: Magination Press.

Gallo-Lopez, L., & Schaefer, C. E. (Eds.). (2005). *Play therapy with adolescents.* Lanham, MD: Aronson.

Gil, E. (2006). *Helping abused and traumatized children: Integrating directive and non-directive approaches.* New York: Guilford.

Gladding, S. T. (1987). The poetics of a "check out" place: Preventing burnout and promoting self-renewal. *Journal of Poetry Therapy, 1,* 95-102.

Gladding, S. T. (1995). Creativity in counseling. *Counseling and Human Development, 28*(1), 1-12.

Gladding, S. T. (2005). *Counseling as an art: The creative arts in counseling* (3rd ed.). Alexandria, VA: American Counseling Association.

Gladding, S. T. (2011). *The creative arts in counseling* (4th ed.). Alexandria, VA: American Counseling Association.

Gladding, S. T., & Gladding, C. T. (1991). The ABC's of bibliotherapy. *School Counselor, 39,* 7-13.

Goh, M., Wahl, K. H., McDonald, J. K., Brissett, A. A., & Yoon, E. (2007). Working with immigrant students in schools: The role of school counselors in building cross-cultural bridges. *Journal of Multicultural Counseling, 35,* 66-69.

Goessling, K., & Doyle, C. (2009). Thru the lenz: Participatory action research, photography, and creative process in an urban high school. *Journal of Creativity in Mental Health, 4,* 343-365.

Gorelick, K. (2005). Poetry therapy. In C. A. Malchiodi (Ed.), *Expressive therapies* (pp. 117-140). New York: Guilford.

Graham, M. A., & Pehrsson, D. E. (2011). Show me your family in the dollhouse activity. In S. Degges-White & N. L. Davis (Eds.), *Integrating the expressive arts into counseling practice: Theory-based interventions* (pp. 16-17). New York: Springer.

Grollman, E. (1993). *Straight talk about death for teenagers: How to cope with losing someone you love.* Boston: Beacon Press.

Grzesik, S., & Vena, K. (2011). "Fashion statements are a fashion choice" activity. In S. Degges-White & N. L. Davis (Eds.), *Integrating the expressive arts into counseling practice: Theory-based interventions* (pp. 84-86). New York: Springer.

Hackney, H. L., & Cormier, S. (2004). *The professional counselor: A process guide to helping* (5th ed.). Boston: Allyn & Bacon.

Hawley, R. C., & Hawley, I. L. (1975). *Developing human potential: A handbook of personal and social growth.* Amherst, MA: ERA Press.

Henderson, D. A., & Thompson, C. L. (2011). *Counseling children* (8th ed.). Belmont, CA: Brooks/Cole.

Hendricks, P. B. (2000). A study of the use of music therapy techniques in a group for the treatment of adolescent depression. *Dissertation Abstracts International, 62,* 107.

Hesley, J. W., & Hesley, J. G. (2001). *Rent two films and let's talk in the morning* (2nd ed.). New York: Wiley.

Hipp, E. (1995). *Help for the hard times: Getting through loss.* Center City, MN: Hazelden.

Homeyer, L. E., & DeFrance, E. (2005). Play therapy. In C. A. Malchiodi (Ed.), *Expressive therapies* (pp. 141–161). New York: Guilford.

Homeyer, L. E., & Sweeney, D. S. (2005). Sandtray therapy. In C. A. Malchiodi (Ed.), *Expressive therapies* (pp. 162–182). New York: Guilford.

Homeyer, L. E., & Sweeney, D. S. (2011). *Sandtray therapy: A practical manual* (2nd ed.). New York: Taylor & Francis.

Huebner, D. (2007). *What to do when your temper flares: A kid's guide to overcoming problems with anger.* Washington, DC: Magination Press.

Humphrey, K. M. (2009). *Counseling strategies for loss and grief.* Alexandria, VA: American Counseling Association.

Ingram, M. A. (2003). Rhyme with reason. *ASCA School Counselor, 42,* 19–23.

Jacobs, E. (1992). *Creative counseling techniques: An illustrated guide.* Odessa, FL: Psychological Assessment Resources.

Jackson, T. (1995). *More activities that teach.* Cedar City, UT: Red Rock.

Jackson, T. (2001). Using bibliotherapy with clients. *Journal of Individual Psychology, 57,* 289-297.

Jakubowski, P., & Lange, A. J. (1978). *The assertive option: Your rights and responsibilitites.* Champaign, IL: Research Press.

Jencius, M. (2011, June). Express yourself. *Counseling Today,* pp. 24–25.

Jensen, K. L. (2001). The effects of selected classical music on self-disclosure. *Journal of Music Therapy, 38,* 2–27.

Johnson, S., & Clark, P. (2001). Play therapy with aggressive acting-out children. In G. Landreth (Ed.), *Innovations in play therapy: Issues, process, and special populations* (pp. 323-333). Philadelphia: Taylor & Francis.

Jones, E. M., & Landreth, G. (2002). The efficacy of intensive individual play therapy for chronically ill children. *International Journal of Play Therapy, 10*(2), 117–140.

Jordan, D., & Jordan, R. M. (2003). *Salt in his shoes.* New York: DDIN Paperbacks.

Joshua, J. M., & DiMenna, D. (2000). *Read two books and let's talk next week: Using bibliotherapy in clinical practice.* New York: Wiley.

Kane, M. (2012, July–August). Beat for peace. *ASCA School Counselor,* pp. 19–23.

Kelsch, D., & Emry, K. (2003, June). *Sharing the counseling program vision: Bibliotherapy using established language arts curriculum.* Paper presented at the annual meeting of the American School Counselor Association, St. Louis.

*Kids write through it: Essays by kids who have triumphed over trouble.* (1998). Minneapolis: Fairview Press.

Kottman, T. (2001). *Play therapy: Basics and beyond.* New York: Guilford.

Kottman, T. (2002). Billy, the teddy bear boy. In L. Golden (Ed.), *Case studies in child and adolescent counseling* (3rd ed., pp. 8–20). Columbus, OH: Merrill Prentice Hall.

Kottman, T. (2009). Play therapy. In A. Vernon (Ed.), *Counseling children and adolescents* (4th ed., pp. 123–146). Denver: Love.

Kramer, E. (1998). *Childhood and art therapy* (2nd ed.). Chicago: Magnolia Street.

Kress, V. E., Hoffman, R., & Thomas, A. M. (2008). Letters from the future: The use of therapeutic letter writing in counseling sexual abuse survivors. *Journal of Creativity in Mental Health, 3,* 105–118.

Kwiatkowska, H. (2001). Family art therapy: Experiments with a new technique. *American Journal of Art Therapy, 40,* 27–39.

Landreth, G. L. (1991). *Play therapy: The art of the relationship.* Muncie, IN: Accelerated Development.

Landreth, G. L. (2002). *Play therapy: The art of the relationship* (2nd ed.). New York: Brunner-Routledge.

Landreth, G. L., Ray, D. C., & Bratton, S. C. (2009). Play therapy in elementary schools. *Psychology in the Schools, 46,* 281–289.

Landy, R. J. (1997). Drama therapy: The state of the art. *Arts in Psychotherapy, 24,* 5–11.

Landy, R. J. (2005). Drama therapy and psychodrama. In C. Malchiodi (Ed.), *Expressive therapies* (pp. 90–116). New York: Guilford.

Lane, C., & Rollnick, S. (2007). The use of simulated patients and role-play in communication skills training: A review of the literature to August 2005. *Patient Education and Counseling, 67,* 13–20.

Lev-Wiesel, R. (2000). The self-revelation through color technique: Understanding clients' relations with significant others, silent language, and defense mechanisms through the use of color. *American Journal of Art Therapy, 39,* 35–41.

Lipson, G. B. (1992). *Audacious poetry: Reflections of adolescence.* Carthage, IL: Good Apple.

Lowenstein, L. (2006). (Ed.). *Creative family therapy techniques: Play, art, and expressive activities to engage children in family sessions* (pp. 33–34). Toronto: Champion Press.

Lowenstein, L. (2010). (Ed.). *Creative family therapy techniques: Play, art, and expressive activities to engage children in family sessions.* Toronto, Ontario, Canada: Champion Press.

MacLean, K. (2009). *Moody cow meditates.* Boston: Wisdom.

Malchiodi, C. A. (Ed.). (2005). *Expressive therapies.* New York: Guilford.

Myrick, R. D. (1997). *Developmental guidance and counseling: A practical approach.* Minneapolis: Educational Media.

Nelson, L., & Finneran, L. (2006). *Drama and the adolescent journey: Warm-ups and activities to address teen issues.* Portsmouth, NH: Heinemann Drama.

Newsome, D. W. (2003). Counseling interventions using expressive arts. In B. T. Erford (Ed.), *Transforming the school counseling profession* (pp. 231–247). Upper Saddle River, NJ: Merrill Prentice Hall.

Nichols, M. (2010). *Family therapy: Concepts and methods* (9th ed.). Upper Saddle River, NJ: Pearson.

Nicholson, J. I., & Pearson, Q. M. (2003). Helping children cope with fears: Using children's literature in classroom guidance. *Professional School Counseling, 7*(1), 15–19.

Nugent, S. A. (2000). Perfectionism: Its manifestations and classroom-based interventions. *Journal of Secondary Gifted Education, 11,* 215–221.

O'Connor, K. (2000). *The play therapy primer* (2nd ed.). New York: Wiley.

Okun, B. F. (2007). *Effective helping, interviewing and counseling techniques* (7th ed.). Pacific Grove, CA: Brooks/Cole.

Oliver, M., Nelson, K. W., Cade, R., & Cueva, C. (2007). Therapeutic letter writing from school counselors to students, parents, and teachers. *Professional School Counseling, 10,* 510–513.

Orton, G. L. (1997). *Strategies for counseling with children and their parents.* Pacific Grove, CA: Brooks/Cole.

Ostertag, J. (2002). Unspoken stories: Music therapy with abused children. *Canadian Journal of Music Therapy, 9,* 10–29.

Palmer, P. (1977). *The mouse, the monster, and me.* San Luis Obispo, CA: Impact.

Pardeck, J. T. (1998). *Using books in clinical social work practice: A guide to bibliotherapy.* New York: Haworth Press.

Pardeck, J. T., & Pardeck, J. A. (1993). *Bibliotherapy: A clinical approach for helping children.* New York: Gordon & Breach.

Payne, R., Lancaster, C., Heil, L., & Pineda, M. (2011). Choice-mobile activity. In S. Degges-White & Davis, N. L. (Eds.), *Integrating the expressive arts into counseling practice: Theory-based interventions* (pp. 71–72). New York: Springer.

Pehrsson, D. E. (2006). Fictive bibliotherapy and therapeutic storytelling with children who hurt. *Journal of Creativity in Mental Health, 1,* 273–286.

Pehrsson, D. E. (2006–2007). Co-story-ing: Collaborative storytelling with children who fear. *Journal of Creativity in Mental Health, 2,* 285–291.

Pehrsson, D. E., Allen, V. P., Folger, W. A., McMillen, P., & Lowe, I. (2007). Bibliotherapy with preadolescents experiencing a divorce. *Family Journal, 15,* 409–414.

Pehrsson, D. E., & McMillen, P. (2005). A bibliotherapy evaluation tool: Grounding counselors in the therapeutic use of literature. *Arts in Psychotherapy, 32,* 47–59.

Pehrsson, D. E., & McMillen, P. (2006). *Competent bibliotherapy: Preparing counselors to use literature with culturally diverse clients.* Alexandria, VA: American Counseling Association.

Pehrsson, D. E., & McMillen, P. (2007). *Bibliotherapy: Overview and implications for counselors* (ACAPCD-02). Alexandria, VA: American Counseling Association.

Pennebaker, J. W. (2004). *Writing to heal: A guided journal for recovering from trauma and emotional upheaval.* New York: New Harbinger.

Peters, J. S. (2000). *Music therapy: An introduction* (2nd ed.). Springfield, IL: Charles C. Thomas.

Potter-Efron, R. (1993). *How to control your anger (before it controls you).* Minneapolis: Johnson Institute.

Prokop, M. S. (1996). *Divorce happens to the nicest kids.* Warren, OH: Allegra.

Ramirez, S. Z., Jain, S., Flores-Torres, L. L., Perez, R., & Carlson, R. (2009). The effects of *cuento* therapy on reading achievement and psychological outcomes of Mexican-American students. *Professional School Counseling, 12*(3), 253–261.

REACH Center. (1993). *REACH Cultural Bingo* [Handout H–G]. Seattle, WA: Author. Retrieved September 30, 2012, from http://www.reachctr.org

Riley, S. (2003). Using art therapy to address adolescent depression. In C. A. Malchiodi (Ed.), *Handbook of art therapy* (pp. 220–228). New York: Guilford.

Rio, R. (2002). Improvisation with the elderly: Moving from creative activities to process-oriented therapy. *Arts in Psychotherapy, 29,* 191–201.

Riordan, R. J. (1996). Scriptotherapy: Therapeutic writing as a counseling adjunct. *Journal of Counseling and Development, 74,* 263–269.

Roaten, G. K., & Schmidt, E. A. (2009). Using experiential activities with adolescents to promote respect for diversity. *Professional School Counseling, 12*(4), 309–314.

Rogers, S. (2005). Play interventions for young children with autism spectrum disorders. In L.A. Reddy, T. M. Files-Hall, & C. E. Schaefer (Eds.), *Empirically based play interventions for children* (pp. 215–239). Washington, DC: American Psychological Association.

Rubin, L. C. (2000). The use of paint-by-number art in therapy. *Arts in Psychotherapy, 27,* 269–272.

Schab, L. (2008). *Beyond the blues: A workbook to help teens overcome depression.* Oakland, CA: Instant Help Books.

Schaefer, C. E. (2002). *Play therapy with adults.* New York: Wiley.

Shallcross, L. (2011a). Big screen therapy. *Counseling Today, 54*(4), 36–40.

Shallcross, L, (2011b). Getting off the couch. *Counseling Today, 54*(6), 28–36.

Shatkin, L. (2011). *The 10 best college majors for your personality.* Indianapolis: JIST.

Shiflett, C. L., & Tang, H. (2011). Felting with family. In S. Degges-White & N. L. Davis (Eds.), *Integrating the expressive arts into counseling practice: Theory-based interventions* (pp. 55–57). New York: Springer.

Silver, R. (2001). *Art as language.* Lillington, NC: Edwards Brothers.

Sloan, G. (2003). *Give them poetry!* New York: Teachers College Press.

Slyter, M. (2012). Creative counseling interventions for grieving adolescents. *Journal of Creativity in Mental Health, 7*(1), 17–34.

Spasaro, S., & Schaefer, C. (Eds.). (2004). *Refusal to speak: Treatment of selective mutism in children.* Lanham, MI: Rowman & Littlefield.

Stevens, R., & Spears, E. H. (2009). Incorporating photography as a therapeutic tool in counseling. *Journal of Creativity in Mental Health, 4,* 3–16.

*Teens write through it: Essays from teens who have triumphed over trouble.* (1998). Minneapolis: Fairview Press.

Thaut, M. H. (2009). *Rhythm, music, and the brain: Scientific foundations and clinical applications.* Philadelphia: Routledge.

Thompson, C. L., & Rudolph, L. B. (2000). *Counseling children* (5th ed.). Pacific Grove, CA: Brooks/Cole.

Thompson, C. L., Rudolph, L. B., & Henderson, D. (2004). *Counseling children* (6th ed.). Belmont, CA: Brooks/Cole.

Thompson, R. A. (2003). *Counseling techniques: Improving relationships with others, ourselves, our families, and our environment* (2nd ed.). Philadelphia: Taylor & Francis.

Vernon, A. (1998a). *The Passport Program: A journey through emotional, social, cognitive, and self-development (Grades 1–5).* Champaign, IL: Research Press.

Vernon, A. (1998b). *The Passport Program: A journey through emotional, social, cognitive, and self-development (Grades 6–8).* Champaign, IL: Research Press.

Vernon, A. (1998c). *The Passport Program: A journey through emotional, social, cognitive, and self-development (Grades 9–12).* Champaign, IL: Research Press.

Vernon, A. (2002). *What works when with children and adolescents: A handbook of individual counseling techniques.* Champaign, IL: Research Press.

Vernon, A. (2006). *Thinking, feeling, behaving: An emotional education curriculum for children.* Champaign, IL: Research Press.

Vernon, A. (2009). *More what works when with children and adolescents: A handbook of individual counseling techniques.* Champaign, IL: Research Press.

Vernon, A. (2011). Rational-emotive behavior therapy. In D. Capuzzi & D. Gross (Eds.), *Counseling and psychotherapy: Theories and interventions* (5th ed., pp. 237–261). Alexandria, VA: American Counseling Association.

Vernon, A. (2013). Creative approaches to counseling. In D. Capuzzi & D. Gross (Eds.), *Introduction to the counseling profession* (6th ed., pp. 256–290). New York: Routledge.

Vernon, A., & Clemente, R. (2005). *Assessment and intervention with children and adolescents: Developmental and multicultural approaches.* Alexandria, VA: American Counseling Association.

Wagenbach, D. (2010). *The grouchies.* Washington, DC: Magination Press.

Wagner, W. G. (2003). *Counseling, psychology, and children.* Upper Saddle River, NJ: Merrill Prentice Hall.

Watts, R. E., & Garza, Y. (2008). Using children's drawings to facilitate the acting "as if" technique. *Journal of Individual Psychology, 64,* 113–118.

White, V. E., & Murray, M. A. (2002). Passing notes: The use of therapeutic letter writing in counseling adolescents. *Journal of Mental Health Counseling, 24*(2), 166.

Wiener, D. J. (2001). Rehearsals for growth: Applying improvisational theater games to relationship therapy. In D. J. Wiener (Ed.), *Beyond talk therapy: Using movement and expressive techniques in clinical practice* (pp. 165–180). Washington, DC: American Psychological Association.

Wigram, T., Pedersen, I. N., & Bonde, L. O. (2002). *A comprehensive guide to music therapy: Theory, clinical practice, research and training.* London: Kingsley.

Wilde, J. (1997). *Hot stuff to help kids chill out: The anger management book.* East Troy, WI: LGR.

Wright, J., & Chung, M. C. (2001). Mastery or mystery? Therapeutic writing: A review of the literature. *British Journal of Guidance and Counseling, 29,* 277–291.

Yarrow, P. (2000). *Don't laugh at me* (CD). Los Angeles: Warner Brothers Records.

Zuzo, C. (2008). *Being Bella: Discovering how to be proud of your best.* Northville, MI: Ferne Press.

# About the Authors

**Ann Vernon,** PhD, RLPC, is Professor Emerita, University of Northern Iowa, where she served as professor and coordinator of the school and mental health counseling programs for many years. During her tenure, she taught courses related to counseling children and adolescents and also maintained a successful private practice where she specialized in working with children, adolescents, and parents. Prior to working in these settings, she was an elementary school counselor. Dr. Vernon has published numerous books, including the Research Press titles *What Works When with Children and Adolescents; Thinking, Feeling, Behaving: An Emotional Education Curriculum for Children and Adolescents; The Passport Program; and More What Works When with Children and Adolescents.* She is the editor of four editions of *Counseling Children and Adolescents,* a popular textbook used in many counselor education programs throughout the country, and is coeditor of *Counseling Theories: Practical Applications for Children and Adolescents in School Settings.* In addition, she has authored numerous journal articles dealing with counseling children and adolescents, developmental counseling, and applications of Rational-Emotive Behavior Therapy (REBT) with children and adolescents.

Dr. Vernon is the recipient of various professional awards and is Diplomate of the Albert Ellis Institute and an American Counseling Association Fellow. She has assumed many leadership roles within the counseling profession on a state, regional, and national level. She is President of the Albert Ellis Board of Trustees and is considered the leading international expert on applications of REBT/CBT with children and adolescents. She currently conducts workshops on a variety of topics related to counseling children and adolescents in Australia, South America, and the United States. She teaches school counseling courses in Romania at the University of Oradea.

**Kathryn L. Barry,** MAE, worked as a professional school counselor for 17 years. She recently retired from Aplington-Parkersburg Schools in Aplington, Iowa. Ms. Barry received both her MAE in school counseling and her BA in music education from the University of Northern Iowa. She has received advanced training in Adlerian play therapy, as well as trauma training from the National Institute for Trauma and Loss in Children and training in the Heartland Autism Model.

Ms. Barry serves on the Iowa School Counselor Association Board and is a member of the Iowa Department of Education's School Counseling Transformation Design Work Team. In 2004, she received the State of Iowa Governor's Award for outstanding service to Iowa's children, and she was awarded the Iowa School Counselor Association's Counselor of the Year award in 2010. Currently, Ms. Barry is an adjunct instructor at the University of Northern Iowa and a frequent presenter on using the creative arts in counseling and dealing with trauma in schools.